Hope for Humanity

How understanding and healing
trauma could solve the
planetary crisis

Hope for Humanity

How understanding and healing
trauma could solve the
planetary crisis

Malcolm Hollick
and Christine Connelly

BOOKS

Winchester, UK
Washington, USA

First published by O-Books, 2011
O Books is an imprint of John Hunt Publishing Ltd., The Bothy, Deershot Lodge, Park Lane, Ropley,
Hants, SO24 0BE, UK
office1@o-books.net
www.o-books.com

For distributor details and how to order please visit the 'Ordering' section on our website.

ISBN: 978 1 84694 443 7

A CIP catalogue record for this book is available from the British Library.

Design: Stuart Davies

Printed in the UK by CPI Antony Rowe
Printed in the USA by Offset Paperback Mfrs, Inc

We operate a distinctive and ethical publishing philosophy in all
areas of its business, from its global network of authors to
production and worldwide distribution.

CONTENTS

List of Tables

This work wonderfully highlights the role trauma plays in the human condition and how this manifests in the many dysfunctional behaviours we see in societies around the world today. In examining the roots of trauma in historical, evolutionary and psychological terms, before exploring the potential solutions, Malcolm and Christine truly give us 'Hope for Humanity'

I found the book thoroughly well written and an excellent overview of the entire field in a very readable and engaging way. I have already started quoting from it to the people I am training and they are asking when it will be published. It is excellent reading for anyone engaging with trauma healing as it gives a wonderful perspective on the whole history of the problem as well as many competing ideas and approaches.

Rob Egan, Trauma Therapist and Co-Founder of Alchemy Healing Techniques

'Hope for Humanity' is a highly readable account of the millennia long process through which humanity has become locked in a crippling cycle, where collective and individual trauma leads to violence and this perpetuates the trauma. It provides a bold, wide ranging and well documented account of what is blocking our flourishing and how this can be changed.

Chris Clarke, Visiting Professor in Applied Mathematics, Southampton University and author of *Weaving the Cosmos*

Acknowledgements

We owe a great debt of gratitude to the many friends, acquaintances, and strangers who contributed their inspiration, support, encouragement, ideas and information during more than two years of gestation, research and writing. We have acknowledged many of these debts in the Notes and References. Others remain anonymous, but nonetheless valuable for that.

We owe special thanks to John Hunt at O Books for his unwavering faith in our project. Also to Trevor Greenfield for his honest criticism of an early draft that sent us back to the drawing board. We are sure the finished book is much better for it.

Our book might never have seen the light of day without the support of Professor Jörg Imberger, Director of the Centre for Water Research, The University of Western Australia. Jörg obtained a 4-month Gledden Visiting Senior Research Fellowship for Malcolm, and provided him with an office and administrative support. This gave us access to a good library, without which much of our research would have been impossible. It also provided the opportunity to share some of our ideas in seminars and public lectures. His subsequent support of Malcolm's appointment as an Adjunct Senior Research Fellow at the Centre for Water Research ensured ongoing access to academic journals from the remote north of Scotland. Our work was also greatly facilitated by the generous gift of a new laptop.

We have never met Riane Eisler, Steve Taylor or James DeMeo, but their ground-breaking works on humanity's 'Fall' from a partnership, matrist culture to a dominator, patrist one started us thinking along the lines that evolved into this book. Another seminal inspiration came from Grant McFetridge's perception that trauma, particularly very early in development, blocks our access to peak states of consciousness.

On a personal level, we have both benefited greatly from the healing methods of the Institute for the Study of Peak States, and Rob Egan, trauma therapist and founder of Alchemy Techniques.

Finally, thank you to all our friends who have encouraged and supported us through the long and sometimes difficult journey. In particular, special thanks to Lisa Parker, George Paul and Rob Egan for reading and commenting on the manuscript.

This work forms contribution 2328 MH at the Centre for Water Research, The University of Western Australia.

Prologue

(M)uch of the violence that plagues humanity is a direct or indirect result of unresolved trauma that is acted out in repeated unsuccessful attempts to re-establish a sense of empowerment.
Trauma Therapist Peter Levine[1]

Trauma is a fact of life. It does not, however, have to be a life sentence. Not only can trauma be healed, but with appropriate guidance and support, it can be transformative. Trauma has the potential to be one of the most significant forces for psychological, social, and spiritual awakening and evolution. How we handle trauma (as individuals, communities and societies) greatly influences the quality of our lives. It ultimately affects how or even whether we will survive as a species.
Trauma Therapist Peter Levine[2]

(A)lmost everyone I have ever met suffers from some sense of incompleteness and emptiness. They sense that parts of themselves are missing and that they are cut off from a deep connection with life. ... Few people are fully at home and some of us have been so badly traumatized that almost no one is at home.
Shamanic Healer Sandra Ingerman[3]

... despite our differences, we're all alike. Beyond identities and desires, there is a common core of self—an essential humanity whose nature is peace and whose expression is thought and whose action is unconditional love. When we identify with that inner core, respecting and honoring it in others as well as ourselves, we experience healing in every area of life.
Joan Borysenko[4]

Do you ever wonder why civilization is faced with so many

1

crises? Why humans seem unable to live at peace with each other? Why we make so little progress in alleviating poverty and suffering? Why we continue to destroy the living systems that support our existence? Why we seem hell-bent on self-destruction despite being so clever? Why some people become monsters like Hitler or Stalin?

In looking for answers to these questions, we have tried to dig down to fundamental causes in human nature and culture. In our view, the problem does not lie in disobedience to God. Nor does it lie in the modern counterpart of original sin—faulty genes. Nor is it an inevitable outcome of the competitive dynamics of evolution. Rather, we believe the planetary crisis is the result of trauma. Trauma runs as a constant undercurrent beneath our psychological, biological and cultural evolution from the emergence of *Homo sapiens*, through prehistory and history, to the present. A brief definition will suffice for the moment. Trauma is "an experience that is emotionally painful, distressful, or shocking and which may result in lasting mental and physical effects."[5] Trauma warps our personality, blights our health, stunts our development, and condemns us to living well below our potential, both as individuals and as a species. Yet it is so widespread and so embedded in human culture that we do not recognize it, and accept our traumatized way of being as normal.

Like other animals, early hominids probably suffered little trauma. Figure 1 illustrates how stresses accumulated over time as humanity spread across the Earth, the climate changed, and our minds, societies and technologies evolved. Yet despite this potential for trauma, the evidence suggests that we maintained a largely peaceful, cooperative and egalitarian "partnership" culture for tens of thousands of years.[6] It was not until about 6,000 years ago that human culture changed. At that time, the climate dried dramatically over a huge belt of latitudes stretching round the globe. In its wake came famine, conflict and trauma, followed by an equally dramatic cultural discontinuity that Steve

Taylor called "The Fall"—a key event to which we will refer frequently.[7] The ancient civilizations of Egypt and Mesopotamia that emerged from The Fall were "dominator" cultures: warlike, competitive and hierarchical. Inherently violent, dominator

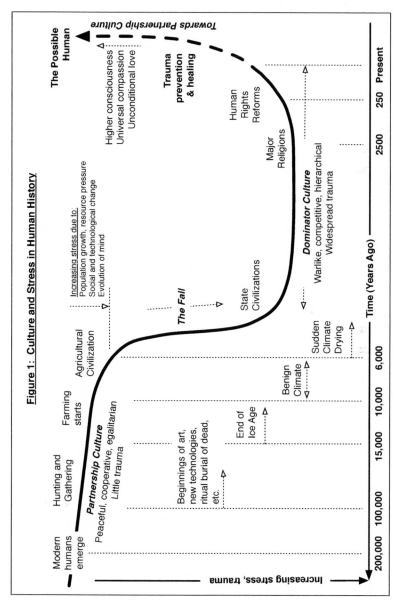

Figure 1: Culture and Stress in Human History

3

cultures are the product of trauma, and perpetuate themselves by traumatizing their own people as well as their enemies, generation after generation. They gradually displaced partnership cultures around the world, as documented by James DeMeo in *Saharasia,* and remain the preponderant way of being today.[8]

Steve Taylor identified two waves of reaction to dominator culture.[9] First, some 2,500 years ago, came the rise of the great religions which sought release from the sufferings of this life by transcending the individual ego, and seeking solace beyond death. Second, was a flood of empathy and compassion that began a mere 250 years ago, and has brought on-going social reforms including democracy, an end to slavery, and universal human rights. These two waves continue to soften the hard edges of the dominator culture, but resistance is strong and progress is slow. Those who are fortunate enough to be at the top of the dominator hierarchy naturally resist any erosion of their power, wealth or status. And even those at the bottom often resist change, preferring to stick with the devil they know.

If human civilization is to survive the present crises, we need to move away from the dominator culture, and do so quickly. With the proliferation of weapons of mass destruction, the acceleration of human induced climate change, peak oil and our voracious consumption of other natural resources, we no longer have the luxury of time. But rapid change is possible if we recognize the problem and take strong, collective action. We can minimize the creation of new trauma, heal existing trauma, and increase resilience to potentially traumatic events. We can consciously push our civilization and species towards a new partnership future in which we transcend the constraints of trauma, and reach towards higher levels of consciousness, universal compassion, and unconditional love for all beings. We can become the possible human.

In this book, we trace the role of trauma through human

prehistory and history, and on into the possible future. We start in Part I with a description of the nature, causes and impacts of trauma, mainly from a psychological perspective. This is followed in Part II by a discussion of the characteristics of the human brain and mind that distinguish us from other animals, and make us more vulnerable to trauma. In Part III, we trace key aspects of the evolution of human culture from hunting and gathering to the establishment of agriculture. The events of The Fall are described in Part IV, together with discussion of its causes and consequences, and reactions to it. Part V examines in detail the incidence of trauma in the world today, from before birth to adulthood, and from the individual to whole societies. Finally, in Part VI we set out a strategy for changing the course of history from domination to partnership, and encouraging the emergence of the possible human.

Writing this book took us on a journey into the darkness and suffering of humanity. At times we found it hard to continue. Our souls resisted the pain, longing to close off and ignore it. As you read, you may find the same reaction at times. But for the sake of the world's children and grandchildren, we hope you will persist through the dark and despair, knowing that there is hope for humanity.

Part I. Understanding Trauma

The magnitude of the trauma generated by the events that are affecting our world exact a toll on families, communities, and entire populations. Trauma can be self-perpetuating. Trauma begets trauma and will continue to do so eventually crossing generations in families, communities and countries until we take steps to contain its propagation.

Trauma Therapist Peter Levine[1]

The profound impact of domestic violence, community violence, physical and sexual abuse and other forms of predatory or impulsive assault cannot be overestimated. Violence impacts the victims, the witnesses and, ultimately, us all.

Bruce Perry of the ChildTrauma Academy[2]

Before we can explore the role of trauma in human evolution and civilization, we must understand what trauma is. This is the subject of Part I.

1. What is Trauma?

Trauma is the most avoided, ignored, denied, misunderstood, and untreated cause of human suffering.
Peter Levine[1]

The Nature, Scope and Incidence of Trauma

The medical profession often refers to physical injuries as trauma, but our interest is in psychological trauma which may or may not be associated with physical injuries. From this perspective, trauma is an emotionally painful or shocking experience that has lasting mental and physical effects.[2] This definition makes no mention of the severity of these effects, but research and therapy tend to focus on victims who are obviously dysfunctional in some way, perhaps suffering from insomnia, nightmares, social isolation, or amnesia.[3] However, we believe trauma forms a spectrum. At one extreme are dangerously violent psychopaths created by a process criminologist Lonnie Athens calls 'violentization'.[4] At the other extreme are people who appear mentally, emotionally and physically normal, but who are unable to achieve their full potential due to mild but chronic fears of not being good enough, or of what other people think of them.

According to trauma therapist Peter Levine, most humans suffer some degree of trauma.[5] Similarly, psychotherapist Dorothy Rowe argues that most psychiatric disorders are actually responses to fear,[6] and back specialist John Sarno concluded that the epidemic of back problems in the western world is due to suppressed rage—a common symptom of trauma.[7] We argue that what is regarded as normal in modern society is actually well below the human potential which includes higher states of consciousness, universal compassion and unconditional love. We believe trauma blocks our access to these states and traps us in competitive, hierarchical, violent ways of being.[8] Despite this broad focus, much of the information on which this book is based relates to the dysfunctional end of the spectrum simply because this is where most data are available.

Trauma may arise after experiencing a threat to our physical or psychological survival or well-being, whether or not that threat is real. Trauma also may occur indirectly, after we witness a loved-one suffer a traumatic experience. Emotional memories of traumatic events surface whenever similar sensations are evoked in the future. When this happens, we react in the same way that we did to the original event. In other words, we develop an automatic response to any incident that our subconscious mind identifies as similar to the original threat. This response is not rational. At times, it may be quite inappropriate, and may even lead to fresh trauma. A child who is locked in a cupboard as a punishment may grow into an adult who cannot ride in the enclosed space of an elevator. And a child who is frightened by an unknown man may find that her adult social life is limited by her fear of strange men. We remain trapped in these unwanted patterns of behavior until the trauma is healed.

The Natural Reaction to a Potentially Traumatic Event

Such reactions are not due to psychiatric disorder, but are a normal effect of the way our brains and bodies respond to threats. Imagine an animal in the wild. When something changes in its environment, it becomes instantly alert: Is it a predator? Prey? A potential mate? Or just the wind? Any delay or mistake could mean death. There is no time for rational thought. The response is instinctive and fast. If there is danger, the animal's body automatically prepares for action—fight or flight, defense or escape. Blood is diverted to the large muscles from non-essential functions such as the skin, digestion, and the immune system. When the action is over and the nervous energy has been discharged, the animal relaxes, blood flow returns to normal, and the base level of arousal is restored.

But suppose the animal is faced with a fight it cannot win, and there is no time to escape. The normal reaction in this situation is to fake death in the hope that it will not be seen, or will be rejected as unfit to eat. The animal becomes immobile, freezing like a rabbit caught in the beam of headlights. In humans, time seems to slow, and there is no fear or pain. But when the danger has passed, the energy aroused is still there, ready for action. Typically, the animal discharges it by shaking and trembling for a while before continuing on its way, apparently untraumatized despite this brush with death. In this way, the original base level of arousal is re-established, and the cycle is completed.

Early humans probably responded to danger much as animals do, discharging the energy of arousal soon after the event. Ancient hunter-gatherers, like modern indigenous peoples, would have had many ways of healing potentially traumatic experiences before they could harden into trauma. Perhaps most importantly, they would have accepted fear, freezing, trembling, nightmares and other symptoms as normal reactions to danger, and allowed their free expression and discharge. By contrast, modern civilization tends to regard them as signs of weakness, forcing us to repress our natural emotional responses, and trapping the energy inside. Until this energy is discharged, we remain aroused, and trauma occurs. This chronic state of arousal causes us to be hyper-vigilant, constantly on the lookout for danger, anxious, tense, and with raised heart and respiration rates. From mild beginnings, the stress can spiral upwards as fresh traumas are experienced until the person becomes dysfunctional. If the process continues, they may eventually turn into an emotional time-bomb waiting to explode in rage, aggression and violence at the slightest provocation.

Trauma and the Triune Brain

The threat-arousal-relaxation cycle is controlled by ancient structures within the brain. Back in 1973, Paul MacLean observed that we have a 'triune brain' with three parts nested one inside the other.[9] The oldest, innermost part is the 'reptilian' brain which is responsible for basic functions such as arousal and sleep, the five senses, instinctive behaviors, and the regulation of temperature, heart rate and blood pressure. In the middle is the limbic system, or brain of a horse. This is associated with our emotions, and with feelings such as sexuality, hunger and fear that guide our behavior, including the response to threat. Wrapped around the limbic system is the newest part. Known as the cortex, this is where voluntary movement originates and thinking takes place, including language, abstract thought and self-reflection.

Our five senses of sight, hearing, touch, taste and smell continually supply the reptilian brain with information. At any given moment, these stimuli form a pattern of sensations that represent, say, an object, a place, or an event. The limbic system compares this pattern with remembered ones. If it is new, or recognized as a known threat, the 'fight, flight or freeze' response is triggered automatically through the rapid release of an array of hormones. There is simply no time for rational thought. But if the current pattern is classified as safe, no action is taken other than to refine the stored patterns in the light of the new information. This ability to associate cues, such as the growl of a dog with the threat of attack, or the smell of cut grass with a happy childhood event, is one of the brain's most remarkable characteristics. It is an ideal system for responding reliably and quickly to danger. But it lacks the intelligence to make considered judgments or respond flexibly to subtly different situations. Hence, the process produces faulty conclusions at times. Someone who has almost died from asphyxiation, for instance, may suffer a panic attack if their breathing is constricted in any way regardless of the actual danger posed. Or a woman who was raped by a man in a red shirt may be terrorized by the sight of a harmless red object.[10]

A key factor in understanding trauma is that the cortex and

limbic system of the mature human brain are able to exert some control over the lower levels. This is what happens when children learn to control instinctive 'reptilian' reactions to frustration, and to regulate their emotions arising from the limbic system. This is also how yogis learn to control their body temperature, respiration, heart beat and other functions. The cortex is not powerful enough to prevent the instinctive response to survival threats, but it can block the discharge of the energy afterwards, thus unintentionally causing trauma. Peter Levine suggests a few reasons why we might do this.[11] One is to gain social approval by appearing tough, and unaffected by traumatic events. Another is fear of what will happen if we let our raging aggression loose. Hence, we turn it inwards on ourselves. Release also may be blocked by our distinctively human fear of death. Freezing feels like death to our subconscious minds, and so we avoid remaining in that state while the energy dissipates.

Failure to release the energy of arousal creates a vicious spiral that becomes more intense with each traumatic experience. In order to cope, we may develop pathological symptoms that provide a safety valve, letting off just enough pressure to enable our system to keep going, but not enough to heal the trauma. These symptoms may become chronic, and become stronger with time. The only way out is to release the energy fully.

The Story of Tom Brown Jr. and a Feral Dog

Tom Brown Jr. is a well-known tracker and teacher of wilderness survival skills. In his extraordinary boyhood, he was taught by an old Native American who was perhaps the last to live in the old ways, wild and free. In this story, he tells of being attacked by a feral dog when he was 10 years old, clearly describing typical symptoms of trauma.[12]

It just came so suddenly out of such dead quiet that the snarl sounded like an explosion that hurled the dog in my face. For a long time the sound of a dog would send that face full of teeth flying at me again out of the bushes, and for years afterward I woke up whimpering and sweating out of the vision of those fangs snapping at my face. I could see that face, with its eyes wide and staring, its ears back, and that long narrow mouth taking bites that could have swallowed my face.

He was a big dog, and the weight of him alone knocked me over backwards. ... He was huge and it was all stringy muscle from running all the time. He felt so incredibly heavy, and I kept kicking and screaming and punching trying to get the knife out. I held his face back by one ear, but ... it jerked my arm forward once and its fangs caught me, ripping through my upper lip.

I got to my knife somehow, and I kept stabbing at it and kicking at it until it fell dead on top of me. I was covered in blood, and I flung it off me and leaped on it, stabbing and stabbing and stabbing at it as if its teeth were still snapping shut on my face. The utter horror of those teeth coming at me so fast and so unexpectedly had put me into a frenzy, and I knelt screaming and stabbing for a long time, until I finally realized it was dead. I knelt there and shook. ...

But for a couple of years ... I had the nightmares. Sometimes a howl far off in the Pines would trigger one, and I would wake up in my sleeping bag with that snarling face melting away as I came awake. ... I must have killed that dog a dozen times in my sleep before he went away and died completely. Even a long time later, that face would come back at me out of nowhere to remind me.

Note how the instinctive will to survive brought an almost superhuman strength and ferocity. But, despite being trained to kill for food, Tom became frenzied with terror, behaving much like the soldiers who run amok in the heat of battle. Also note that for a long time afterwards the sound of a dog would trigger a flashback or nightmare in which he re-enacted the experience over and over again. This is typical of trauma, particularly Post-Traumatic Stress Disorder.

2. The Causes of Trauma

Potentially Traumatic Events

We are all exposed to experiences that could cause trauma as shown in Table 1. For convenience, we refer to these as Potentially Traumatic Experiences, or Events (PTEs). Whether or not a PTE actually results in trauma depends on two factors: the nature and severity of the event, and our response to it. What is a traumatic event for one person may be a welcome challenge and stimulus for another. Some people are vulnerable, and easily traumatized, whereas others are resilient and able to shrug off much more severe threats. No matter how vulnerable or resilient we are, we all need to face challenges and succeed in meeting them in order to grow, develop and remain emotionally and mentally healthy. When we do so, we feel exhilarated, alive and energized. Without them, we may lose vitality and fail to engage fully with life.[1] Note, however, that in modern society we face many PTEs that do not require an active physical response, either because of the nature of the threat or because it is the responsibility of government agencies such as the police. In these cases, there is no channel for the discharge of the flight or fight energy aroused, and it can easily build up unless we find other ways to release it.

Table 1a: Some Age-Related Traumatic Events

In utero	Stinging eye disinfection	Genital mutilation
Maternal stress	Separation from mother	Medical procedures,
Smoking, alcohol, drugs	Denial of breast	surgery
Diet	Death of mother	
Infection (e.g. German		*Adulthood*
measles)	*Infancy*	Rape
Environmental toxins	Neglect	Oppression of women
Loud noises	Lack of touch	Sex slavery
Injury to fetus (During	Swaddling	Domestic violence
sex, accident)	One of multiple births	Divorce
Excessive heat or cold	Physical or sexual abuse	Violent crime: murder,
Restricted fetal oxygen	Schedule feeding	mugging
supply	Bottle feeding (due to	Burglary, property theft
Multiple fetuses	lack of touch, smell,	Job loss or
	antibodies, etc)	unemployment
Birth	Fostering or orphanage	Slavery or economic
Umbilical cord round	Separate bedroom	exploitation
neck		Homelessness
Oxygen deprivation	*Childhood*	Bereavement
Placenta previa	Physical or sexual abuse	Imprisonment, solitary
Breech presentation	Frequent change of	confinement
Umbilical cord cut too	caregiver	Humiliation
soon	Corporal punishment	
Held upside down and	Teasing, bullying	
smacked	Boarding school	

Defining a Potentially Traumatic Event

Each of us has a fuzzy but unique threshold beyond which challenge becomes damaging trauma. At one end of the scale are those who may be traumatized by what appear to be trivial events, such as the sight of a spider. Often the terror and panic

Table 1b: Examples of Traumatic Situations

War and political violence	Environmental impacts	Health
International war	Air, water, soil pollution	Food additives
Revolution or civil war	Noise pollution	Toxic residues in foods
Terrorism	Nuclear radiation	Iatrogenic illness
Genocide	Electromagnetic radiation	Drug side-effects
Political oppression	Desertification	Diseases
Torture and impris-		Allergies
onment	Economic &	Auto-immune diseases
Refugees	Technological	Surgery
Cultural memory of past	Displacement for devel-	Chronic or acute pain
events	opment	
	Slum clearance	Accidents
	Cyber crime	Motor vehicles
Natural disasters	Credit card fraud	Workplace
Drought, famine	Identity theft	Domestic
Hurricane, typhoon,		Sporting and leisure
cyclone		
Earthquake, tsunami		
Volcano		

are a re-enactment of an earlier trauma, and the trigger—in this case the spider—may be symbolic rather than a literal part of the original event. At the other end of the scale are people who appear invulnerable, or at least extraordinarily resilient. An example is Viktor Frankl's ability to find deep meaning among the horrors of a Nazi concentration camp.[2]

This diversity means there is no clear dividing line between an event that causes trauma and one that does not. In this book, we have included both physical and psychological injuries, and the absence of desirable events as well as the presence of harmful ones. Hence, a PTE could be a life-threatening physical injury which has psychological effects, or the purely psychological impact of watching a loved-one being beaten or raped. Similarly, failure to nurture an infant is a PTE, just as much as active child abuse. Nor are PTEs necessarily severe or dramatic. Psychoanalyst Boris Cyrulnik argues that our identity may be shaped in childhood by a raised eyebrow, a shrug, or even a smile. "(T)his chronic violence … probably (has) a devastating effect on personalities that are still developing, and their effects may be more long term than acute traumas, which are easier to talk about."[3] We become the boy who made men laugh, or the humiliated girl. Medical procedures, especially surgery, are a common cause of trauma, particularly in young children who cannot understand what is happening. Even as adults, our minds may accept the need for the operation, but, despite the anesthetic, our bodies still register the cutting of flesh and bone as a life-threatening wound.[4]

Often, too, we may be unaware of a traumatic experience. This is particularly true of injuries in the womb or during infancy before conscious memory develops. It applies to children who forget the disapproving frown while embodying its message, and to adults who suffer amnesia—a common effect of trauma. It occurs when we cannot detect the cause of injury, such as many environmental pollutants or other invisible factors. Similarly, we are generally unaware of traumas passed down the generations from our ancestors through upbringing and culture. But in all these cases, our bodies may store 'memories' of the trauma in tissues or organs, in individual cells, in the balance of hormones, or even in the expression of genes. These 'memories' in turn can affect the development of our brains and psyches, particularly during infancy. When, as adults, we react more strongly to events than seems justified, we may suspect the presence of replayed trauma. We may feel helpless, overwhelmed, and unable to cope or integrate associated thoughts and emotions. Similarly, we may be aware of persistent, unwanted behavior patterns such as rage or panic that are triggered by emotional 'buttons' set off by certain types of event.

A further complication is that the impact of an event depends on the culture in which it occurs. During childhood, we learn which events are considered stressful in our society, and how to respond appropriately.[5] If an event is regarded as normal and acceptable, it is less likely to cause psychological trauma than if it is regarded as illegitimate and humiliating, despite causing the same physical injuries in both cases. Evelin Lindner goes so far as to argue that: "Victimhood and trauma apply only when victims become consciously aware that they have suffered victimhood and trauma."[6] Hence, for example, if the moral law encourages husbands to beat disobedient wives, a woman will suffer less from such abuse than one in a society where women are autonomous. Many women in western societies are beaten, but few regard it as legitimate, and most suffer significant psychological distress as a result. By contrast, in 2005, 94% of Egyptian and 91% of Zambian women thought beating was acceptable.[7] This mental attitude lessens their conscious emotional distress, but does not eliminate their physical injuries or the associated subconscious emotional and psychological impacts. Similarly, many of the most significant traumatic events occur in infancy before there is any understanding of cultural traditions. These subconscious traumas not only affect individual behavior, but also foster cultural norms that perpetuate re-creation of traumatic events.

These complexities mean that there can be no universal definition of the kinds of event that may cause trauma. Nevertheless, some types of event are more likely to be traumatic than others. One that is repeated and frequent, such as child abuse or torture, is more likely to be harmful and harder to heal than an occasional or one-off event like a car accident or mugging.[8] An event that threatens our life or the integrity of our body or self is more traumatic than one that does not. This includes threats to our psychological identity such as the experience of humiliation.[9]

Destruction by humans due to war or terrorism is typically more traumatic than similar devastation due to a natural disaster. Events that we perceive as beyond our control, and which induce a feeling of helplessness and impotence are more likely to overwhelm us than situations in which we have some power. Sudden, unexpected events also create high levels of stress, particularly when they are novel and we cannot rely on past experience to cope with them. Finally, there may be a combination of PTEs, none of which would be sufficient to cause trauma on its own. For example, a change of employment, moving house or catching 'flu do not normally cause trauma individually, but might do so if they all happened at once.

A Story of Courage and Resilience from the Democratic Republic of Congo

Christine lives in the Democratic Republic of Congo. Her story, told in Amnesty International's magazine, is a remarkable illustration of resilience and courage in the face of potentially traumatic experiences.[10]

Christine's husband was killed and she and two of her daughters were raped by armed group fighters who broke into her home in September 2002.

After this, she decided to become a counselor to help other rape survivors to cope with their experiences. In July 2007 Christine was accompanying a group of women rape survivors from Masisi territory to Goma for medical care. She left the road at one point and heard someone moaning softly. She told Amnesty:

"I saw a girl tied up by her hands and feet. I started to untie her. She had been raped by soldiers who had pushed a piece of wood into her. She was telling me that she was going to be married on Saturday and had just returned from receiving marriage instructions. I freed her and started to carry her back to the road.

"Then a group of CNDP soldiers came out from the trees. They beat me and I let the girl fall to the ground. Then four of them then took turns to rape me, in front of the other women I was with. When they stopped, I was bleeding heavily and my arm and leg were badly swollen. We were about to leave to get help when we saw that the girl had died. We buried her there. My clothes were stained with blood, but we walked to a health centre. Then we continued to Goma, where I spent two weeks in hospital.

Despite her experiences, Christine continues with her work, travelling to rural communities to identify survivors and arrange for their care. Fear, stigma and shame often prevent rape survivors from coming forward – but when Christine tells her personal story, it encourages other women to seek help. ...

At the time of Amnesty's visit, Christine was caring for 28 women, including seven survivors aged from 12 to 50 who had arrived the previous day, some apparently suffering from fistulas or collapsed uteruses. She said she continues to get threats from armed groups, and this now prevents her from working in certain locations. 'I am trying to forget, but it is difficult', she says. 'I have such anger.'"

Christine's anger is thoroughly justified. It is also a common response to the terror of traumatic experiences. Soldiers who are in constant fear for their lives are particularly prone to outbursts of rage; and parents will often explode after a child has a narrow escape. Such anger re-surfaces whenever the traumatic experience is triggered later in life.

3. The Response to Potentially Traumatic Experiences

Resilience and Vulnerability

Whether or not a potentially traumatic experience causes trauma depends on the response to it, and responses vary hugely. Some people may remain overwhelmed, defeated and terrified, unable to conquer their fears and re-engage with life. Others may have no enduring symptoms, even after an extreme event. Unresolved trauma can make us excessively cautious and inhibited, destroy relationships, and lead to compulsive, perverse, promiscuous or inhibited sexuality.[1] It also can create perpetual victims who precipitate the reactions they fear through hostility, blaming, complaints, anger, baseless accusations, and personal attacks. Such behaviors may stem from a combination of fear with anger at their humiliation. Evelin Lindner argues that there are three possible responses to such experiences. A person may turn her anger inwards and become depressed, anxious or addicted. Alternatively, he may turn it outwards, exploding in destructive rage, or, like Hitler, seeking revenge by humiliating those who humiliated him. Thirdly, he may use the energy of his anger constructively, like Nelson Mandela.[2]

If we have dealt successfully with a particular type of PTE in the past, we will face similar experiences in the future with greater confidence. If we have an optimistic, hopeful outlook on life, we are less likely to be stressed by challenging events. If we have strong support from friends and family, we have a better chance of pulling through a PTE without trauma. Similarly, it helps if we have ways of releasing pent-up emotional energy, such as telling friends about it, vigorous exercise, or religious practices. Other factors that may affect our response include our health, general stress level, fatigue, nutrition, physical fitness and age.

An unhealed trauma may make us more vulnerable to similar events in the future. This applies particularly to traumas experienced in the womb, at birth or in infancy when our ability to cope is very limited. What seems like a minor event to an adult, such as missing a meal, may be a significant trauma for a new-born baby. As adults, past trauma may cause us to respond to a new challenge with anger and aggression, accompanied by tension, and denial of what has happened. Alternatively, if trauma has beaten us down, we may resignedly and apathetically accept the situation.

Often, the concept of resilience (or its opposite, vulnerability) is used to explain these varying responses to PTEs. In his book on the subject, psychoanalyst Boris Cyrulnik describes resilience as the ability to succeed despite stress and adversity; to roll with life's punches and bounce back. "Misfortunes are never wonderful. A misfortune ... forces us to choose: we can either give in to it or overcome it. Resilience defines the spirit of those who, having suffered a blow, have been able to get over it."[3] But, Cyrulnik stresses, resilience is not invulnerability, as we discover when a minor event triggers a painful memory. Rather, resilience reflects our sense of self-identity, and the ego's ability to adapt and evolve.

Stress occurs when the demands of life stretch us; trauma happens when they stretch us to the limit or beyond. Even the most courageous, most 'together' person has a limit beyond which they will break. The term 'trauma' is often reserved for those extreme situations that overwhelm our ability to cope — times when we feel totally helpless, knowing that no-one can save us or protect our loved ones; times of primal fear when our physical and psychological integrity is breached, and our world lies shattered.[4] Many of us carry subconscious experiences of this kind due to birth traumas, or events in early infancy. But in this book, as already noted, we include within the ambit of trauma any experience that reduces the victim's ability to achieve their full potential in the long run. Similarly, psychotherapist Piers Bishop argues that trauma may lead to a spectrum of effects ranging from anxiety, through depression, to Post-Traumatic Stress Disorder (PTSD) and psychosis.[5]

Transformation and Breakdown

It is important to recognize that even a traumatic breakdown can be a growth experience. Many people testify that their lives were transformed by a life-threatening illness, the loss of a loved-one, or the break-up of their family. Survivors often report greater confidence, competence and strength of character; increased empathy, altruism and self-understanding; better relationships with their family, friends and community; a deeper sense of the meaning and purpose of life; and new goals and priorities.[6] As Boris Cyrulnik expressed it, the beauty of wounded souls "may even have been enhanced, despite the splinters of wood, the fading of the colors and the rotten knots."[7] The key to transforming trauma into growth appears to be deep and sustained self-reflection about the event and its meaning until we can integrate it into a new worldview.[8]

In most cases, the obvious effects of a traumatic experience dissipate within a few weeks, and the victim's life appears to return to normal. However, there are often long-lasting impacts that may not be recognized as being caused by trauma.[9] These include moderate depression, anxiety and stress—conditions with which the sufferer can cope but which nevertheless disrupt their careers, relationships, sleep, memory, concentration, or other aspects of their lives. Sub-clinical trauma is particularly important in young children as it can impair development of the brain and emotional system.

More severe trauma may lead to long-term mental health problems, and trauma can be the underlying cause of virtually any psychiatric illness.[10] If specific symptoms continue for more than a month, the person may be diagnosed as suffering from

Post-Traumatic Stress Disorder (PTSD) (See Appendix A for a summary of the diagnostic criteria.) Despite its name, PTSD is not a mental illness, but a normal defensive response to an extreme threat. As therapist Peter Levine put it: "I do not view post-traumatic stress disorder as a pathology to be managed, suppressed, or adjusted to, but the result of a natural process gone awry."[11] PTSD is a debilitating condition that adversely affects the immune system, physical growth, reproductive hormones, emotions and memory.[12] It also has been shown to increase the risk of death following surgery.[13] Sufferers have persistent frightening thoughts and memories of their ordeal, and feel emotionally numb, especially with people to whom they were previously close. Normally trivial stimuli such as a color, sound or smell may trigger flashbacks into the full horror of the event, and cause anxiety, panic, weakness, exhaustion, muscle stiffness, poor concentration, and disturbed sleep. Sufferers are left feeling that the traumatic event has not finished, and any new stress may cause fresh trauma. Rather than being relegated to a memory of the past, the event keeps intruding unbidden into the present.[14]

After a traumatic event, the victim tries to make sense of it. This may be difficult because the memories are often distorted, and the experience may have been very different to past ones. The event is replayed in the mind again and again, and the story may be told over and over to patient friends. Rational thought may be swamped by intrusive images and sensations, such as hearing a dead person's voice, or seeing them in a crowd. Normally, these phenomena fade within a few weeks as the frozen residue of energy trapped in the nervous system is discharged. But victims of PTSD may not be able to complete the process. They may remember little or nothing about what happened, be unable to make sense of it, and be plagued by inappropriate emotional and physical reactions to normal life events. Sometimes, these develop into extreme fears, such as claustrophobia.

Coping Strategies and Defense Mechanisms

People use many conscious and unconscious strategies for coping with potentially traumatic situations as shown in Table 2. These psychological defense mechanisms are often regarded as problems to be overcome, but trauma therapist Babette Rothschild argues that they should be seen as positive resources for dealing with PTEs.[15] They are only a problem when they become limiting. For example, withdrawal from the world is not a problem in itself—we all need to withdraw at times. It is a disadvantage only if it prevents us from ever interacting with others. At the other end of the spectrum, a person who is afraid to be alone and cannot enjoy solitude is equally handicapped.

Dissociation is one of the commonest defense mechanisms, and may be the mind's way of escaping an intolerable situation, as freezing is for the body.[16] Dissociation is a splitting of awareness so that part of our ego can isolate itself from the traumatic experience. It often results in amnesia, or a gap in memory. Those who retain conscious memories of the experience report that time slowed, or they ceased to feel pain or emotions due to the release of natural opiates. These effects protect us from the pain and terror of immanent death, and help us cope with unendurable events such as being hit by an automobile, raped, or sliced by a surgeon's knife. Frequently, dissociation is accompanied by an out-of-body experience in which the victim watches the event as if they were an external observer. In its mildest form, dissociation brings a 'spacey' feeling, memory lapses, and distortions of time and perception. In extreme cases, children may withdraw into a fantasy world, and adults may develop multiple personality disorder in which a whole persona splits off.[17]

The dissociated state normally dissolves slowly, but sometimes the energy fails to discharge, and there is a long-term fragmentation of identity, and re-enactment of the trauma in flashbacks. When this happens, victims may feel disembodied

Table 2: Strategies for Coping with Stress and Potentially Traumatic Experiences
(Adapted from Harms 2005)

Conscious Strategies

Confrontative: Angry, emotional, direct response to a problem

Distancing: Making light of the situation, minimizing the threat

Self-controlling: Keeping feelings to oneself

Seeking social support: Telling someone

Accepting responsibility: Criticizing, lecturing or blaming oneself

Avoidance: Wishing the situation would go away

Problem-solving: Making an action plan and following it

Positive re-appraisal: Finding personal benefits in the situation

Unconscious Strategies

Dissociation: A splitting of awareness; a partial or complete separation from the traumatic event

Repression: Keeping unwanted thoughts and feelings out of awareness

Reaction formation: Repressing a conscious impulse and replacing it with its opposite

Projection: Attributing unacknowledged feelings to others

Isolation of affect: Repressing emotions associated with a particular context, or ideas associated with particular emotions

Undoing: Nullifying an unacceptable act

Regression: Returning to an earlier developmental phase

Introjection: Turning feelings inwards, rather than express powerful emotions

Idealization: Overvaluing another person, place, family or activity

Denial: Not accepting important aspects of reality

Somatization: Converting anxiety into physical symptoms

Reversal: Changing feelings or attitudes to their opposite

Sublimation: Changing a socially unacceptable aim into an acceptable one

Continued on next page

Table 2 Unconscious Strategies continued

Intellectualization: Thinking about an experience or emotion rather than feeling it directly

Rationalization: Using reason to justify certain ideas

Displacement: Shifting feelings about one person or situation onto another

Withdrawal: Avoiding engaging with others, or the world

Mental illness: depression, addiction, phobia, obsession or psychosis

for months or years, and often talk about their souls being stolen. In shamanic terms, the soul is our vital essence, or spiritual life principle; the seat of our emotions and feelings. Healer Sandra Ingerman claims that splitting the soul is an intelligent response to the pain of trauma, but can result in a part of the soul becoming permanently lost in another realm of reality. She continues: "almost everyone I have ever met suffers from some sense of incompleteness and emptiness. They sense that parts of themselves are missing and that they are cut off from a deep connection with life. ... Few people are fully at home and some of us have been so badly traumatized that almost no one is at home."[18] Shamans are trained to use altered states of consciousness to travel into these other realms of reality to retrieve soul parts for their clients.

Boris Cyrulnik describes how young children use various defense mechanisms.[19] They may dissociate, dividing their ego into socially acceptable and secret identities. Or they may withdraw from reality, creating an invulnerable space inside. They may deny their traumatic experiences, making light of the dangers of the world, or the pain of a wound. They may use beautiful daydreams to escape their desolate reality, or intellectualization and abstraction to depersonalize the issue. Frequently, too, they may transform an oppressive tragedy through the power of humor. Cyrulnik claims that all children who survive trauma combine intellectualization and dreaming. Intellectualization tells them why they suffer, while dreams provide a safe hiding place in which they can be happy. One of us, Christine, is aware that this strategy has been operating all her life, and is still mildly active despite many years of healing work. This dissociation from reality is a triumph of the human spirit for those who manage to rise above their sufferings and lead a normal life. But many remain permanently dissociated. They become dysfunctional to a greater or lesser extent, and often feel that a part of themselves is missing. On the other hand, Cyrulnik observes that children who fail to escape reality in this way are overwhelmed by their bleak and meaningless world.

Whatever defense mechanisms we use, locking traumas away takes a lot of energy, and saps our vitality. Thus, even those who emerge from traumatic experiences apparently unharmed are actually impaired unless the energy of arousal trapped by these defense mechanisms is released. They may not suffer from diagnosable disorders, and may lead apparently normal lives, but frequently develop emotional and behavioral patterns that limit their lives.[20] Truly resilient people do more then merely survive their ordeals. They are able to reintegrate their fractured selves by discharging the energy of trauma.

Trauma and Fear in the Modern World

On the face of it, there may seem to be no reason why most of us who live in the peaceful, affluent democracies of Europe and North America should be traumatized and live in terror. However, as infants many of us experienced separation from our mothers soon after birth, schedule feeding, and being left to cry ourselves to sleep. This was, and often still is, standard practice. But, from the infant's point of view, it is terrifying to be apart from its mother, and life-threatening not to be fed when hungry, or held when distressed. Such experiences have serious effects on brain development, and set lifelong patterns of response to stress.

Parents are not to blame for these traumas. They mostly do their best with inadequate training by following social customs and imitating the way they were brought up themselves. Often, mothers are anxious, stressed out, and struggling with their own traumas, while the fathers are emotionally and/or physically absent. As a result, many parents feel hostile, angry and resentful towards their children, sometimes leading to neglect, or emotional, verbal, physical or sexual abuse. All-too-many children are punished for minor 'offences', humiliated, criticized, beaten or raped. Layer upon layer of trauma and fear is built on these foundations throughout childhood and adolescence through bullying, sexual harassment, teasing and other torments.

Later, adolescents must make their way in the adult world, often without family support. They may repeat their parents' patterns of abusive relationships, or experience demeaning and exploitive work. They may have to cope with serious illness or disability, death of loved ones, a natural disaster, or other catastrophe. Our deepest fear is of annihilation, not so much of the body, but of who we are, of our sense of identity. As Sue Gerhardt expressed it: "The essential aspect of trauma is that it generates doubts about surviving – either as a body, but equally as a psychological self."[21] Modern civilization is a particularly threatening environment for the core self. Our individualistic, competitive world lacks strong family or community support structures, or even stable employment opportunities, and our intimate relationships are expected to bear more than they can carry. We are left to sink or swim in the tide of mass society.

Julia's Experiences in Baghdad

Julia spent a year in military service in Baghdad, but for 6 months after her return she did not sleep well, was filled with rage at friends and family, and fought the impulse to commit suicide—all symptoms of PTSD. This extract from her story is taken from an article by Paula Caplan.[22]

"Iraq was terrifying because I had no idea how to explain my feelings," Julia said. "There were all those explosions, and my regular assignment was doing pat down searches of Iraqis who might have been friends or might have been wearing explosives. If a pat had located a bomb," she explained, "before my mind registered it, I'd have been dead. And it was rough when this larger-than-life soldier we all loved died from a roadside bomb. But I keep thinking how many thousands of soldiers have gone through this and been just fine. Not a single soldier in Iraq ever told me they were scared or angry or crazy. They were sad when the big guy died, but nobody lost control."

The thought of "maybe if I kill myself, I'll stop feeling so angry and will be able to get some sleep" churned constantly through her mind. Julia considered therapy but feared "seeing a military shrink, because that could wreck my plan to retire on a nice pension when my twenty years in the Army National Guard are up." ...

Private therapists are expensive, but for six weeks, Julia saw "a very nice psychologist" and talked about her emotional numbness, which alternated between rage and despair. The therapist encouraged her to let her guard down. But Julia clung to the numbness, believing it protected people from her irrational anger. She also thought, "If I'm redeployed, I can't have my feelings exploding all the time."

Military ethos discourages soldiers from talking about their fear, frustration, helplessness, and uncertainty about the progress of the war. Julia only once told someone about her feelings. While doing pat searches, she had said to a soldier, "Any of those people could kill us." He responded, "Aw, no, they won't!" Never again did she say anything less than gung-ho about her work. In no official or unofficial instruction did her sergeant or commanding officer say these reactions were normal. Someone would occasionally say that anyone who felt depressed or anxious should tell their squad leader who would send that person to a chaplain or counselor, but the nonverbal message was that needing help was unsoldierly. For the men, it was unmanly. For the women, it proved that women should not be soldiers."

Healing began unexpectedly when Julia spoke about her experiences to a college class who showed compassion and wanted to understand.

4. The Symptoms and Effects of Trauma

The Range of Effects

Trauma occurs when the arousal due to a threat or stress fails to return to base level once the event is over. Thus, chronic hyper-arousal is a fundamental symptom or effect of trauma. Another way of looking at this is that trauma happens when our emotional responses to an event are stored in the brain and body, ready to be reactivated by similar future events, instead of dissipating and leaving us with only the cognitive memory of what happened. These emotions may be held as patterns in the brain, as tensions in muscles and organs, in the balance of hormones, or even in the expression of genes. We survive, but at a cost in emotional and physical energy that impacts on our psychological, emotional and physical well-being.

The effects of trauma can be dramatic and severe, including dangerous violence, insomnia, nightmares, and phobias. But the majority of people process PTEs without suffering clinical disorder. They remember and talk about what happened, make sense of it, have appropriate feelings about it, and appear to put it behind them. But this does not necessarily mean they do not suffer long-term harmful effects. It may simply be that the effects remain below the threshold for diagnosing a disorder, and they are able to continue functioning more or less normally. Most, perhaps all, of us hold some traumatic memories which surface from time to time in broken sleep and nightmares, inappropriate and embarrassing outbursts of anger or aggression, addictions, or in other ways. Many people's careers and relationships are significantly disrupted by such unwanted patterns of behavior and emotional triggers. Further, we believe that what is regarded as 'normal' is significantly biased by the large fraction of the population whose behavior is affected by such sub-clinical trauma.

Trauma in early life can impair the development of our brains and psyches, with lifelong consequences. Later, it can shatter trust in others and the world. It can prevent us fulfilling our dreams and ambitions, and block access to higher states of consciousness. It can wreck our intimate relationships and social networks, leaving us feeling isolated and abandoned. In extreme cases, it can lead to suicide. Some of the more specific symptoms and effects of trauma are listed in Table 3.[1] Note that many of them correspond to problems in the world today. This does not mean that trauma is the direct cause of everything that is wrong in the world. But the results of many studies clearly show that it is a significant contributory factor in many of the issues we face.

Traumatic Reality

Peter Levine describes at some length what it is like to suffer severe trauma.[2] Some of the energy of hyper-arousal is channeled into a persistent, compulsive search for the source of the threat, even when there is none, causing muscle tension in the head, neck and eyes. As the compulsion builds in intensity, the brain may interpret any change as a threat. Even sexual arousal, or a caffeine shot may set off fears that appear paranoid. Unable to unwind, we become overloaded and confused, incapable of taking in new information, learning or breaking out of dysfunctional patterns. Ordinary situations may become nightmares of frustration, anger and anxiety, leaving us helpless and unable to participate fully in life. Any new event tips us into frozen immobility, not able to see or take advantage of any opportunity to escape. Besides feeling helpless, we may experience anxiety, rage, terror, panic, shame, numbness, depression, and a loss of identity. The stress of keeping the energy contained may lead to psychosomatic illnesses including blindness, deafness, inability to speak, paralysis of limbs, chronic back and neck pain, chronic fatigue, bronchitis, asthma, gastrointestinal problems, migraines and many others. Victims

Table 3: Some Symptoms and Effects of Trauma

Developmental	Excessive fear of death	*Behavioral*
Stunted brain	Feelings of isolation,	Violence and aggression
Learning difficulties	alienation	Abusive behaviors
Repression of sexuality	Emotional outbursts	Low stress tolerance
	Muted emotions	Insomnia
Psychological	Abrupt mood swings	Inflexibility, lack of
Psychological armoring	Guilt, shame	spontaneity
Repression of emotions	Lack of empathy and	Fussiness
Acute sensitivity to light	compassion	Phobias (Claustrophobia,
and sound	Emotional dependency	agoraphobia, etc)
Post-Traumatic Stress	Inability to express	Sexual inhibition or
Disorder	emotions	exaggeration
Denial of problem	Emotionally cold	Suicidal tendencies
Blaming others	relationships	Critical, judgmental
Amnesia, mental blanks		Inability to cooperate, or
Nightmares	*Health*	share
Flashbacks	Stress	Antisocial; excessive
Panic attacks and phobias	Muscular tension	shyness
Low self-esteem, self-	Migraine headaches	Destructive intimate
confidence	Frequent 'viral' illnesses	relationships
Depression	Back pain, arthritis and	Substance abuse
Schizophrenia	other physical problems	Overeating
Bipolar disorder	Digestive problems	Excessive consumerism
Attention Deficit	Immune and endocrine	Gambling
Hyperactivity Disorder	system disorders	Attraction to danger
Hyper-vigilance	Allergies	Patterns of behavior that
	Auto-immune diseases	create repeated trauma
Emotional	Some cancers	Excessive infant crying,
Excessive, unjustified	Chronic fatigue, low	distress
anger	energy	Hyperactivity
Aggression		Child misbehavior,
Unreasonable fear,		including ADHD
anxiety		Traumatize own children

may deny that they have such problems, not because they are dishonest, but because denial is an important survival mechanism for them.

These symptoms may constitute a living hell, as Levine imaginatively portrays:[3]

I don't know of one thing I don't fear. I fear getting out of bed in the morning. I fear walking out of my house. I have great fears of death ... not that I will die someday, but that I am going to die within the next few minutes. I fear anger ... my own and everyone else's, even when anger is not present. I fear rejection and/or abandonment. I fear success and failure. I get pain in my chest, and tingling and numbness in my arms and legs every day. I almost daily experience cramps ranging from menstrual-type cramps to intense pain. I just really hurt most of the time. I feel that I can't go on. I have headaches. I feel nervous all the time. I have shortness of breath, racing heart, disorientation, and panic. I'm always cold, and I have dry mouth. I have trouble swallowing. I have no energy or motivation, and when I do accomplish something, I feel no sense of satisfaction. I feel overwhelmed, confused, lost, helpless, and hopeless daily. I have uncontrollable outbursts of rage and depression.

In her monumental work, *Beyond Fear,* psychologist Dorothy Rowe goes further. She argues persuasively that most mental disorders are actually strategies for dealing with fear, and the consequent stresses of life.[4] In this category, she includes depression, anxiety, obsessive-compulsive disorders, bipolar disorder, phobias and schizophrenia. Even the rising levels of autism have been tentatively linked to overwhelming fear based on a study of rats.[5] Further, in an article in New Scientist magazine, Rowe forcefully pointed out that the symptoms of Attention Deficit Hyperactivity Disorder (ADHD) are essentially the same as those of fear.[6] In other words, the millions of children being treated with powerful drugs for this 'disorder' may simply be "very afraid." Similarly, Bruce Perry of the ChildTrauma Academy claims that many of the children diagnosed with ADHD or learning difficulties are suffering from trauma. Millions of them have been "literally incubated in terror."[7] With their brains in a terrified hyper-vigilant state, they are jumpy and simply unable to sit still and focus on intellectual learning.[8] In one of his many papers Perry wrote: "Terror, chaos and threat permeate the lives of too many children—millions of children across the globe each year have tiny pieces of their potential chipped away by fear. Fear inhibits exploration, fear inhibits learning, and fear inhibits opportunity."[9]

Psychosomatic Disorders

As already noted, trauma and associated emotions such as fear and anger can cause physical diseases as well as psychiatric disorders. John Sarno is a back specialist at the New York University School of Medicine.[10] He has concluded that the epidemic of back pain in the USA is not due to physical deterioration, but is caused by repressed emotions, particularly rage. He decided he would only treat someone if they could accept that this might be true for them. Amongst this select group of about half the applicants, he achieves a 90% cure rate. Sarno argues that repression of traumatic experiences, fear and other unacceptable emotions is responsible for other painful conditions such as repetitive strain injury, sciatica, neck pain and headache, as well as many digestive, respiratory and reproductive disorders, allergies, skin conditions and other complaints. Trauma therapist, Babette Rothschild concurs: "It is possible that certain unexplainable physical symptoms that puzzle doctors and plague patients may be incidents of somatic (i.e. bodily) re-enactment (of a traumatic experience)".[11]

This association of trauma with physical and psychiatric disorders is supported by Wilhelm Reich's theory of psychological armoring.[12] Little-known today, Reich was a prominent student of Freud, and an important figure in the development of psychoanalysis. He believed that our deepest biological drives are to seek pleasure and avoid pain, as expressed in the infant's desire to suck, his pleasure in defecation and genital play, her joy in loving physical contact, and in the sexual urges of the adolescent and adult. If this sensuality is repeatedly punished or neglected, the child learns to associate her natural impulses with pain. The result is repression of his desires, and anger against the cause of repression. The blocked drives do not disappear, however. They become overlaid with secondary drives associated with anxiety, fear and anger that corrode the individual from within, or eventually explode in violent, antisocial, sadistic, destructive and deceitful behaviors.

In Reich's opinion, repression of sexuality is of particular importance because blocking this powerful drive often leads to violence when the pent-up inner tension can no longer be contained. He concluded that full discharge of sexual energy at orgasm is only possible when the feelings of both tender love and erotic excitement are present. When intercourse is accompanied by fear, anxiety, anger, aggression, or a lack of feeling, there is a residual frustration, and undischarged sexual tension.

The energy of a repressed impulse or emotion is held in the body by chronic tensions in the muscle groups which normally express that drive. Such tensions are visible to the trained eye in our posture, mannerisms and gestures, and in the way we move and talk. In other words, every psychological problem has a corresponding physical expression. Common symptoms identified by Reich include shallow breathing, stiffness in the pelvic region, back pain, tight stomach, poor muscle tone, and reduced physical sensation. Reich called this repression of the primary drives 'armoring' to reflect the stiff carapace of tense muscles, the defensive attitudes, and the resistance to feeling or expressing emotions. When we experience repeated traumas, this armoring becomes permanent, and "we live as mere shadows of our deeper selves, the armor sapping our strength, pleasure and joy in life."[13] Reich found that specific emotions can be released by applying gentle pressure to the muscle groups that hold them, after which the posture changes, breathing deepens, and secondary behaviors cease.

How could we possibly live in a society so permeated by fear, and other negative emotions without realizing it? With regards to children, Dorothy Rowe argues that psychiatrists simply do not know enough about the lives of their young clients to understand what is going on, parents are often oblivious, and children are too afraid of adults to open up. It is easy to blame psychiatrists who have focused almost exclusively on a medical approach that identifies symptoms, pigeon-holes clients with diagnoses, and treats them with drugs that relieve the symptoms. It is similarly easy to blame parents for neglect and abuse of their children when most are doing their best with inadequate training and social support, while coping with the effects of their own traumas. But we all share responsibility by our willingness to accept the level of fear and trauma in society without protest.

Billy Connolly's Childhood

Scottish comedian Billy Connolly was severely abused as a child, as his wife, Pamela Stephenson, relates in her biography.[14] At 4, Billy's mother deserted him and his sister. They were taken in by two aunts, one of whom took out her frustrations on Billy.

At first it was verbal abuse. She called him a 'lazy good-for-nothing', pronounced that he would 'come to nothing', and that it was 'a sad day' when she met him. She soon moved on to inflicting humiliation on Billy, her favorite method being grabbing him by the back of his neck and rubbing his soiled underpants in his face. She increased her repertoire to whacking his legs, hitting him with wet cloths, kicking him, and pounding him on the head with high-heeled shoes. She would usually wait until they were alone, then corner and thrash him four or five times a week for years on end.

Billy, however, had been in a few scraps in the school playground and had decided that a smack in the mouth wasn't all that painful. The more experience he had of physical pain, the more he felt he could tolerate it. 'What's the worst she could do to me?' he would ask himself. 'She could descend on me and beat the shit out of me ... but a couple of guys have done that to me already and it wasn't that bad ... I didn't die or anything'.

In fact, the more physical, emotional and verbal abuse he received, the more he expected it, eventually believing what they were telling him: that he was useless and worthless and stupid, a fear he keeps in a dark place even today.

Bruce Perry, of the ChildTrauma Academy, argues that kids like Billy can escape becoming violent criminals if there is some element of hope in their lives.[15] In Billy's case, hope came from the love of his older sister, the Scout movement, and teachers he admired who were funny and smart, and encouraged his own humor.

5. Collective and Generational Trauma

Individualism and Collective Trauma

So far we have focused on individual trauma, such as childhood abuse or an accident. But many traumas are collective, arising from experiences common to a family, a community, an ethnic group, a nation, or even our species. We have devoted relatively little space to this aspect, not because it is unimportant, but because most trauma research comes from individualistic western cultures. From their perspective, society appears to be an assemblage of individuals, and collective trauma tends to be seen as little more than the sum of individual traumas. We interact with each other, changing the world and being changed by it, but we see ourselves as independent beings, pursuing our own destinies. We see ourselves as playing out our personal dramas in the context of the world, rather than being integral, inseparable parts of it.

Despite this viewpoint, many traumatic events do affect the community or society as a whole—even in the USA, the heartland of individualism. The Vietnam war did more than traumatize individual returned servicemen. It had a deep impact on a whole generation of American society and its values. Hurricane Katrina did not simply disrupt the lives of the citizens of New Orleans. It transformed the city's character and way of being. Mass shootings at neighborhood schools do more than distress grieving parents. They change the community in fundamental ways. After the 9/11 attack on the World Trade Center, most people coped as individuals, many with support from their families and therapists. At the collective level, fear led people willingly to trade valued freedoms for a greater sense of security. But the basic fabric of society was not torn. There was no need to rebuild American culture and society.

Communal Cultures and Collective Trauma

Communal cultures view the world quite differently to individualistic ones, as shown in Table 4.[1] To them, personal identity is inseparable from the family, community and society, just as an organ is inseparable from the body. The boundary between the self and other is blurred, with the family and community forming part of a person's self-identity and consciousness. Individuals derive their sense of meaning and purpose from the group, and trauma is experienced through it. Such peoples tend to cope with trauma through cooperation and mutual support, and by finding a common meaning for their plight. When the

Table 4: Individual v. Communal Ways of Thinking

(Adapted from Ratnavale 2007)

Individual	*Communal*
Thinks in terms of 'I'	Thinks in terms of 'we'
Emphasizes uniqueness	Emphasizes commonality
Independent self	Inter-dependent self
Self and immediate family	Extended family, community
Individual ownership	Shared resources
Competes with or controls nature	Cooperate with nature
Confrontational	Yielding
Speak one's mind	Speak one's mind with caution
Narcissistic	Self-effacing
More extroverted	More introverted
Adventurous, self-starter	Group initiative
Encourages risk-taking	Exercises caution
Single God	Multiple gods

group recovers, the individual tends to improve as well.[2]

Shared loss and grief often unite a community in cooperative efforts to rebuild. Equally, collective trauma can fracture traditional bonds so that the society disintegrates into chaos as

Table 5: Symptoms of Collective Trauma

(Adapted from Ratnavale 2007)

Deep mistrust of self, others, even family	Loss of traditional values, desecration of land and institutions
Fear and anticipation of betrayal	A conspiracy of silence; attitude of secrecy
Shame and humiliation	
Violence against women	Substance abuse
Self-directed violence: suicide, risk-taking	Unremitting grief
	Intergenerational conflict
	Sexual abuse
	Leadership vacuum

indicated by the symptoms in Table 5. The fate of the nomadic Ik people of East Africa provides a graphic example, as told by Colin Turnbull in *The Mountain People*.[3] Forced from their land and struck by drought, this happy, cooperative tribe descended into appalling barbarism. Such collective trauma occurs when the continuity and integrity of a society is threatened. The culture may be literally shattered, and the individual's sense of identity, meaning and purpose lost along with it. When this happens, the society can no longer explain what is happening, nor bring any meaning to their suffering. Daya Somasundaram describes collective trauma as wounding or tearing the social fabric, with negative impacts on social bonds, processes, networks, relationships, institutions, functions, dynamics, practices, capital and resources. He goes on to argue that individual trauma in traditional cultures can be understood only within the context of the family, group, village, community and society.[4] This is illustrated by the impact of the Exxon Valdez disaster in 1989 on native Aleuts in Alaska. Mary de Young describes how the massive oil spill killed fish, birds and animals that lay at the heart of the community's identity, social structure and ideology, and that symbolized their culture for future generations. Not surprisingly, the Aleuts suffered twice the level of psychiatric disorders as other inhabitants of the area.[5]

Collective Trauma and Cultural Memory

Daya Somasundaram notes that most modern wars are about control and assimilation of minority groups into the dominant culture of a nation. The fighting occurs in occupied areas, and 90% of the casualties are civilians. Intimidation and terror are increasingly used as weapons.[6] The result is cultural disintegration as in Bosnia, Rwanda, Sri Lanka and many other places. In the words of Mary de Young, cultures are reduced to "meaningless customs, pointless rituals and vague collective memories." Trust gives way to suspicion and paranoia. Aggression replaces nurturance and support. And the loss of identity and meaning opens the door to fierce nationalism, tribalism, fundamentalism and other regressive forces.[7] In the words of Peter Levine:[8]

Trauma is among the most important root causes for the form modern warfare has taken. The perpetuation, escalation and violence of war can be attributed in part to post-traumatic stress. Our past encounters with one another have generated a legacy of fear, separation, prejudice and hostility. This legacy is a legacy of trauma no different from that experienced by individuals — except in its scale.

Traumatic re-enactment is one of the strongest and most enduring reactions that occurs in the wake of trauma. Once we are traumatized it is almost certain that we will continue to repeat or re-enact parts of the experience in some way. We will be drawn over and over again into situations that are reminiscent of the original trauma. When people are traumatized by war, the implications are staggering.

When we have been traumatized, we become hyper-vigilant,

looking for an enemy, and desperately searching for the source of the threat. If peoples living in the same area have different languages, colors, religions or ethnic traditions, the 'cause' of the threat is obvious. Out of fear, they slaughter each other and "destroy each other's homes and dreams. ... they kill their own futures."[9]

Cultural memories of collective trauma may go back centuries. Kept alive in myths and ceremonies, they are passed from generation to generation. They feed the desire for vengeance, block the path to reconciliation, and continue to fuel conflicts today. Israeli aggression against the Palestinians and neighboring countries can be traced to the collective trauma of the Holocaust; the ghettos, pogroms and forced conversions of history; the diaspora of Roman days, and even to Old Testament tales of captivity and oppression thousands of years ago. Similarly, the memory of the Serbs' defeat at the battle of Kosovo more than 600 years ago was used to unite them against a modern 'enemy'. The troubles in Northern Ireland had their roots in the historical relationship between England and Ireland stretching back to the 17th century and before. And the genocidal frenzy of the Hutus in Rwanda was a response to centuries of domination by the Tutsis.

Not all collective memories of trauma involve war and domination. Many are of long-gone volcanic explosions, earthquakes, famines, plagues and other disasters that still deeply affect their worldviews, attitudes to life, and social structures and norms. Similarly, not all collective traumas are ancient. Many new ones are being created almost daily, the memories of which will have unimaginable consequences for the future of humanity. As we write in mid-2009, 2 million refugees from the Swat region of Pakistan are fearfully trickling back home after the proclaimed defeat of the Taliban in their homeland. In Afghanistan, untold numbers continue to be traumatized by conflict, and seemingly indiscriminate bombing. Millions of Tamils in Sri Lanka are beginning to rebuild their lives after decades of bitter civil war. The suffering continues in Darfur, Somalia, and too many other conflict zones. Elsewhere, communities are struggling to recover from natural disasters: the 2004 tsunami in south-east Asia, the 2008 hurricane in Burma, and earthquakes in Pakistan, China, Italy and elsewhere. In yet other places, indigenous peoples worldwide are fighting for their lands and their lives, and whole towns and villages are being displaced to make way for dams, mines, industrial developments, tourist resorts, and commercial plantations.

Generational Transmission of Trauma

Once a people has been traumatized, that trauma is often passed from generation to generation in self-perpetuating cycles that are hard to break. A war veteran with PTSD may withdraw and be emotionally remote at times. At others, his rage may terrorize his wife and children. When they grow up, his children may unwittingly re-enact their trauma, and the patterns of family relationships they have learned. [10] As a result they damage their own offspring, and the trauma passes to the next generation through family traditions of child-rearing, ways of relating, and associated beliefs and stories. Research is also slowly revealing that trauma may be inherited through epigenetic modification of gene expression—a topic we will discuss later in the book.

Beyond the family, traumatic events experienced by many people may become embedded in the collective psyche of the community or society. We pass them to our descendants in the form of myths, stories, histories, poems, dramas, songs, proverbs, 'common sense', cultural beliefs, rituals, ceremonies, norms of behavior, and even in laws and social institutions. As a recent example, the Al-Qaeda attacks mean that American and European children now grow up in an atmosphere of increased fear and distrust, particularly of Moslems and those of middle-eastern appearance. This is reflected in laws and institutions that support obsessive security precautions, increased surveillance of public places, monitoring of some private communications, and reduced freedoms. These responses to collective trauma have already changed the western democratic way of life, and are likely to have further significant impacts on future generations.

Societies are normally conservative. They change their basic worldview, beliefs, moral code and norms of behavior only slowly with time. And the store of recorded history, art and literature teaches us about our ancestors' experiences, including their traumas. Hence, the culture we absorb in childhood carries with it the legacy of past generations upon which we can build the future. But all too often today societies are so fragmented by trauma that this foundation is lost. Many cultures have broken down, or are breaking down, under the destructive pressures of war, ethnic cleansing, genocide, suppression of minorities, displacement of populations, famine, extreme poverty, HIV, natural disasters, technological and economic change, and other collective traumas. Whole generations are growing up immersed in violence, and without the guidance of a traditional culture. Somehow, out of this social chaos they have to create new homes, new livelihoods, and new ways of relating to each other, and to their enemies. But the only models they have to work with are those of violence, destruction and chaos.

One Morning in Afghanistan

It takes little imagination to understand the depth of the collective trauma suffered by the village in Afghanistan that is the subject of this brief, heart-rending story. It happened in December 2008.[11]

It was 7.30 on a hot July morning when the plane came swooping low over the remote ravine. Below, a bridal party was making its way to the groom's village in an area called Kamala, in the eastern province of Nangarhar, to prepare for the celebrations later that day.

The first bomb hit a large group of children who had run on ahead of the main procession. It killed most of them instantly.

A few minutes later, the plane returned and dropped another bomb, right in the centre of the group. This time the victims were almost all women. Somehow the bride and two girls survived but as they scrambled down the hillside, desperately trying to get away from the plane, a third bomb caught them. Hajj Khan was one of four elderly men escorting the bride's party that day.

"We were walking, I was holding my grandson's hand, then there was a loud noise and everything went white. When I opened my eyes, everybody was screaming. I was lying meters from where I had been, I was still holding my grandson's hand but the rest of him was gone. I looked around and saw pieces of bodies everywhere. I couldn't make out which part was which."

Relatives from the groom's village said it was impossible to identify the remains. They buried the 47 victims in 28 graves.

6. Healing Trauma

What is Healing?

Traumas form a spectrum. At one end are severe disorders such as PTSD and other mental illnesses and at the other are people who are normal but prevented from achieving their full potential or higher states of consciousness. Not surprisingly, therefore, there are different levels of healing. All trauma therapies focus on returning dysfunctional people to normal life. Healing enables them to cope with the demands of daily living, a job, and relationships with family and friends without being triggered into disruptive violence or phobias, nor into outbursts of anger, fear or other strong emotions. Many therapies also recognize the importance of existential healing—that is, helping clients to find meaning in their suffering, integrate it into their worldview, and create a new sense of personal identity. In our view, however, the ultimate goal of healing is to remove the barriers to self-actualization, or to what many spiritual traditions call enlightenment. This is the level of healing which will empower humanity to overcome the crisis of civilization, and open the way to evolution of the possible human. There are relatively few therapists who are able to act as guides at this level, which is traditionally the domain of spiritual teachers and practices such as meditation and service.

What does it mean to be healed? In essence, it means that unwanted and disruptive emotional patterns and behaviors due to past traumatic experiences cease to happen. The alarm buttons that used to trigger automatic responses to certain stimuli are inactivated. The person who suffered from claustrophobia no longer panics when entering an enclosed space. The war veteran no longer hits the deck when a firework goes off. The husband no longer explodes with rage when his wife is late with dinner or his infant cries. They become free to respond rationally and appropriately to such situations.

Conscious memories of a traumatic experience are not usually affected by healing. We can still recall the event and think about it when we wish. But its emotional power to affect the present goes, together with any associated physical symptoms. However, many people do not remember the original traumatic events—amnesia being one of the commonest symptoms of trauma. In these cases, repressed memories may be opened up by healing, or they may remain hidden. The latter is particularly likely when the trauma occurred in the womb or early infancy before cognitive memory developed. Most of us hope for explicit memories and the self-understanding that may come with them, but they are not necessary. Indeed, Peter Levine argues that the cortex's drive to explain and understand may obstruct the reptilian brain's impulse to heal by releasing the energy of arousal. To escape hyper-arousal, we need to suspend thinking, and allow the lower brain to act.[1]

Trauma Healing in Wild Animals and Humans

Wild animals do not seem to suffer from trauma to the extent that humans do. They tremble and twitch as they emerge from the immobility of the freeze response, thus releasing the energy aroused. Afterwards, they appear to return to normal. Similarly, young animals may playfully re-enact a narrow escape to sharpen their survival skills and diffuse the terror of the experience.[2]

Shamanic hunter-gatherer societies used similar strategies. They recognized the reality of traumatic stress, and accepted fear, trembling, nightmares and other symptoms as normal. Emotional and spiritual wounds were acknowledged, sufferers were encouraged to share their pain, and the tribe performed healing ceremonies. Energy discharge was facilitated by trance states induced by storytelling, dramatic re-enactment, ritual, dancing, singing, drumming and, sometimes, by psycho-active herbs. During this process the sufferer trembled and shook. When necessary, a shaman would travel into the spirit world to retrieve lost parts of the sufferer's soul.[3]

In contrast, ever since The Fall, most cultures have sung the praises of the great hero, bloody but unbowed in the face of overwhelming odds. Often, too, they have frowned on any expression of natural feelings after a potentially traumatic experience, particularly by men. To cry or express fears, to admit to insomnia and nightmares is to be seen as inadequate. We still tend to admire a stiff upper lip, and discourage the weakness of trembling. But this bold front comes at the cost of trapping trauma, with its physical, psychological and social consequences.

Healing Collective and Generational Trauma

In some ways, healing collective trauma is not that different to healing individual trauma. After all, those involved have their own personal histories of pain and loss that must be healed. Until this individual rage and desire for revenge is released, it is impossible to reach reconciliation, forgiveness and justice at the collective level. Also, collective healing becomes easier as individuals start to heal, and become more willing to share and discuss their common feelings, fears, pain and loss. And as the collective slowly heals, growing awareness and sharing of their common suffering provides a supportive context for individual healing, too.

Thus, the two levels of healing intertwine and are complementary. But there are also differences that demand different approaches. The sheer scale of the problem when thousands or even millions of individuals suffer the aftermath of a natural disaster, war or genocide make it impossible to heal all such traumas one by one. There are also major differences in the nature of the healing required. A whole village and way of life may have been destroyed, and need rebuilding. Cultural beliefs, values, attitudes, and norms of behavior may have been shattered, leaving a void which must be filled by new under-standings, meanings, myths and rituals. Deep fear and distrust of other religions, races or ethnic groups may need to be faced and resolved so that co-existence and cooperation can be re-established. Often, these are generational as well as collective traumas, and centuries of conflict, exploitation and prejudice may need to be overcome.

Collective traumas vary widely in scale and impact. Some, such as a playground shooting, have a severe impact on a small group. By contrast, millions were involved in the Rwandan genocide and the Sri Lankan war, often becoming destitute refugees. Whole peoples, such as Native Americans and Australian Aborigines, have suffered collective and generational trauma for hundreds of years. And the German nation is still coming to terms with the trauma of responsibility for two world wars and the holocaust. Each of these events demands a different approach to healing, which we will discuss in Part VI.

The Healing of Tom Brown Jr.

In Chapter 1, we quoted Tom Brown Jr.'s account of being attacked by a feral dog. In the years that followed, he had other encounters. Once, he was trapped by a pack up a tree for days before he found a way to escape. This second extract from his book tells of another adventure when he and his friend Rick escaped by scaling the wall of a deep excavation, leaving a pack of 15 ravenous dogs trapped in the bottom. Tom tells how this led to healing of his trauma.[4]

We sat ... looking down at the dogs who were now at our mercy as I had been at theirs when I was in the tree. ... I sat looking at them and what came to mind was ... that face of fangs that had come leaping at me out of the bushes years before. The terror had long since turned to smoldering anger, and I looked down at the dogs with a hatred and rage I had never let myself feel before. ...

All the fear ... that came to the surface only in dreams, welled up in me, and I lifted a huge log above my head and stood looking down at the dogs. I hated them at that moment in a way I could not understand then, though I have come now to realize that hate is just fear worn inside out, and it was my fear, not my hatred, that drove me.
...
I heaved the log with all my strength.
It fell in the middle of the dogs ... but it did not hit any of them. I turned to pick up another. ... The dogs were trapped, they had no chance. It did not seem right to slaughter them like that. But ... that ghost dog leapt snarling at my face ... I picked up a piece of cinderblock ... There would be no random miss this time.
But as I lifted the cinderblock, the dog looked up at me with his head cocked and the anger drained out of me. He looked not like a wild dog but like my own dog. I let the cinderblock drop and turned away. ... When I looked back down at the dogs I saw them in a new way, ... doing their job in the pattern of things ... There was no killing them after that. But there was no leaving them there either.

Tom and Rick dropped food to the dogs, and rubble to make a ramp so they could climb the side of the pit. The final piece was an old refrigerator. Tom dropped it over the edge and then ran for his life before the dogs could catch him. He continues his story:

The dogs sounded as if they were right on top of me when I noticed that they were running along with me. ... I was so surprised that they hadn't attacked me, that I stopped running and drew the machete. But the dogs stopped when I stopped, and pranced around wagging their tails. I couldn't believe it. They trotted around nice as house dogs.

Closure to Part I

This introduction to trauma leaves us with many questions.

- Why do humans suffer so much from trauma?
- Why do we so often block natural healing mechanisms?
- How do we manage to repress our trauma so effectively?

- How has the course of human history been shaped by our experience of trauma, our attitudes to it, and our ways of dealing with it?
- Why have civilizations since The Fall repressed trauma?
- Why do most humans today suffer from some degree of trauma?
- What impact does trauma have on the world today?
- What is trauma's role in the current crisis of civilization?

- How can we as individuals and as a civilization become aware of and open to the reality of trauma?
- How can we overcome the denial that prevents many people from acknowledging their trauma?
- How can we prevent the transmission of trauma between generations?
- How can we minimize the creation of fresh trauma?
- How can we heal trauma in ourselves as individuals?
- How can communities, ethnic groups, nations and our civilization prevent and heal collective trauma?

These are the subjects of the rest of the book. We cannot answer all of these questions—no-one can—but at least we can open some of the key issues to the air and light.

Part II. The Human Brain and Mind

We start our search for answers about the role of trauma with an inquiry into the nature and evolution of the human brain and mind.

- How do they differ from those of other animals?
- When did those differences appear?
- What effects did they have on the evolution of culture and civilization?
- What implications do they have for the future?

There are written records for only a tiny fraction of the time that humans have walked the Earth, and archaeological evidence for the earliest times is sparse. Also, the interpretation of archaeological data is riddled with uncertainty. Even the best scientific methods of dating cannot tell us the exact sequence of events. Still more challenging is working out the significance of many finds. We can only conjecture why a cave wall was painted, and what the images meant to the painters. Sometimes, we can only guess what they represent. Inevitably, we interpret the factual archaeological evidence in the context of our own culture, and our observations of modern indigenous societies.

In his carefully argued book, *The Origins of Human Society,* Peter Bogucki wrote: "Archaeological data are frequently cited as having "proven" something about life in the distant past, but these claims should be examined critically. Archaeological data are in themselves objective and concrete. Yet all interpretations of them, no matter how grounded they are in scientific method and social science theory, are always subject to revision." Later he commented that "archaeology relies on imaginative reconstruction and many intuitive leaps-of-faith in the interpretation of its data."[1]

The stories we tell in this book should be understood in this light.

7. The Evolution of the Brain and Mind

The human story began in Africa 7 million years ago when our genetic line separated from our close cousins, the chimpanzees and bonobos. Over the ages that followed, we left our forest home for the open spaces of the savannah; we started walking upright; and our brains became larger. By 2.5 million years ago we were making simple stone tools. Half a million years after that, our ancestor Homo *ergaster* exploded out of Africa. Its descendants dominated the Homo scene for over a million years, evolving into H. *heidelbergensis* in Africa, H. *erectus* in East Asia, and H. *neanderthalensis* in Europe. Homo *sapiens*, appeared some 500,000 years before present, and genetic evidence indicates that fully modern humans, Homo *sapiens sapiens*, emerged from a small group in Africa just 200,000 years ago.[1]

Another 100,000 years passed before our ancestors began to leave tell-tale traces in the archaeological record that suggest the presence of modern human minds—traces such as pendants, beads, and bone as well as stone tools, lumps of ochre, and animal parts buried with their dead. This marked the beginning of what archaeologist Steven Mithen called the 'Big Bang' of human culture, and biologist Jared Diamond referred to as the 'Great Leap Forward'.[2] This was an era of extraordinary cultural change and creativity from 60-30,000 years ago—well after our brains reached their maximum size. It was in full swing by the time of the second exodus from Africa about 50,000 years ago, following which modern humans rapidly occupied all habitable corners of the globe, displacing H. *erectus* and the Neanderthals in the process.

For almost all these millions of years our forebears lived by foraging. They gathered a wide variety of wild plant foods from many species: leaves, roots, tubers, fruits, seeds and nuts. They supplemented this vegetarian diet with meat, initially scavenged from carcasses, and later from animals they killed themselves. Meat became the primary diet in cold regions, where human bands moved constantly with the seasons, the migrations of the herds, and the changes of climate as the Earth swung in and out of ice ages. It was not until a mere 15,000 years ago that some groups began to settle in one place, and start the slow process of domesticating plants and animals that eventually led to farming.

It is clear from this time frame that hunting and gathering is the lifestyle for which evolution fitted us. The period since we became farmers and, later, city-dwellers is too short for there to have been any significant genetic evolution, and there are no signs of change in brain size and shape. Whatever sparked the explosion of cultural development and geographical expansion is not apparent in the archaeological record. Researchers are reduced to theorizing about what might have happened.

The Early Human Brain and Mind

The brain is a physical organ of the body, part of the nervous system. By contrast, the mind consists of non-physical phenomena such as thoughts, emotions, perceptions, memories, choices, and consciousness. Most scientists believe the brain is the site and source of mind, and often conflate the two. But there are reasons to believe that mind may exist independently of individual brains, and it is useful to maintain a clear distinction between the two.[3]

The evolution of the brain, or at least its size and shape, can be traced in the skull cavities of our fossilized ancestors. It had achieved its modern volume and form by 200,000 years ago. By contrast, the mind leaves no anatomical signature to reveal how it changes. In what ways are our thought processes different now from when we parted company from the other great apes? How and when did we gain our capacities for advanced language, mathematics, logical reasoning and analysis? Our artistic and technological creativity? Our ability to break the mould of old ideas, and to make connections between discrete areas of knowledge? Our curiosity, intuition, imagination and vision? Our sense of identity, meaning and purpose? Our emotions and the ability to prevent release of the threat-arousal energy that make us so vulnerable to trauma? These questions are of vital importance to our understanding of ourselves, and the planetary crisis. They cannot be answered with certainty, but we can glean hints from the anatomy of our ancestors' brains, and their tools and ways of life; from observations of the behavior of other great apes and the way their brains work; and from research into the structure and functioning of the modern human brain and mind.[4]

When the hominid line first parted from the other great apes, our minds would have been little different to theirs. On this basis, we can conclude that our forebears knew what was safe and good to eat, and where the best fruit trees were in their locality at each time of year. They made simple tools for fishing insects from their holes, cracking nuts, and similar tasks. They were curious and playful, and sometimes discovered new ways of doing things by accident. But their ability to solve new problems was limited, and they were unable to teach their skills to their young who often took years to learn them by imitation. Like us, early humans were social animals, and understood the nuances of social status, and how to maintain amicable, cooperative relationships with other members of their group. But they were also smart enough to use cunning and deceit to get food, sex and other desirable things. Mutual grooming was the most important form of social communication, but they also used a wide range of simple speech sounds.

From these beginnings, human brains and minds would have co-evolved with their habitat and way of life. As their brains became bigger, our ancestors were able to handle the complexities of social relationships in bigger groups, which helped them survive attacks by predators. But as their brains became bigger, their need for meat to feed them also grew. Before they learned to hunt and kill for themselves, that meant being clever enough to reach dead or wounded animals before other scavengers. Then, they had to dismember the carcass quickly, and carry parts to the safety of their camp or the branches of a tree before other animals arrived. They would have found sharp broken stones useful for this, and later discovered how to shatter them to make nodules that fitted their hands for cutting sinews, smashing marrow bones, or crushing roots. Sharp flakes, produced accidentally at first, would have been good for cutting and sharpening sticks. Despite these advances, it was a million more years before our ancestors were able to work out how to make an imagined shape from a flint nodule. But once they developed this skill, 1.5m years ago, they began to make stone handaxes with carefully sharpened edges. These require a highly sophisticated production process. The sequence of blows must be planned with just the right force, direction and position, followed by finishing with soft hammers of unshaped bone or wood.

Even at this stage, however, their minds had serious short-comings compared with modern humans. For another million years, they made only a few types of general purpose tools. Unlike H. *sapiens sapiens*, they failed to invent special-purpose stone blades and points, or carve bone, antler or ivory into tools such as needles and fish hooks. They never thought to fix shaped stones in shafts to make arrows, spears and axes. They made no personal ornaments or cave paintings, carved no figurines, and did not bury their dead with rituals and grave goods. All these came later at the Great Leap Forward. In our efforts to under-stand why, we need first to look at the way the human mind works.

The Modular Mind

As neuroscientists probe ever deeper into the workings of the brain, they are revealing that many specific tasks are performed in dedicated areas. Many of these modules are located in the more primitive parts of the brain which handle a wide variety of subconscious mental activities. These include receiving information from our external and internal senses, memory recall, regulation of bodily functions, and the 'flight, fight or freeze' reaction to danger. These modules are fixed by our genes, work fast, and cannot normally be switched off. They interact little with each other (e.g. sound with vision, or body temperature with taste), and their communication with the conscious mind is also limited.[5] This system is ideal for responding reliably and quickly to hazards such as a predator or a fast-moving automobile. But it lacks the intelligence to make considered judgments, or respond flexibly to complex situations.

The conscious mind is associated with the cortex, the most recent part of the brain to evolve. It integrates information from the lower levels in order to create a holistic picture of the world, think, solve problems, and plan. This processing takes time, and the cognitive mind is too slow to deal with emergencies. Hence, the activities of the conscious and subconscious minds complement each other. Like the subconscious, the cognitive mind appears to be modular. Howard Gardner has identified nine discrete types of intelligence associated with specific brain areas, and other researchers have suggested that there may be a few more.[6] They include verbal-linguistic, logical-mathematical, visual-spatial, body-kinesthetic, musical-rhythmic, interpersonal, intrapersonal, naturalist and existential. These intelligences do not impart particular skills or knowledge directly, but are innate abilities which facilitate specific types of learning. Further details are given in Appendix B.

When we think of intelligence, we normally associate it with intellectual abilities such as language, mathematics, reason, logic, and science. But some intelligences 'think' and communicate quite differently. Music uses pitch, rhythm, harmony, timbre and so on. Art uses visual images. The subconscious mind uses processes of which we are unaware to solve problems in the background. The heart, or limbic system, thinks in sequences of emotional feelings, and the body, or reptilian, brain in associations of physical sensations.[7] Our culture values cognitive intelligence above all others, and yet it has been demonstrated clearly that we cannot make decisions without emotions, and that we make better decisions on complex issues when we rely on our intuition, or 'gut feelings'.[8] These various intelligences may not always agree with each other, and we may be literally in two (or more) minds about something. For example, we may be sexually attracted (reptilian brain) to someone we do not like (limbic system, or heart) and feel confused (cortex, or rational mind).[9]

Steven Mithen suggests that the skills and information we learn may be stored in 'knowledge modules' associated with the corresponding intelligences.[10] For example, each language may have its own knowledge module linked to the linguistic intelligence; and information about the environment may be held in modules associated with the naturalist intelligence. Howard Gardner argues that everybody has all the multiple intelligences, but that some are normally better developed than others. Which intelligences become stronger depends on our genetic inheritance, and our formative experiences. As a child's brain develops, the intelligences that it uses are strengthened, and those which remain unused atrophy. Of particular importance is the resulting balance between the cortex, limbic system, and reptilian brain which determines our ability to regulate our emotions and instincts. We will return to this topic later.

The Evolution of the Mind

We cannot be sure how the modular mental structure and processes evolved, but Steven Mithen hypothesizes that there may have been three phases.[11] In the earliest phase, the mind was dominated by a multi-purpose general intelligence module that drew information from many sources. All learning happened through this general intelligence, and there were no specialized intelligences. This was slow and inefficient compared to the modern mind, but led to the gradual accumulation of knowledge on a wide variety of subjects. At this stage, knowledge about plants, say, would have been divided amongst discrete modules for identification, palatability, toxicity, time of ripening, location and other topics. In the second phase, knowledge modules based on similar types of intelligence may have begun to communicate and interact. As a result, the modules relating to plants may have become integrated under a naturalist intelligence, thus making learning faster and more effective. In a similar way, improvements in social relationships might have occurred by combining knowledge of how to identify individuals, understand their feelings, and behave sexually towards them within an interpersonal intelligence.

Steven Mithen argues that by the early stone-age, humans had developed at least verbal-linguistic, interpersonal, naturalist and physical intelligences, with their associated knowledge modules. However, their technology and culture stagnated for a million years because these intelligences did not communicate with each other. Each intelligence and its associated knowledge modules operated independently, so that ideas and information originating in one intelligence were not normally available to others. An alternative explanation of the failure to progress, suggested by Steve Taylor, is that early stone-age people did not yet connect cause and effect. To them, the world was still a magical place inhabited by nature spirits who controlled events and had to be placated through rituals and ceremonies. Hence, they never thought that they could change their world directly through their actions.[12] According to modern theories, however, even young infants have an innate ability to create 'causal maps' that enable them to predict the effects of their actions.[13] A third perspective comes from the observation that the cortex was not as strongly developed as in modern humans.[14] As a result, they would have been less able to control their emotions and instinctive behaviors, and their lives would have been governed more by instincts and feelings, and less by conscious, rational thought than is the case today.

Perhaps all these factors contributed to the lack of innovation by early stone-age humans. However, things began to change within 100,000 years of the emergence of H. *sapiens sapiens*. Mithen believes this was because the doors between specialized intelligences swung open, the connection between cause and effect was made, and rational action became more possible. Skills, knowledge and ways of learning began to be shared and integrated across intelligences, and thought became more holistic. This 'cognitive fluidity', as Steven Mithen called it, had far-reaching consequences. Our ancestors began to use their tool-making skills for social purposes by making jewelry. Similarly, combining their naturalist and physical intelligences with tool-making led to the invention of new types of hunting weapon. Cognitive fluidity also may have been the source of higher mental functions such as symbolic communication, grammatical language, and religion. More generally, the ability to mix sources of information and different types of mental process enabled them to 'think outside the box', leading to a surge of creativity.

What caused this cognitive fluidity? Mithen claims that language was the essential ingredient that made inner communication possible. Without language we cannot discuss strategies, plans, or ideas; share knowledge and experiences; communicate complex ideas to others; or coordinate more than the simplest group actions. With complex language, our thoughts and reflections can move beyond the concrete realms of images, feelings and sensations to become an inner conversation that includes abstract ideas, and logically constructed arguments. In similar vein, Jared Diamond suggests that a great advance in intelligence came with physical changes to our vocal tracts that enabled us to make subtle sounds. As he expressed it:[15]

(A) tiny change in anatomy resulting in capacity for speech would produce a huge change in behavior. With language, it takes only a few seconds to communicate the message, "Turn sharp right at the fourth tree and drive the male antelope toward the reddish boulder, where I'll hide to spear it." Without language, that message could not be communicated at all. Without language, two protohumans could not brainstorm together about how to devise a better tool, or about what a cave painting might mean.

This argument has force, but may be over-stated. Humans and other animals communicated in many ways before the Great Leap Forward, and continue to use non-verbal as well as verbal means. These include gestures, body language, grooming and dance (body-kinesthetic intelligence), symbols, icons, logos, maps, diagrams and other images (visual-spatial intelligence), and sounds such as talking drums and melody (musical intelligence). From this, it seems likely that complex internal communication between intelligences may have been common before the advent of language. In other words, language may not have initiated cognitive fluidity, but heralded a jump to more complex and abstract inner communications.

This conclusion is supported by research on vervet monkeys which showed that they have an extensive vocabulary of calls with distinct meanings. Amongst these are warnings to other members of the troop that distinguish between snakes, eagles and leopards, and evoke appropriate avoidance behaviors.[16] This indicates that vervet language connects a few different intelligences. Identifying the predator requires a detailed knowledge of nature. Issuing a warning call clearly involves both verbal-linguistic skills and interpersonal intelligence related to cooperation and survival of the troop. And taking appropriate evasive action brings the body-kinesthetic intelligence into play.

Whatever the exact evolutionary history of the human mind may be, Steven Mithen's theory provides a valuable model as we move on to examine what happened at the Great Leap Forward and afterwards.

8. The Great Leap Forward and Afterwards

The Great Leap Forward

As we have seen, the ways of life and technologies of early modern humans changed little for hundreds of thousands of years. But things speeded up once Homo *sapiens sapiens* appeared on the scene. The first archaeological evidence of a dramatic mental transformation is indicated by new tools, jewelry, lumps of ochre, and the burial of animal parts with human bodies. By 50,000 years ago, these sparse signs had become a veritable blizzard of innovation which blew our forebears out of Africa for the second time, to colonize all corners of the Earth within a few tens of millennia.

This transformation appears in the archaeological record as a sudden explosion of innovation dubbed the 'Great Leap Forward.'[1] It happened in a blink of the evolutionary eye, but would have been imperceptible to those who lived through it. Our ancestors did not suddenly find that their children were geniuses, and they were living in a brave new world. Rather, new abilities would have been gained bit by bit over hundreds of generations. Generation after generation they would have experienced the slow rise of new mental powers and ways of thinking; a smoldering desire to experiment, try new things and explore new ideas; a steady flow of technical and cultural innovation; a growing urge to discover what lay beyond the edge of their known world.

Archaeologists tend to date the end of the Great Leap Forward at 30,000 years ago, but it may be that it has never ended. This burst of creativity was not a flash in the pan, and the pace of change is actually accelerating today with the emergence of new mental skills—such as 'living' an alternative life as an avatar in the virtual reality of Second Life—as well as lightning-fast technological and social innovation.

Before the Great Leap Forward began, our ancestors were highly conservative. If something had been done a particular way in the past, they would do it the same way again. They lacked the critical faculty to ask why it was done that way, and the imagination, reason and logic to experiment or think about other ways they might do it. After the Great Leap Forward, these barriers to innovation were gone. From 60-30,000 years ago, they created a boxful of specialized tools crafted from bone and antler as well as stone. They made personal ornaments for the first time— pendants, bracelets, and necklaces. They began to express their artistry in realistic carvings and paintings of the animals around them. They built durable shelters, and sewed clothes with bone needles and twine. They invented new hunting strategies, and designed weapons suited to each type of game. They forged larger bands, and built more complex social relationships. They began to bury their dead with rituals, and to honor their ancestors. Later, they invented pottery, agriculture, the wheel, and metallurgy; mythology and religion, writing and mathematics. And in time we created the whole panoply of technologies, arts, and social institutions that constitute modern civilization. Thousands of generations have built their innovations layer upon layer on the knowledge, ideas and skills of our forebears.

It is remarkable that this jump in mental ability happened at all, and even more remarkable that it happened when it did. This was not a time of abundance, when our ancestors would have had leisure to experiment, or indulge in art, religious speculation and ritual. Rather, it was a period of challenging change and hardship. Our species was leaving its African womb, adapting to new habitats, and confronting a planet that was sliding ineluctably into the last ice age. Indeed, the magnificent cave art of Europe was created in the depths of the ice age which peaked 20,000 years ago.

Steven Mithen's theory of cognitive fluidity provides a

coherent explanation of what may have happened. When our ancestors associated cause and effect, and their physical intelligence merged with tool-making, they began to turn flint nodules into a range of complex, specialized tools. When this skill mingled with their wealth of knowledge about nature, they would have realized that bone, antler and ivory can do things stone cannot, like forming needles and fish-hooks. Further links with musical and kinesthetic intelligences could have led to the creation of simple instruments and music; and combining visual-spatial and kinesthetic intelligences with tool-making would have opened up the world of art. Empathy with fellow humans may have emerged from communication between intrapersonal and interpersonal intelligences. The addition of naturalist intelligence may have extended that empathy and understanding to other animals, thus increasing success in the hunt. When tool-making skills coalesced with social intelligence they would have seen how personal decoration could carry information about band membership and social status. And pondering the mystery of death may have led them to provide gifts for the departed, and to honor their memory.

Over millennia, in ways such as these, we can imagine our forebears gradually integrating knowledge from many modules and intelligences, opening up new ways of thinking, new subjects of thought, and a new curiosity, creativity and consciousness. In sum, the power of the cortex exploded as cognitive fluidity opened new channels of communication. As a result, the cortex began to control older emotional and instinctive parts of the mind.

Cognitive Fluidity and Emotional Intelligence
The mental revolution of the Great Leap Forward has carried us from primitive stone-age hunting and gathering to our advanced scientific civilization. But this cognitive power has not been an unmixed blessing. On the one hand, it has given us extraordinary

cleverness. It enables us to think more complex thoughts, reason more logically, hold a more objective perspective, act more rationally, and to be less influenced by irrational fears and outdated survival instincts. On the other hand, we believe it has made us more vulnerable to trauma, and may be responsible for the lack of wisdom that threatens our very survival.

The cycle of energy arousal and discharge in response to danger is normally automatic, and controlled by the reptilian brain. But the human cortex is powerful enough to interfere with this process. We cannot prevent arousal in the first place, but we can deliberately prevent release of the energy.[2] Once trapped, this energy causes trauma, and so cognitive fluidity gave us the ability to traumatize ourselves! Another way of looking at this is that the balance between our emotional and rational minds changed. As we focused more on the intellect, we became less aware of our emotions, and less willing to express and release them. Instead of healing our emotional and psychic wounds soon after we received them, we may have begun to ignore them and hide them from others as well as ourselves. Simultaneously, our ability to repress unwanted feelings increased, and we may have chosen to do this on occasion rather than take the time and suffer the discomfort of processing them. But these traumatic emotions cannot be buried without cost. Keeping them locked in with muscle tensions constantly drains vital energy, and they resurface periodically to disrupt our lives.

After the Great Leap Forward, we were more curious and more willing to experiment and innovate. Hence, we exposed ourselves to more novel and potentially traumatic events (PTEs). It seems likely that we also became better able to anticipate the future and remember the past, increasing our ability to learn from experience, plan and innovate. However, the uncertainty of imagined futures naturally creates fear, including fear of death, pain and injury. Also, clearer memories and enhanced inner reflection may lead to guilt, shame, grievances and a desire for revenge. All such negative emotions make it more likely that a PTE will actually cause trauma.

The imbalance between our cognitive and emotional intelligences affects us in other ways too. Our culture places a high value on rational thought, and is only slowly becoming aware of the importance of emotions. Emotions shape our perceptions, direct our attention, help us set goals and priorities, and enhance our memory. They also steer us in directions that evolutionary experience indicates are more likely to be useful than random leaps, or prolonged rational analysis. In practice, we seldom evaluate all options in detail, but focus on those to which we have a positive 'gut reaction.' These instinctive feelings have been shown to be more reliable guides to action than reason in complex situations. Similarly, people with impaired emotional minds have difficulty making choices at all.[3] In other words, emotional intelligence, or EQ as Daniel Goleman called it, is of vital importance, and is actually a more reliable predictor of success in life than IQ.[4] But we have suppressed it in favor of intellectual intelligence.

Most emotions trigger a state of readiness, and an impulse to act.[5] This suggests that, over evolutionary time, the basic 'fight or flight' response may have been elaborated into the primary emotions of fear, anger, sadness, enjoyment, love, surprise, disgust and shame. The sensations of pleasure and pain, drives such as hunger and thirst, and states of consciousness such as awe and bliss may have similar origins.[6] Each basic emotion is associated with a specific trigger. Fear, for instance, being aroused by immediate, concrete danger. Similarly, each emotion induces a universally-recognized facial expression, and has a unique function. Thus cooperation is fostered by love and gratitude, and supported by guilt after a violation, anger against cheats, and sadness when social bonds are broken. Similarly, fear and disgust help us to avoid danger, while curiosity and excitement aid the search for resources.[7]

Most of the time, we keep our emotions on a short rein with reason. But reason is hijacked in emergencies, or when sexual desire floods the system. EQ is about balancing emotion and reason, and preventing emotional distress from swamping thought. According to Daniel Goleman, it involves five key skills:[8]

- Self-awareness, i.e. recognizing and understanding our own feelings as they arise.
- Management of our emotions so that they are appropriate to the situation, including soothing ourselves, and shaking off negative feelings.
- The ability to delay gratification and control impulses in order to achieve our goals.
- Recognition of, and empathy with, the emotions of others.
- The ability to handle relationships with and emotions in others—skills that form the basis of popularity, leadership and inter-personal effectiveness.

EQ is not innate, but is learned by experience, and there are windows of opportunity in infancy and childhood during which the right experiences must be available. If the parent lacks empathy, she cannot tune in to her infant's needs. As a result, her child will grow up unable to empathize with her own children, and thus pass the problem down the generations. Similarly, a parent low in EQ may have little control over his emotions, leading to frequent outbursts of rage and other emotions. These can be terrifying for the child, leaving her traumatized even when there is no physical abuse.

Ideally, EQ and IQ work in harmony and balance, with the emotional mind helping to inform rational decisions, and reason modulating our emotional responses. But the Great Leap Forward opened the way to a greater emphasis on the intellectual mind. This has resulted in extraordinary cleverness and creativity at the expense of trauma, and a serious deficit in wisdom.

Cognitive Fluidity and the Ego

Before the advent of cognitive fluidity, the sense of self-awareness must have been extremely limited. It would have been confined to whichever intelligence was active at the time, and would have lacked an integrated sense of identity. As cognitive fluidity opened up, however, the different intelligences started to communicate with each other. We would have begun to hear different inner 'voices' conversing in the 'languages' of the various intelligences: images for the visual-spatial intelligence, tone and rhythm for the musical intelligence, feelings for the intrapersonal intelligence, words for the verbal-linguistic intelligence, and so on. Ideally, these voices would harmonize into a coherent, integrated view of the world. In reality, experience, particularly when we try to quiet the mind in meditation, suggests it is normally more like an argument. The need to make sense of this babel of voices may have provided the impulse for evolution of an inner sense of self-identity, variously known as the ego, psyche or 'I', and the emergence of the observing self or witness which seems to watch all we do.

For an animal, survival is simply a question of the body, and the fight, flight or freeze reaction is triggered by any threat to it. But, once the ego has emerged, we can also be threatened with destruction of our self-identity; with psychological annihilation. Indeed, such threats begin to loom larger in our minds than physical ones. We live in fear of humiliation, criticism, judgment, ridicule, and other forms of attack, and many of the defense mechanisms we use against trauma are actually aimed at protecting the ego, not the body. They include dissociation, projection, denial, regression, intellectualization and others listed in Table 2. In other words, cognitive fluidity and the Great Leap Forward introduced a major new category of trauma that affects most of our lives deeply.

Closure to Part II

According to the archaeological record, human minds began to diverge from those of other great apes about 100,000 years ago. But it seems likely that this divergence actually began with the genetic birth of Homo *sapiens sapiens*, twice as long ago. We cannot be sure what happened, but it is clear that there was a dramatic increase in human cognitive abilities that led to unprecedentedly rapid technological and cultural innovation, and that set humanity on the road to the digital age. As there was no change in brain size or shape at this time, it seems that there must have been a radical shift in the way the cortex operates. One persuasive theory is that this may have been due to the opening of communication channels between previously discrete intelligence and knowledge modules.

With hindsight, we can see that this mental revolution has been a mixed blessing. Cognitive fluidity not only brought us reason, abstract thought, and creativity, but also may have given rise to our sense of individual identity, or ego. As far as we can tell, this is a distinctively human characteristic which leads to the fear of psychological death, and makes us uniquely vulnerable to psychological trauma. The increased power of the cortex also brought the ability to control our emotions, making it possible to suppress emotional intelligence and trap the energy of arousal in the form of trauma. Despite these vulnerabilities, however, trauma does not appear to have become a major factor in human society until The Fall, a mere 6,000 years ago, as Parts III and IV make clear.

Part III. From the Golden Age to Agricultural Civilization

When I look at history, I am a pessimist ... but when I look at prehistory, I am an optimist.

J.C. Smuts[1]

The idea of a Golden Age is controversial, but, like many ancient myths, it contains an element of historical truth. As the Earth warmed from the last ice age and the glaciers retreated, there was a period of abundance that lasted several thousand years. As Neil Roberts wrote in his environmental history of the Holocene:[2]

> *If ever there was such a 'Golden Age' then surely it was (10,000 years ago), when soils were still unweathered and uneroded, and when (hunter-gatherers) lived off the fruits of the land without the physical toil of grinding labor ... Human life ... was adjusted to the movement of deer or salmon, the autumn harvest of fruits, nuts and berries, and other rhythms of nature.*

Many other scholars have associated the transition to agriculture with the expulsion of Adam and Eve from the Garden of Eden. According to the Biblical story, God cursed the ground and ordained that "in toil you shall eat of it all the days of your life; thorns and thistles it shall bring forth to you ... In the sweat of your face you shall eat bread."[3]

There is no question that life for hunter-gatherers was often hard, dangerous and short. And there is little doubt that the transition to farming was accompanied by shortages of food, ill-health, physical hardships and social tensions. Nevertheless, a quality of harmony, peace and cooperation echoes down the ages in what

Riane Eisler called a partnership culture. This quality has been missing since the advent of urban civilizations at The Fall, and the rise of dominator cultures.[4]

9. Hunters and Gatherers

We are foragers at heart. This remained our way of life for 7 million years after hominins separated from the other great apes. Modern humans have walked the Earth for only 3% of this time, and farmers have existed for less than 0.2%. In other words, hunting and gathering is in our blood; it is what we evolved to do. If we want to know who we are, and what our nature is, we must seek to understand our hunter-gatherer forebears. But interpretations of the evidence from archaeology, observations of our ape cousins, and anthropological studies of modern hunter-gatherers vary widely, particularly with regards to violence and warfare. This is not the place for a detailed discussion of these differences, and we have chosen instead to present a coherent picture that we believe is consistent with the evidence, and is supported by many scholarly interpretations of it.[1] But, like all such descriptions, it is an imaginary reconstruction rather than fact.

The Hunter-Gatherer Lifestyle

It is hard to generalize about hunter-gatherer lifestyles as they varied a lot over time and between habitats. Early hominins would have been little different from our nearest relatives, the chimpanzees and bonobos who share 98% of our genes. But our later ancestors probably lived more like modern hunter-gatherer tribes. In the early days they mainly roamed the savannah, but, by the time farming began, humans occupied habitats ranging from frozen tundra to burning deserts. From various strands of evidence, it seems that they formed bands of 30-150 members. These bands consisted mainly of nuclear families, but probably were linked more by friendship than blood ties. People could swap bands easily, and so relationships were generally harmonious. Band members cooperated in foraging, and shared the few possessions they could carry. At first, grooming was their main means of social communication and bonding which limited the size of the groups. But as their brains became bigger and spoken language developed, they were able to handle the complexity of relationships in larger bands.[2]

Most bands were mobile, moving with animal migrations, and the availability of water, fruits and seeds. Few had the luxury of permanent camps, although seasonal bases were common. However, food gathering typically occupied only a few hours a day, so our forebears had plenty of time for leisure and social activities. Once or twice a year, too, several bands probably gathered in a sacred place to meet old friends, hold rituals and ceremonies, arrange marriages, exchange gifts, trade goods, and generally have a good time. Their diet was typically diverse and nourishing, and they were healthier, taller and longer-lived than the first farmers. However, they were not without health problems. For instance, Steven Mithen observed that in tropical environments the edible plants often wore their teeth "right down to the gums ... simply leaving little crescents of enamel round the edge."[3]

Hunter-gatherers lived very close to nature, and had to be highly attuned to their local environment to survive. They ate hundreds of different plants, and knew the medicinal uses of many more. They identified deeply with many animals—particularly their totems or spirit guides—and could think and move like them. They saw themselves as integral parts of their landscape, and were able to read its subtlest signs in order to find food and water at all times. Often, they regularly re-enacted the creation of their land, keeping it alive through rituals, songs, stories and art. However, they lacked our modern knowledge of ecology, long-term changes in animal populations, and satellite images that show the big picture. They had no way to know, for instance, that mammoths were vulnerable to predation because they reproduced so slowly. Unfortunately, such ignorance, combined with the needs of growing populations, sometimes led to extinctions and land degradation.

Cooperation and Sharing

Hunter-gatherer societies were deeply cooperative, sharing all food and possessions equally, even amongst unrelated band members. This way of life was supported by the belief that they were not isolated individuals, but integral parts of one whole, like organs in a body. From this perspective, failing to share or cooperate would injure a part of yourself. Such behavior is also evident amongst the great apes. Chimpanzees become distressed when a member of their group is hurt. They cooperate, share food, groom each other, and care for aged and disabled individuals. And violent conflicts usually end in reconciliation, often initiated by the aggressor.[4] Human infants similarly display empathy and altruism at an early age. Alison Gopnik describes how fourteen-month-old children will try hard to help someone else. "If they see an experimenter straining for a pen that is out of reach, for example, … they'll toddle all the way across the room and clamber over a couple of cushions to get there to help. They will not only get upset when they see someone in pain, they will also try to help, petting and kissing and trying to make it better."[5]

These findings suggest that cooperation is genetically determined—a conclusion that is supported by research which shows that successful cooperation results in the release of 'feel-good' hormones in the brain. Recent studies on altruism have revealed that we also have an innate sense of fairness. Most of us are willing to sacrifice some personal gain to punish unfair behavior, such as failure to cooperate, even when we are not directly affected.[6] Cooperation is further enhanced by social factors. People are more likely to cooperate if they know they will meet again, and those with a cooperative reputation more often receive help when they need it. Mutual trust is also important, as is the ability to identify and punish 'free-riders' who try to gain the benefits of group membership without contributing fully. All these conditions undoubtedly existed in close-knit hunter-gatherer bands, and the desire for social approval and peer pressure would probably have been sufficient to keep free-riding to a minimum. As Evelin Lindner put it, "cooperating is the most intelligently selfish strategy people can employ."[7]

Despite this evidence, and the fact that modern civilization depends on willing cooperation amongst huge numbers of strangers, scientists still argue that we are self-serving individualists, out to get the most we can for ourselves—or at least for our blood relatives. In this vein, philosopher Mark Rowlands argues that the evolution of the large human brain was driven by our efforts to deceive, manipulate and exploit each other for personal gain.[8] Similarly, evolutionary theorists struggle to explain how altruism towards unrelated people could have evolved through natural selection because it does not appear to increase the chances of reproducing our own genes. But the fact remains that cooperation and altruism are parts of human nature.

Hunter-gatherer Social Relationships

From studies of modern hunter-gatherer societies, it seems that most bands had no permanent leaders or chiefs, and barred anyone who sought power from leadership. Boastfulness was discouraged, and the arrogant and domineering tended to be ostracized. Decisions were generally made by discussion and agreement amongst respected adults, and the person best able to deal with the situation would take charge when a leader was needed. In this way, the experience, intelligence and skills of all band members could be tapped without concentrating power in the hands of one individual. Born leaders naturally gained respect and responsibility, but not privilege, wealth or power.

This egalitarian social structure is surprising because it is generally thought that a hierarchy with the strongest male at the top is normal, as in chimpanzees and many other animals. However, our other cousins, the bonobos, are quite different. They do not have permanent leaders, and cooperation between females enables them to dominate the individually stronger males. Their social hierarchies are less strong, and the status of males reflects that of their mothers. Adolescent females often move to another band where they gain acceptance by bonding sexually with other females.[9] These observations indicate that we have the potential for either egalitarian or hierarchical structures.

Gender relationships in hunter-gatherer bands also tended to be quite egalitarian, although men and women performed very different roles. Women naturally bore and raised infants. They also cared for the elderly and sick, gathered staple plant foods, tended the fires, prepared the food, built shelters, sewed clothes, and helped make tools. But in other ways women generally were accepted for their personal qualities alongside men, and they sometimes joined the hunt when not pregnant or nursing.

Sexual relationships seem to have changed a lot over time.[10] Early hominins probably behaved similarly to bonobos and chimpanzees. Bonobos do not mate for life, and indulge their sexual feelings freely with whoever attracts them, regardless of age or gender. Sexual encounters are frequent but brief, and include tongue-kissing and genital rubbing as well as copulation. Together with grooming, this open, frequent sex forges emotional bonds, strengthens the unity of the band, and helps defuse conflict as the following examples illustrate. When bonobos find a tree laden with ripe fruit, they celebrate with sex before eating, thus reducing competition. After two bonobos have quarreled, one will often make a sexual advance, and the other will respond. Similarly, when two bands confront each other, female bonobos may intervene by seducing the males of the opposing band. It is hard to fight while making love![11]

By contrast, chimpanzees are sexually receptive for a shorter part of the estrous cycle, and their sexuality is more constrained in other ways too. Dominant males mate with whoever they choose, and more lowly males may have to make do with less attractive females, resort to subterfuge, or do without. Chimpanzees also indulge less in sex for pleasure or conflict management. We cannot be sure how our early ancestors behaved, but humans evolved to be sexually receptive for even longer than bonobos. As a result, human sexuality has ceased to be primarily for reproduction, and is more about pleasure, intimacy and social bonding. This hints that perhaps early humans were more like bonobos than chimpanzees. Of course, human sexuality today is also associated with exploitation, manipulation, pain, domination and violence flowing from repression of this powerful drive—but it seems likely that these traits are a product of The Fall, and mostly came after we had stopped hunting and gathering.

Some hunter-gatherer societies continued with relatively open sexuality right down to modern times, but most tribes gradually introduced some form of marriage. From anthropological studies of many such cultures, it seems that polygamy was rare. However, extra-marital relationships were often tolerated, and it was relatively easy to change partners in many tribes. Both sexes usually had similar freedoms, and children were often allowed to explore their sexuality without restraint. Virginity and paternity were not important, particularly where descent was traced through the mother. However, despite this freedom, it seems that sex was still a common cause of disharmony, even murder.[12]

Child-Rearing

One of the greatest challenges faced by hunter-gatherers was the fact that a woman could carry only one child while foraging, and the men needed to be unburdened for the hunt. This meant spacing offspring at least four years apart. Fertility was typically limited by extended breast feeding, and the use of herbal contraceptive and abortion agents.[13] Mental control of ovulation also may have been used.[14] For instance, some Australian Aborigines believed that they would conceive only if they slept beside a birthing stone, and similar Celtic beliefs are reflected in ancient British fertility customs that were still practiced until recently. If all else failed, many hunter-gatherers societies killed or abandoned infants they could not support.[15]

Children in contemporary hunter-gatherer societies, Israeli Kibbutzim, and other communes are raised by the community and not by their biological parents. Mothers and children belong to the whole group, like one big family, and all adults share responsibility for their safety and well-being. This generally benefits the child who is not dependent on the variable moods of two adults, but can move freely amongst many 'aunts' and 'uncles'. Parents, too, are freed from the stress of full-time child care. In such societies, there was always someone willing to comfort or befriend a child, and men shared child-care with the women. As with other aspects of life, child-rearing practices varied widely amongst hunter-gatherers. But on the whole they loved and cherished their children, and emphasized the importance of non-violence and cooperation.[16] Most tribes carried their infants everywhere, and children were part of communal life. Misbehavior was generally tolerated, and, when needed, discipline was firm but non-violent. Far from 'spoiling' their offspring by encouraging them to be demanding and manipulative, these practices generally produced well-behaved and respectful children.

Managing Conflicts

Just as in any group, there were personality clashes, breaches of the band's code of behavior, and eruptions of sexual jealousy. Such disputes were handled in various ways. In some cases, the rest of the band might choose to ignore the issue unless it became too disruptive, in which case one party might be asked to move to another band. Alternatively, elders or a council of adults might seek to make peace between the parties, and to collectively enforce their judgment.

The relationships between neighboring bands were usually cooperative. Australian Aborigines, for example, had networks of mutual obligations that sometimes extended for hundreds of kilometers. They were cemented by the exchange of gifts, inter-marriage, and regular gatherings in sacred places for celebrations and ceremonies. These relationships were not just about keeping the peace, but were vital to survival in hard times when the tribes might need to share resources. When disputes did occur, they were generally resolved by one band moving to another area, or through mediation or arbitration. The commonest causes of violence were murder by a member of another band, and terri-torial disputes. In the case of murder, it was widely accepted that justice required a death for a death, and the victim's family would seek vengeance on the perpetrator, or another member of his family or band. The violence seldom escalated further.

Each band normally had a home territory, but the boundaries were not fixed and disputes sometimes broke out. Whether or not these became violent depended largely on the abundance of the resources involved and the reliability of their supply. In practice, bands only fought over land that was sufficiently abundant and reliable that they could settle permanently in one place. Once settled, they tended to identify with 'their' land, and its richness made it worth defending. However, the scarcity of such lands meant that conflict was actually quite rare.[17] In his global prehistory from 20-5,000 BC, Steven Mithen conveys an overwhelming impression of peaceful coexistence, describing only three cases of violent conflict. Two of these were caused by the loss of an abundant resource due to climate change, and the third was a rich area surrounded by arid lands.[18]

Are humans innately violent?

There is a long-established belief in the violent nature of humans which often biases interpretations of the evidence. For example, when scientists found broken hominin skulls, they jumped to the conclusion that they had been deliberately hit with a large bone. But more recent examinations concluded that the damage was more likely to have been caused by geological processes, or even by laboratory accidents. And the twin holes in some skulls were probably made by the canine teeth of an extinct leopard.[19]

Other scientists point to the violent behavior of chimpanzees as an illustration of human nature. They sometimes murder members of their own band, kill male intruders on their territory, and occasionally engage in what looks like guerilla warfare against an adjoining band—seemingly in order to take over their territory.[20] However, we cannot be sure why such acts occur. It may be that the pressure of contemporary human activities on chimpanzee territory has disrupted their normal behavior patterns. Also, no-one has seen bonobos, our other ape cousins, commit murder. They remained peaceful even when two groups were merged—a situation that would have caused a bloodbath amongst chimpanzees.[21] As primatologist Frans de Waal wrote:[22]

Had bonobos been known earlier, reconstructions of human evolution might have emphasized sexual relations, equality between males and females, and the origin of the family, instead of war, hunting, tool technology, and other masculine fortes. Bonobo society seems ruled by the "Make Love Not War" slogan of the 1960's rather than the myth of a bloodthirsty killer ape that has dominated textbooks for at least three decades.

Another strand of evidence sometimes put forward in support of innate human violence is the disappearance of the Neanderthals soon after modern humans came on the scene. At times there may have been skirmishes and killings when the two met, but these were probably not the reason why the Neanderthals became extinct. When two similar species share the same habitat, one is usually more successful than the other. Ultimately, the more creative and innovative minds of modern humans gave them the edge in a harsh environment. A small example illustrates this process well. Homo *sapiens* invented bone needles and thread, enabling them to sew skins into warm clothes. The Neanderthals did not.[23]

There continues to be a steady flow of books arguing that humans are warlike by nature despite mounting evidence to the contrary. Why is this? One deep-seated psychological reason may be that we cannot be held responsible for our bloody history as a species if violence is encoded in our genes. Nor do we need to make the effort to change, because it would be futile. Another reason why so many scholars take this line is that they conflate warfare with feuding and even murder. In his book, *The Human Potential for Peace*, Douglas Fry drew a careful distinction. Feuding involves limited revenge killings in reprisal for murder, as already described. By contrast, warfare is organized, indiscriminate armed combat between communities. Many analyses of anthropological data count feuds and even individual murders as warfare. More discriminating analyses, however, show that many cultures do not wage war. There are even 20 nations today that have not been to war for over 100 years.[24] Many archaeologists and anthropologists have drawn similar conclusions to Fry, that there is little or no evidence for warfare before the rise of agriculture, 10,000 years ago. As John Horgan stated: "A growing number of experts are now arguing that the urge to wage war is not innate, and that humanity is already moving in a direction that could make war a thing of the past."[25]

Overall, the evidence does not support the argument that humans are innately aggressive, violent and warlike. There is no doubt that we are capable of appalling violence, but we are equally capable of cooperation, peace, compassion and love. History and the media record the acts of violent, powerful, domineering people. They ignore the reality that the vast majority of humans co-exist peacefully, or would do so given a chance, and that most disputes are settled without violence.

10. The First Farmers

The last ice age reached its peak 20,000 years ago, following which the climate slowly warmed, and the ice retreated. This was a time of growing abundance, and by 15,000 years ago permanent human settlements were appearing in some places. At first the settlers continued to forage for wild plants and hunt local game. But slowly they became farmers. By 10,000 years ago, farming was widespread in west Asia, and it extended right across Europe by 5,000 BP (Before Present). The first farmers were horticulturalists who cultivated small gardens of fruit and vegetables with digging sticks and hoes. After a few years the soil would become worn out or weed infested, and they would clear and burn a new patch. The old garden would be left to return to nature and regenerate naturally for 20-30 years. This practice of slash-and-burn or shifting cultivation is sustainable indefinitely provided the population is low enough that the land has time to recover fully. It is still practiced in a few areas. Agriculture was a later development in which grain is grown in relatively large, permanent fields which are cultivated by plowing.[1] For convenience, we refer to both horticulture and agriculture as farming.

The transition to farming was not easy or quick. After some hunter-gatherers became sedentary and lived off abundant local resources, the next step was domestication of plants and animals. This was probably a matter of serendipity rather than deliberate invention in most cases. Once they had mastered these skills, hunter-gatherers still had to be convinced that it was worth changing their ancient way of life. The Biblical story of Adam and Eve's eviction from the Garden of Eden suggests that this was not an immediately attractive proposition.

Settling Down
The most likely reason that some hunter-gatherers became

sedentary was that climate change made it possible. In Europe, forests spread northwards, replacing the frozen tundra with ecosystems rich in plants and animals. Meanwhile, in North Africa, the Middle East and west Asia, extreme aridity was replaced by seasonal rains, wetlands and woodlands. The survivors of the Ice Age found themselves in an abundant world, with the area of habitable land expanding faster than their population. In some places, it became possible to live permanently off the resources within a day or two's travel.

Humans had faced this kind of opportunity many times before as the Earth swung in and out of ice ages over the previous two million years. So why did they not seize the opportunity to become sedentary much earlier? One possible answer is that they did, but were forced to become mobile again with the onset of the last ice age. Another possible explanation is that this was the first opportunity since the Great Leap Forward in mental ability. As a result, they were more willing than their forebears to experiment and change, and their enhanced creativity enabled them to exploit wild resources more effectively. They could harvest the seeds of wild grasses with stone-bladed sickles, and grind them into flour in hollow stones. They could pound hard roots with mortars and pestles, and catch fish on bone hooks suspended on twine. And spear-throwers and bows and arrows increased their success in the hunt. These new inventions also may have made the idea of settling down attractive for the first time. They could not carry grinding stones, carved bowls and other heavy implements with them, and had to store them at their seasonal camps, or do without altogether.

It is unlikely that the decision to stay in one place was made all at once. It probably came about as a gradual extension of seasonal camps, or gatherings of the bands in sacred places. Such gatherings would have been times of intense communal life with feasts, rituals, storytelling, drumming, singing, dancing, sex and marriages. As resources became more abundant, people may simply have stayed longer and longer until they never left.[2] But being sedentary would not have been all roses. Sometimes they would have overstressed and degraded their environment, and impoverished their diet. Similarly, lack of understanding of the need for sanitation could have resulted in disease.

Once a band settled and became dependent on a particular area, they may have become less willing to share its resources with other bands. This would not have been a big issue when the human population was low and the area of habitable land was growing. But as population pressure increased, their conflict management skills would have been taxed to the full, and violence would have become more common. Similarly, living together all year round would have raised social tensions, and conflicts would have broken out more often between band members. This situation would have been exacerbated by bands becoming less open in order to protect their resources from newcomers, thus making it harder to change band to avoid conflict. A good example of this is the Murray river in Australia. Resources were abundant and reliable close to the river, but sparse beyond this zone. Bands of Aborigines divided the river's riches amongst themselves, and jealously guarded their territories. Amongst other ways of doing this, they made the appearance of band members distinctive by deforming the skulls of infants, or knocking out a prominent tooth.[3] In other words, these tribes developed a closed membership and were hostile to strangers, in contrast to the open and hospitable networks of desert bands.

Domestication of Plants and Animals

When our ancestors first settled in one place, they would have used their intimate knowledge of the environment to feast off a wide range of greens, tubers, grains, nuts, fruits, fish and game. They would naturally have chosen the ones that tasted best and were easiest to harvest. And so began an accidental process of plant selection and breeding.

Imagine a wild grass, perhaps the ancestor of wheat. Its seeds ripen at different times, and gradually fall from the head to the ground. Now imagine the seeds are harvested. Some ripe ones have already fallen to the ground and are lost. But any that are not ripe or have stayed in the head are collected. So the harvested grains include more late-ripening and non-shedding seeds than normal. Some of these collected seeds are lost around the camp, end up in waste dumps, or are excreted nearby. When they grow, they produce more late-ripening and non-shedding varieties than in the wild population. The people naturally harvest these convenient plants, and so the process is repeated. Year by year there would be more non-shedding and later-ripening plants. This selection process would have accelerated when people started deliberately to sow stored seeds. It is possible to fully domesticate wild grains in this way within as little as 2-300 years. Once domesticated, they are no longer able to reproduce naturally because all the seeds stay in the head instead of falling onto the soil where they can germinate.[4]

In a similar way, our ancestors would have picked the biggest and tastiest fruits. Over the years, these plants also would have grown around their camps, and become bigger, juicier and sweeter. Once this accidental garden had been established, it would have been a simple step to start tending the plants by removing competing weeds, and watering them in dry weather. Later, seeds of these selected varieties would have been deliberately sown, and good seeds would have become a valuable commodity for trade with other bands and tribes.[5] Once these first steps were taken into horticulture, our ancestors would have invented new technologies to make it more efficient, such as digging sticks and hoes to loosen the ground, and ways of collecting scarce rainfall and channeling it to plant roots.

Animals probably were domesticated in semi-accidental ways as well. Our forebears might have tempted grazing animals within striking distance with food or salt licks. Then, instead of killing them all at once, they might have begun to capture some alive to eat later, and raised orphaned young. They would have kept the calmer, more malleable and more productive beasts for wool, milk and breeding, and killed the less tractable for meat. In this way, they unconsciously began to breed more docile herds.

The Adoption of Farming

Even when domesticated plants and animals were available, farming generally spread slowly. Our ancestors had evolved as hunters and gatherers, and mobility was in their blood. Australian Aborigines still feel the call to 'go walkabout' from time to time, and Steven Mithen wrote of Papua New Guinean hunter-gatherers that "Living in one place is not in their nature."[6] Even for those who chose to become sedentary, farming would have held few attractions. It required hard work to clear and cultivate the land, sow seeds, water the plants, remove weeds, and tend livestock. Then, at the end of the growing season, the produce had to be harvested, processed and stored for the lean months ahead. Sometimes, too, the work-load increased as local supplies of firewood and game ran short. The reward for all this labor typically was more food per hectare of land, but a less nutritious diet, an increase in degenerative conditions such as arthritis, and more infectious diseases due to poor sanitation and transmission from domesticated animals.[7] With their reliance on a few staple crops, early farmers were also more likely than hunters and gatherers to experience shortages due to adverse weather, and crop pests and diseases. Not surprisingly, skeletons reveal that early farmers grew less tall, and died younger than contemporary hunter-gatherers.

With all these disadvantages, it is hardly surprising that farming spread slowly from its birthplace in west Asia. Farmers and hunter-gatherers lived alongside each other for at least 1000 years in some areas, and farming advanced only 1km a year across Europe. It took over 4,000 years to spread from the Near East to Britain and Scandinavia, and it was not fully established in all parts of the continent until 5,000 years ago.[8] As biologist Jared Diamond put it: "That's hardly what you can call a wave of enthusiasm."[9] But there are other interpretations. Faced with the same data, archaeologist Steven Mithen wrote that "the new farmers travelled westward at a remarkable rate, covering 25 kilometers a generation. ... Such speed reflects more than the success of their lifestyle – it implies an ideology of colonization."[10]

It is likely that farming spread for two reasons. Hunter-gatherers slowly and reluctantly adopted it, and they were also pushed out of their lands by frontier farmers. In Europe, a mosaic of lifestyles and land uses developed as colonizing farmers from the east took the fertile valley soils, and left the hills and forests to the foragers.[11] Generally, the two coexisted reasonably peacefully, often trading with each other. However, the decline of foraging may have been hastened by the farmers taking wives from among them.

Hunter-gatherers probably accepted farming for a combination of social reasons and because the age of abundance came to an end. Being sedentary loosens the constraints on both possessions and population. Once settled, our ancestors were no longer limited to what they could carry, and they began to build more durable shelters, dig food storage pits, and collect artifacts—a range of hunting weapons, grinding stones, mortars and pestles, baskets, earthenware pots, sculptures and carvings. For the first time, too, they could have as many children as they could feed, stop infanticide, and let their population grow. These trends were fine while the abundance lasted, but they were faced with a stark choice when it ended. Either return to a mobile lifestyle, abandoning their possessions and infants they could not carry, or find ways to grow more food locally than nature provided. This dilemma is sometimes referred to as 'the point of no return' beyond which the adoption of farming became inevitable.[12]

Unfortunately, farming does not work well with the band social structure. Hunter-gatherers traditionally shared all food immediately, but at harvest farmers must store food for the rest of the year and keep some grain for seed. Hence, Peter Bogucki argues that farming only became possible with the emergence of smaller, more tightly bonded family groups.[13] Families would have had a stronger incentive to risk innovation because they could keep what they grew. And without a supportive, sharing band they would have been motivated to find ways to reliably produce plentiful harvests. This shift to family structures also would have led to the concept of tenure, or ownership, of a particular piece of land and its resources, thus strengthening the resistance to becoming mobile again. These social changes may have created new demands on the food supply as well. Families and villages may have competed to put on the most lavish feasts, and gift exchange probably continued to be an important means of maintaining cooperative relationships. Also, the custom of endowing the bride with wealth at her marriage may have begun at this time.[14]

Steven Mithen suggests that the real motivation to adopt farming may have been quite different: to accumulate the wealth, status and power that come with the control of land, water and food storage facilities. In other words, the transition may have been driven by the rise of individualism, greed and competition rather than necessity.[15] However, this seems unlikely as significant inequalities of wealth and status do not appear in the archaeological record until 4,000 years after farming began.

The rise of religion is another possible influence. Near where domesticated wheat is thought to have originated in Turkey is a remarkable site. Over 11,000 years ago, using flint tools and living off wild foods, the people of Göbekli carved giant T-shaped pillars from the limestone bedrock. Ten of these, up to

2.5m tall and weighing 7 tonnes, were erected in circular hollows, and carved with images of animals and enigmatic symbols. We will never know the significance of these structures, but Steven Mithen believes they reflect fear and the danger of the wild. What is clear is that they required a huge amount of labor, and the need to feed the workforce would have provided a powerful incentive to start farming.[16]

Besides these social factors, farming was encouraged by the end of abundance. As the population grew, so the demand for resources outstripped the sustainable production in some places. In consequence, the environment became degraded, reducing the supply of firewood, and timber for construction and furniture, as well as food. However, these pressures were probably overshadowed by climate change. Two millennia of warm, wet conditions in North Africa, the Middle East and west Asia ended abruptly around 12,800 BP when the temperature dropped 7⁰C in a decade or so. The Younger-Dryas, as climatologists call this period, brought cold and drought for the next 1,000 years.

The history of the Natufian culture near the Jordan Valley illustrates its impact. As early as 14,500 years ago, permanent settlements were established in woodlands which augmented foraging with gardening.[17] Hit by the combined effects of over-population and climate change, the woodlands died out, and plants and animals became less abundant. During the Younger-Dryas, these settlements were abandoned, and the people returned to a mobile way of life. But they could not go back to life as it had been as hunters and gatherers. Their population was larger, they had new technologies, and their relationships with nature, the land and dwelling places had changed. They had even begun to develop concepts of ownership that clashed with the old value of sharing. They adapted to scarcity by hunting a wider range of animals, and intensifying production. As the wetlands and rivers shrank, they moved from the hills to newly-accessible alluvial soils in the valleys. Perhaps they carried precious seeds of domesticated plants with them. In 11,500 BP, the Earth's temperature rose again as suddenly as it had dropped. Woodlands returned. Wetlands were rejuvenated. Wild plants and animals became abundant again. And the Natufians returned to their old lands—this time as farmers, not gardeners.

11. Agricultural Civilization

Was the Agricultural Era a Civilization?

Our focus in this chapter is primarily on developments in Europe, west Asia, the Middle East and Mesopotamia between 10,000 and 6,000 years ago—the period and region where agriculture first became the dominant way of life. In historical terms, this is a huge stretch of time—similar to that which separates us from the builders of Stonehenge in Britain or the pyramids in Egypt, and twice as long as the Christian era. The earliest cultures that are normally recognized as 'civilizations' arose at the end of this period in Mesopotamia and Egypt about 5,500 years ago. The millennia of agricultural society which preceded them tend to be glossed over, at least partly because they left no written records or monumental structures. This neglect is slowly being remedied with the help of modern archaeological research, and a picture is emerging of a far more complex and sophisticated culture than previously suspected.

Table 6: Characteristics of Civilization
(Sources: Mithen 2003, Brooks 2006, Bogucki 1999, DeMeo 2006)

Complex, highly organized Centralized state authority and power with expansionist tendencies	An established religion with a priesthood
	Taxation and wealth accumulation
Urbanization	A professional army
Monumental architecture	Writing
Extensive trade	Bureaucracy
Specialization of production	Artistic expression
Centralized irrigation systems	Predictive science
Social stratification with a ruling class	

But was it a civilization? It certainly did not include most of the characteristics commonly associated with the concept, as listed in Table 6. In fact, the only ones that fit are extensive trade, specialization of production, artistic expression, and a modest amount of urbanization.

However, the term 'civilization' is also used in a more normative sense to describe a society which is not barbaric, savage and violent. According to the Shorter Oxford Dictionary, to civilize means to convert a society from a rude, wild, cruel 'barbarian' state to one that is orderly, well governed, educated, decent, humane and gentle. On criteria such as these, early agricultural society was in many ways more civilized than the 'civilizations' that followed. The evidence suggests that it did not engage in warfare, had no standing armies, and no slaves or gross inequalities, but it was similarly inventive and creative. In other words, it lacked what a friend of ours calls 'the 4C's of civilization': coercion (military), control (bureaucracy), conditioning (priesthood) and commerce (monopoly trade).[1] Early agricultural society was also more civilized than many modern 'civilizations' such as Hitler's Germany, Stalin's Russia, and Mao's China, not to mention the widespread violence, corruption and poverty in modern democratic, capitalist societies. In short, we believe that prehistoric agricultural society, particularly in its later stages, deserves to be recognized as a different form of civilization.

Agricultural civilization ultimately extended over an immense area, and life varied widely from northern Europe to Mesopotamia. There was no central political power, or unifying religion. Rather, it was a decentralized, self-organizing network of coexisting sub-cultures that was very different to the later civilizations of Egypt and Mesopotamia. These diverse peoples left no written records, and few palaces, temples, city walls or irrigation schemes for archaeologists to discover. Our understanding of them depends on the notoriously difficult interpretation of more subtle evidence. Personal and cultural bias is hard to avoid, but we have attempted to create a reasonably objective overview.[2]

Many of the seeds of change sown by the transition to farming blossomed in this period. The most important changes were probably in social organization, but these did not happen in isolation. They were part of more general changes that included new settlement patterns—including the first towns—the establishment of long-distance trade routes, the invention of new technologies, and the emergence of new religious beliefs and practices. The changes varied significantly across the region, but a few broad similarities can be identified that led Riane Eisler to call it a partnership culture.[3]

The Rise of the Family

Hunter-gatherer bands probably began to change when they became sedentary. The ties that bound them would have started to weaken, and new ideas would have arisen about belonging in a particular place, having rights to a particular piece of land, and owning possessions. Such thoughts may have led people to compare their land and possessions to those of others, thus sowing the seeds of competition for the wealth, status and power that they could bring. As the band structure weakened, sedentary communities began to divide into households based on family relationships. Such households are evident in the first permanent settlements, which often consisted of a cluster of separate dwellings, each with its own hearth and food storage pits. In some places, they even buried their dead beneath the floor, thus linking themselves to their ancestors in a new way.

These arrangements indicate that each household may have grown, processed and stored its own food. Archaeologist Steven Mithen sees "the household as the key social unit; it made its own decisions and sought to maintain its independence, while remaining ultimately reliant upon others in times of need."[4]

Similarly, Peter Bogucki argues that the household made production decisions, and was the focus of reproduction, social life and obligations.[5] If these interpretations are correct, this represents a major shift from the communal life of hunter-gatherer bands. Combined with new technologies that boosted food production, these changes reduced the need for cooperation and sharing, thus undermining core hunter-gatherer values.

Researchers cannot be sure of the composition of the households, but they probably would have centered either on an extended family of three generations, or on siblings with their partners and offspring. Either way, people would have belonged for the first time to a genetically-related family associated with a particular piece of land, who owned dwellings, pots, tools and animals. Instead of relying on their band, security would have come from producing surplus food, getting more land, and obtaining favors and obligations from other households.

The rise of the household would have been accompanied by other social changes. Early farmers worked harder than hunter-gatherers, had a poorer diet, and suffered more disease. As a result, they would have often been tired and debilitated, with less time and energy for play, group bonding, leisure activities, and attuning to wild nature. Socializing outside the household would have been more constrained than in the old bands, and living permanently in close proximity would have increased social tensions. Mobility between groups would also have been reduced, and so it would no longer have been possible to defuse tensions simply by joining another household. It is possible that sacred rituals grew out of the need to forgive and forget by acting out hostilities and tensions.

Awareness of family identity may also have changed relationships between the generations and genders. Hunter-gatherers generally were not concerned about paternity, but kin relationships became important with the rise of the family household. Eventually, most cultures switched from matrilineal to patrilineal descent, following the father's line. At this point, strict marriage customs and the control of women's sexuality would have become important to ensure correct paternity. The final step in this process was abandonment of gender equality in favor of patriarchy, or male power. Family structures also brought a new significance to the dead, reflected in more elaborate burial rites and ancestor worship. Families also may have begun to think more about future generations, and how to pass land and possessions to them.

The Tension between Equality and Hierarchy

The shift to households placed great pressure on the old values of cooperation and sharing. Inevitably, some families did better than others because they were smarter, luckier, worked harder, or had better land. The less fortunate would have looked to them for support in hard times. However, as families gained a sense of ownership of the plants they grew and the animals they raised, they may have begun to resent propping up those who were lazy, stupid or luckless. They may have become less willing to share their surplus with those who had not shared the work, and to ask for something in return, such as help in their fields, or in building a new house. Over time, these differences would have been accentuated as the more successful families passed on wealth to succeeding generations, and the poor inherited debts and obligations.

Communities would have respected and listened to the advice of successful families, thus giving them status and influence. Sometimes, they may have been asked to oversee the distribution of food surpluses to the needy, and at others they may have hosted feasts and celebrations. But such 'Big Men' in contemporary cultures have no formal power, and no police or army to protect them or enforce their will. Their power is derived from their generosity, oratory, charisma and management skills, and their positions are not hereditary. Typically, they use their wealth to throw parties, give gifts—including dowries for their daughters—strengthen alliances, and preserve peaceful cooperative relationships between families and villages.[6]

It is possible that the step from Big Man to Chief was taken in some agricultural societies, driven by personal ambition and greed, or community need for central coordination. Unlike a Big Man, a Chief has formal power to order things to be done. He can distribute produce, organize trade, manage a complex irrigation system, or represent the community in negotiations with neighboring villages. While Chiefs have no army to back up their power, they tend to accumulate privileges such as wealth, a large house, exemption from manual labor, special clothes, and hereditary status.[7]

Hierarchical structures such as these could have emerged from differences in ability and luck, without the need for competition or a desire to control and dominate others.[8] Despite the social pressures, the archaeological evidence indicates that agricultural civilization remained relatively egalitarian throughout its 4,000 year history, without obvious hierarchies of wealth, status or power. The similar sizes of most dwellings indicate that differences in wealth were limited. Burials, too, varied little in the wealth of grave goods, at least compared to those of later times. There were no palaces or fortifications of powerful chiefs or kings, and no massive monuments to great leaders. On the whole, people appear to have been valued more or less equally, and women seem to have entered most areas of life on equal terms with men.

The picture is similar with regards to religion, and priestly hierarchies. Most archaeological sites from this period show few signs of organized religion. There were various rituals and practices in burying the dead. The people left many carvings and clay images of animals and humans—particularly of pregnant women—and some that are half animal, half human. There are wall paintings with similar themes that include symbols like pictograms. And there are rooms with the skulls and horns of wild bulls. Only a few sites and buildings are more obviously associated with religious beliefs and practices, but their meaning is unclear, and interpretations differ widely. Some scholars see them as symbolic of a widespread cult that worshipped a Great Goddess, source of all creation. Others argue that there was a pantheon of gods and goddesses. Some hold that the artifacts reflect a more primitive nature worship, whilst others see them as representing a growing fear of wild nature. Yet others believe that many of these creations had no religious significance, and were simply decorations, toys or communications of some kind. At this distance, we cannot be sure.[9]

Throughout these thousands of years, the old hunter-gatherer values of cooperation, sharing and peaceful coexistence seem to have remained strong enough to limit the development of inequalities. A social structure seems to have emerged in which individuals and households varied in occupation, skill, artistic talent, ceremonial functions, rights and obligations, but had similar status and power with limited differences in wealth. As in hunter-gatherer bands, leadership may have rotated depending on experience, skills, knowledge and the needs of the moment. Such heterarchies can handle complex situations through cooperation and self-organization without the need for central authority. Indeed, they work better than a power hierarchy in challenging situations. In these ways, the pressures for change could have been accommodated by allowing the emergence of individual and family differences while maintaining the old ethic of equal value and status.

Specialization and Economic Exchange

As farming became more productive, a family could grow more food than it needed, and it was no longer necessary for everyone to be a hunter, forager or farmer. Instead, they could become skilled artists and craftspeople, trading their skills and products for food. As a result, technological innovation surged. Agricultural peoples invented many new tools, including hoes, sickles, ploughs, grinding stones, mortars and pestles, weaving looms, and the wheel. They began to make fired pottery, and work with metal ores, particularly copper and lead. They learnt to make furniture, rugs for the floors, and pots for cooking and storage. They wove cloth and sewed it into comfortable clothing. They displayed beautiful artistry in sculptures, carvings, paintings, murals, decorated pottery, jewelry, and more. And they created the first scripts for recording and communicating information.

Living in one place, generation after generation, they were able to build solid, rectangular stone dwellings, often with plastered and decorated walls, and with safe places to store food between harvests. In some towns they planned the layout, paved the streets, and installed drains, but seldom built larger public buildings and temples. Their land was often improved, too, with terraces to hold the soil in place, and structures to collect meager rainfall, and guide it to the plants.

These new technologies required raw materials: timber for furniture, doors and other artifacts; firewood for cooking, firing clay and warmth; stone for buildings and making tools; lime for plaster; salt for preserving meat; clay for pots and minerals for decorative glazes; pigments for paints; ores for metallurgy; wool for spinning and weaving, and animal skins for leather. Seldom were all these resources found in one place, and seldom did a village, or even a town, have all the crafts necessary to work them. And so trade blossomed. Villages would swap their surpluses for the things they needed: foods, seeds, domesticated animals, salt, obsidian, marble, metals, tools and artifacts of all kinds. In time, local networks grew into long-distance trade routes traveled by professional merchants. Accounting started as long as 8,500 years ago, using small clay spheres, discs and pyramids to tally the goods.[10] Places that were rich in a valued resource, or that lay on a busy trading route, became wealthy and grew into towns, some with several thousand inhabitants.

War and Peace

Despite all these developments, agricultural civilization appears to have remained remarkably peaceful, as evidenced by several factors. The villages and towns were not built on easily defended hilltops, nor did they have defensive walls. Archaeologists have found no weapons of war, and there are none of the layers of destruction typical of settlements that have been attacked. Similarly, their art fails to record battles and war heroes — most probably because there were none.

Once again, a lot hangs on the interpretation of archaeological evidence. The Bible describes how the walls of Jericho fell down when Joshua's followers blew their trumpets. A few hundred years after Jericho was founded, a massive stone wall was built on the west side, with a big circular tower inside it. These were the first structures of their type, and for a long time it was assumed that they were remains of the defenses destroyed by Joshua. But awkward questions remained. Why was there no sign of a similar wall on the east side of the town? Why had the wall not been rebuilt when it became buried in debris after only 200 years? Why did no other settlements in the region at that time have similar defenses? And who were the enemies the wall was designed to keep out? Today, the widely accepted answer is that the wall was not for defense against invaders, but to deflect flood waters and debris pouring down the adjacent wadi — a gully that carries flash floods when it rains. The tower remains a puzzle, but is thought to have been used for public ceremonies of some kind.[11]

Catal Huyuk

Catal Huyuk is a world-famous site of an early town which illustrates many of the issues discussed above, and many of the challenges of interpreting prehistory. It was founded about 10,500 BP, and was at its peak for an astonishing 1,500 years from 9,000 years ago. During this time it was a thriving town of 7,000 inhabitants set in the midst of farm fields and woodlands.[12] The size and wealth of the town was partly due to farming, but primarily stemmed from control of trade in obsidian from nearby deposits that was in much demand for making the finest stone tools.

Catal Huyuk was surrounded by a wall without gates that was formed by joining the perimeter buildings. Laborers had to scale the wall to reach the fields and woods, and all supplies had to be carried up ladders. It is a mystery why such an inconvenient structure was built. It seems unlikely that it was a defense against attack as the first signs of violent conflict do not appear until 7,000 years ago when the city was well past its prime. It was finally destroyed 200 years later. Also, no weapons have been found amongst the grave goods, and no battles are depicted in the city's art. We simply do not know if the wall was intended to keep wild animals out, to protect the people from the fearsome wilderness outside, or, like Jericho, to protect the town from floods.

Inside the wall, the town was well laid out with solidly constructed buildings that varied little in size or design. Consistent with the need to scale the outer wall, the town's streets ran across the roofs. Holes allowed entry to the dwellings which had plastered and painted walls. There were no large temples, palaces or even public buildings, but there were some larger rooms, possibly used as shrines. Social organization seems to have been strong, but with no powerful leaders, priests or priestesses. This is reflected in the graves which differed little, and the absence of monuments to famous leaders. The citizens were ethnically mixed, and there appears to have been little discrimination by gender, occupation or ethnicity. The people were innovative and creative. Their houses had furniture, rugs and other household goods. Their clothes were woven and sewn.

They worked cold copper, cast lead into ornaments and tools, and created beautiful pottery and wall paintings.

Perhaps the biggest mystery at Catal Huyuk is its art. There are many figurines, predominantly of female figures with exaggerated breasts and genitalia, some pregnant and others giving birth. In one room, a female figure sits on a throne with each hand resting on the head of a lioness sitting beside her. There are male figures too, some with an erect phallus, and clear indications that these people understood the connection between copulation and birth. Bulls' heads and horns are everywhere, and the dwellings are dominated by murals depicting bulls, and, in some cases, vultures attacking headless people. We cannot know why these images and figures were created, or what they meant to the inhabitants of Catal Huyuk. They may have represented a pantheon of gods and goddesses.

More controversially, these creations may have formed part of a cult of the great Goddess, believed to be the fount of all life. There are still remnants of such religions today, including the elevation of Mary, the mother of Jesus, to Mother of God. This interpretation appears to be inconsistent with the predominance of bulls and horns, which are normally taken to represent male power. However, some scholars argue that they symbolized the power of nature, and thus of the Goddess. This view is possibly supported by a figurine of a woman giving birth to a bull. It is also possible that male and female were not polarized, but seen as complementary principles in an integrated whole—a view that may have been reflected in gender equality. From this holistic perspective, the art of Catal Huyuk reveals the integration of the secular and the sacred; religion was life, and life was religion.

Most visitors respond positively to Catal Huyuk, but archaeologist Steven Mithen reacted with horror and a sense of oppression. To him, the bulls "seem to threaten all of human life within the room," and "are always shocking." He describes some scenes as showing giant deer and cattle surrounded by "tiny frenzied people." And, in one room where the nipples of a pair of breasts have split open to reveal animal skulls: "motherhood itself violently defiled." Mithen concluded that the people of Catal Huyuk were "trapped within a bestiary from which they cannot escape" and "seem to fear and despise the wild." "It seems as if every aspect of their lives had become ritualized, any independence of thought and behavior crushed out of them by an oppressive ideology manifest in the bulls, breasts, skulls and vultures."[13]

Closure to Part III

Reconstructing the lives of prehistoric peoples is fraught with challenges. Inevitably, the pictures are colored by personal and cultural biases, and the limitations of research techniques. The portraits of hunter-gatherer bands and early farmers presented in this Part are broad generalizations that mask great diversity of lifestyles, as well as wide differences in scholarly interpretations of the data. Nevertheless, they are not wild fantasies, but have a solid basis in the research literature.

We may conclude that, on the whole, the lives of our hunting and gathering forebears were not 'nasty, brutish and short' as Thomas Hobbes claimed. They survived for millions of years in a tough, dangerous world by cooperating and sharing with each other in small bands living close to nature. This evolutionary heritage suggests that we are better-suited to life in small, cooperative groups than to competitive mass society. However, we also evolved to be flexible and adaptable, able to survive anywhere from burning deserts to icy poles or the urban jungle. Although we have been peaceful and cooperative for most of our history, we are capable of being aggressive, bloodthirsty, and competitive. Our genes endow us with the potential to develop in many different ways, depending on our life experiences, particularly of potentially traumatic events (PTEs).

It is impossible to know for sure if hunter-gatherers suffered more or less from trauma than modern humans, but our guess is that they suffered significantly less. One reason is that they faced a far less complex array of PTEs then we do, mainly stemming from natural disasters and hazards. More importantly, we believe they accepted trauma and death as normal parts of life, and supported each other to release the energy of arousal through their social lives and healing practices. Rather than repress and hide their fear and trembling, they probably defused potentially traumatic experiences regularly, preventing them from becoming trapped as trauma. Also, they did not have the history of generational trauma that modern humans suffer from war, genocide, abuse, brutality, exploitation, displacement, and more.

As human culture evolved beyond hunting and gathering to farming and agricultural civilization, so the pressures for change grew, and the potential for trauma increased. Perhaps the most important source of stress was climate change. Had it not been for abundance after the ice age, we might have remained mobile hunters and gatherers for longer. Had it not been for the sudden return to cold, dry conditions in the Younger-Dryas, we might not have made the transition to agriculture then. Several factors besides climate change probably helped tip the balance in favor of farming. These included the accumulation of possessions, population growth, weakening of the band structure, and the increasing importance of kin relationships. It appears that our ancestors did not make a conscious decision to become farmers, but drifted into it until they reached a point of no return.

This transition was also a time of potential trauma. The risk of crop failure from flood, drought, insects and diseases fed fears for the future. Climate change brought famine, and forced people to leave their homes to become refugees. Many died of strange diseases caught from their livestock, and arthritis from heavy labor often made life painful. Infant mortality was high. Sometimes violent conflict broke out between communities struggling to survive. Also, the old ways of releasing the energy of potentially traumatic experiences may have been lost, thus increasing the amount of trauma.

As the hunter-gatherer social structures crumbled, the seeds of ownership, competition, and male hierarchies of power, wealth and status were sown. However, it was to be another four millennia before they blossomed. With a few exceptions, farmers and hunter-gatherers coexisted reasonably peacefully and cooperatively between 10,000 and 6,000 years ago. Somehow, the old egalitarian values held, and war was not even a shadow on the horizon for most of this time. It was only with the birth of the so-called civilizations of Mesopotamia and Egypt, during yet another change in climate, that war and gross inequalities became institutionalized.

Perhaps the most important message of this Part is that we humans are not competitive, greedy, aggressive, warlike, violent, hierarchical, and male dominated by nature. It appears that we lived for many thousands of years in a state of relative peace and equality as hunter-gatherers, farmers and towns-folk. We must look elsewhere than our genes for the causes of our destructive behavior. We believe the answer is trauma, as the rest of the book seeks to demonstrate.

Part IV. The Fall

So far we have painted a mostly positive picture of human nature and culture covering more than 100,000 years. Suddenly, this enduring peaceful, egalitarian, cooperative and sharing approach to life was swept away. In little more than a millennium, between 6,000 and 5,000 years ago, it was replaced by warlike, male dominated, hierarchical civilizations in Mesopotamia and Egypt. In the millennia that followed, this new type of culture spread like a disease until it dominated the world. Undefended towns and villages were transformed into walled cities with standing armies of professional soldiers. Harmonious relationships were fractured by battles, conquest, mass slaughter, genocide and rape. Grassroots democracy was replaced by bureaucrats serving autocratic kings and high priests. They ruled over lesser mortals ranging from nobles and merchants at the top to peasants and slaves at the bottom. Sexual freedom was abandoned as women became the chattels of powerful men. Loving nurture of children was displaced by strict, authoritarian child-rearing. Unity with nature gave way to alienation and the worship of High Gods.

This transformation cut much more deeply than the changes brought by agriculture. It seems to reflect a transformation in the very nature of humanity, of our minds and psyches, giving rise to new beliefs, new values, new ways of relating, and new ways of being. Riane Eisler first drew attention to this transformation in her classic work, *The Chalice and the Blade*.[1] There, she referred to it as the shift from a partnership to a dominator culture. In similar vein, James DeMeo in *Saharasia* wrote about the change from matrism to patrism.[2] And Steve Taylor called it *The Fall* in his book of the same name.[3]

The Fall. The term evokes images of tumbling off a cliff and plunging to destruction. For Jews and Christians, it represents disobedience to the will of God, and the entry of sin into the world. It signifies a loss of grace and blessedness, God's curse, and the beginnings of collective insanity. And so it seems when we look at the events of this time and since. 'The Fall' also conveys the implication that hunter-gatherer and agricultural societies were an ideal, and that the transformation brought nothing but negative effects. Neither is true. We have described already some of the shortcomings and challenges of pre-Fall societies. Now our focus is mainly on the negative impacts of The Fall, but it is important to bear in mind that there have been positive changes too. As Steve Taylor points out, in the wake of The Fall came written language and mathematics, modern science and technology. Whether or not these would have arisen without The Fall is an open question beyond the scope of this book.

12. The Great Drying

Visualize a belt of land about 1,600km (1,000 miles) wide stretching from the Atlantic coast of north Africa, through the Middle East, and Asia. Jumping the Pacific, it continues across southern North America. Today, this strip contains most of the true deserts of the world including the Sahara, Arabian, Negev, Thar and Gobi, linked by semi-arid areas. But it was not always so. From 10,000 to 6,000 years ago, *Saharasia*, as James DeMeo called it, was relatively wet and warm with the exception of a few drier centuries around 8,000 BP. During those millennia, what we know as the Sahara Desert was well-watered savannah, with woods and lakes supporting a substantial human population.[1] This equable climate began to change around 6,000 years ago, and within a millennium or so had created today's great deserts. The drying did not happen all at once, nor everywhere at the same time. The long-term trend included shorter fluctuations, and regional variations. But once the drying was complete, water was plentiful only along the rivers and around oases. Since then the climate has remained relatively stable but dry for 4 or 5 millennia. Outside this belt of latitudes, climatic conditions remained more stable.

City-States Based on Irrigation

As the climate dried, remaining hunter-gatherers needed more land, but there were few vacant areas available. In desperation, some probably resorted to raiding, and expelling their neighbors. Others abandoned their old ways and became farmers. But farmers, too, were under pressure. Increasingly frequent and more severe droughts turned their land to dust, and dried their water holes. Many hung on, adapting their lifestyles and inventing new methods of production. In marginal areas, they began to harvest water from sporadic rainfall, and channel it to their trees and crops. But in the long run, many settlements were abandoned.

Some migrated to wetter places which became crowded, with many of their inhabitants crammed into towns and cities as the drying persisted. It seems likely that the existing occupants sometimes would have exploited the desperation of refugees, forcing them to become laborers or slaves in exchange for food. In other cases, aggressive tribesmen swept in from the deserts, conquering and enslaving the original inhabitants. And so violence, social stratification, exploitation and oppression grew out of environmental disaster.

As natural lakes and oases dried, their occupants dug sloping tunnels called qanats or foggaras into the hillsides to tap remaining groundwater. And along major rivers they diverted seasonal floods along irrigation channels to their fields. But such schemes were often too large and complex for individual households or villages to build. Centralized management and control were needed to design, build and operate them. New occupations arose to meet these needs, including irrigation engineer, slave master and food distributor. With them came bureaucratic hierarchies.

The first city states appeared in Mesopotamia where the drying climate turned large swamps into fertile soil. From 6-5,000 years ago, the Uruk culture built new towns with central temples, or ziggurats, large food stores, and big residences for the elite. Surrounded by networks of irrigation canals, some had defensive walls indicative of conflict over the rich land. Uruk society was strongly stratified, with a mix of religious and secular authorities. These were supported by administrative centers that collected and redistributed food, oversaw the construction of buildings and canals, supervised the work of craftsmen, and used clay tokens to record trade in scarce commodities such as timber, stone and metals. Uruk also saw the birth of pictographic writing on clay tablets. Eventually, various warring Mesopotamian city states were united in the Akkadian, and later the Babylonian empires.[2]

Civilization in Egypt was preceded by a long period of agricultural settlement in which a string of competing chiefdoms developed along the Nile. Social stratification grew, temples and large tombs began to appear, and an elite took control of trade. Then, about 5,000 years ago, these chiefdoms were united into a single state ruled by a Pharaoh with dynastic capitals at Memphis and Thebes, and administrative centers at the seats of local chiefs.[3] In both Egypt and Mesopotamia, the ruling castes appear to have been immigrants from the deserts, possibly descendants of nomadic invaders.

Pastoralism and Nomadic Invaders

An alternative response to increasing aridity was to turn from farming to nomadic herding, dependent on cattle where conditions were not too harsh, or sheep and goats in drier areas. Always moving with the seasons and the rains, the herders went wherever there was pasture and water—a sustainable way of life that continues even today. In some areas, herdsmen and marginal farmers found ways to live in harmony. With arrival of the seasonal rains, the herdsmen would follow the flush of green into the desert, and camp by replenished waterholes. Then, as the grass was eaten down and the waterholes dried, they would return to graze the stubble of the farmers' crops and manure their land. Over the centuries, these peoples developed a deep understanding of the land and climate that guided their movements and resolved disputes. Such coexistence continued in the Sahel, on the southern edge of the Sahara, until the last few decades, only to break down with the introduction of modern technologies and economics.[4]

In other areas, however, farmers and pastoralists never discovered how to coexist. The nomads looked with hungry eyes at surviving villages, and prospering settlements along rivers and around oases. The more aggressive, ambitious males took the lead. They encouraged their fellow tribesmen to go raiding, thus opening a new era of violence. As Bruce Lerro noted: "Herdsmen the world over tend to be capable of great aggressiveness and violence because of their vulnerability to losing their primary resources, their animals."[5] In contrast to the peoples they conquered, these nomads seemed to revere war rather than nature. Their art was full of battles and weapons, and they worshipped male warrior gods. They were patriarchal and patrilineal, burying their leaders in rich graves, sometimes accompanied by their women.

Some tribes undertook long migrations in search of more hospitable lands, as graphically recounted in the biblical stories of the Israelites, a Semitic people from Ethiopia. They escaped captivity in Egypt only to wander for long years in the desert before reaching the Promised Land. The Bible describes in the following passage how they savagely butchered, raped and enslaved the peoples they conquered. They claimed to be obeying their god's commands, perhaps as a way to assuage their guilt.[6]

The LORD said to Moses, "Take vengeance on the Midianites ..."
So Moses said to the people, "Arm some of your men to go to war
against the Midianites and to carry out the LORD's vengeance on
them." ... Moses sent them into battle, a thousand from each tribe ...

They fought against Midian ... and killed every man. Among
their victims were ... the five kings of Midian. ... The Israelites
captured the Midianite women and children and took all the
Midianite herds, flocks and goods as plunder. They burned all the
towns where the Midianites had settled, as well as all their camps.
They took all the plunder and spoils, including the people and
animals, and brought the captives, spoils and plunder to Moses ...

Moses was angry with the officers of the army ... "Have you
allowed all the women to live?" he asked them. ... Now kill all the
boys. And kill every woman who has slept with a man, but save for

yourselves every girl who has never slept with a man. ...

The LORD said to Moses, ... Divide the spoils between the soldiers who took part in the battle and the rest of the community. From the soldiers who fought in the battle, set apart as tribute for the LORD one out of every five hundred, whether persons, cattle, donkeys, sheep or goats. Take this tribute from their half share and give it to Eleazar the priest as the LORD's part. From the Israelites' half, select one out of every fifty, whether persons, cattle, donkeys, sheep, goats or other animals. Give them to the Levites, who are responsible for the care of the LORD's tabernacle." ...

The plunder remaining from the spoils that the soldiers took was 675,000 sheep, 72,000 cattle, 61,000 donkeys and 32,000 women who had never slept with a man.

Kurgans from the steppes of central Asia similarly swept westward into south-west Asia and south-east Europe as far as the plains of Hungary. Like the Semites, they destroyed defenseless villages, slaughtering the men and children, and often keeping the women as concubines and slaves. They probably were the first to domesticate the horse, giving them unprecedented mobility and a truly formidable weapon with which to launch the first blitzkrieg. Although controversial, this interpretation of events is supported by recent research on the history of the horse,[7] and horseback raiding remained a way of life in the Sudan until recently.[8]

In response to such raids, townspeople began to build their settlements on hilltops surrounded by fortifications, cooperate militarily, and make weapons of war. They raised armies with hierarchies of command dominated by men, the more aggressive and ambitious of whom became chiefs, kings and emperors. The emerging city-states of Mesopotamia and Egypt began to produce great art, but the beautiful artistry and craftsmanship of the agricultural civilization of southeast Europe were buried in the ruins of their towns.[9] In this way, civilizations emerged that had forgotten the ancient peaceful, cooperative, egalitarian ways. And from this Saharasian heartland of Egypt, the Middle East and Mesopotamia, warlike, aggressive, hierarchical, dominator cultures spread around the world until they became the norm.

The European Chiefdoms

In northern and western Europe, the climate remained relatively stable throughout this period, and the region lay beyond the reach of invaders from the steppes. Here, the social pressures generated by the agricultural revolution continued their slow work. The egalitarian network of villages evolved into a more hierarchical network of chiefdoms, and European society was clearly stratified by 4,500-3,500 years ago. The landscape from that period is littered with burial mounds full of rich grave goods which mark the presence of chiefs in what was clearly a patrilineal society. Individual chiefdoms waxed and waned depending on the qualities and ambitions of their leaders, but the overall system proved remarkably stable, continuing as late as the iron age in western Europe. It is impossible to be sure if these leaders were simply the heads of successful households in an otherwise egalitarian farming society, or if they ruled by coercion, demanding tribute from their subjects. However, the discovery of weapons in some graves, and several mass burials of people killed by arrows or blows reveals that relationships between chiefdoms were not always peaceful.[10]

The Human Tragedy

Concealed beneath these factual descriptions is a human tragedy of almost unimaginable proportions. For generation after generation, century after century, the peoples of this vast region of Saharasia were subjected to drought after drought. They experienced famine, starvation, displacement, war, destruction, exploitation, oppression and death with all the suffering and trauma that this implies.

We see the same tragedy unfolding today on our TV screens as burgeoning populations outstrip degraded local resources, and the climate changes once more. We see the straggling lines of refugees in search of food, water and shelter; the grief-stricken, emaciated women clutching dead infants; the big-eyed, pot-bellied children; the dusty hopeless refugee camps; and the trucks of food aid. And we see the armed conflicts often sparked by desperate need in Eritrea, Darfur and so many other places.

But back then there were no refugee camps, no food aid, no UN peacekeepers; and scant welcome from those who already occupied surrounding lands. For generation after generation, multitudes must have suffered and died without hope. And those children who did survive would have grown up physically, psychologically and emotionally damaged. Lacking loving nurture themselves, they would have been unable to be loving parents to their own children, and thus unwittingly passed their trauma down the generations.

Imagine ...
You've lived all your life in this village with your family and friends. The drought is not so severe here, and you can still produce enough food with the help of water harvesting. Travelers bring tales of troubles far off towards the rising sun— stories of fearsome invaders killing and burning the villages— but so far life here remains peaceful.

Then, early one morning, as you're making your way to work in the fields, you see a dust cloud in the distance. You stand and watch as it grows rapidly, until you can make out strange looking creatures, half man, half animal—an animal the size of your cows but moving much faster. Scared, you turn and run back to the village to warn the others.

The people scramble from their huts as the newcomers circle the village to prevent escape, blood-curdling yells and the thunder of hooves shattering the morning peace. No-one knows what to do, frozen into immobility. They have only farm tools with which to defend themselves.

Suddenly, the invaders leap from their horses, brandishing weapons and torches. They stab and hack; blood spurts; guts spill; heads are smashed; limbs are severed. Smoke and flames rise from the huts. Almost before you realize what's happening, your family are lying dead around you, the other villagers piled beyond.

You and other young girls are the only ones spared, if spared is the right word. Having finished their butchery, the attackers have time for pleasure. Blood-covered and reeking of death and smoke, they seize you and hold you down. And one by one they rape you, tearing and bruising your tender flesh until death seems a welcome alternative.

Having had their fun, laughing and joking, they tie you girls together with a rope attached to one of the horses. Rounding up all the village's animals, they leap back onto their mounts and set off again so fast that you can barely keep up. But if you fall you'll be dragged along the ground and bring down your friends. ...

Imagine ...
Your little village, no more than a cluster of households, is struck by drought. You had enough food stored to survive one bad harvest. But then there was another, and another. Your children are hollow-eyed, their bellies swollen. Your father and mother sit, listless bags of skin and bone, near death. You yourself have little energy left, and find it harder and harder to be patient and kind to your children. The youngest is grizzling quietly in your arms, hungry for milk you don't have. Others in the village are in similar plight, and you feel guilty because you're breaking the ancient bonds of sharing by hiding what you have left for your own family.

It's time to leave. Time to leave this land where you belong.

*Time to leave this place where the bones of countless genera-
tions of your ancestors lie buried. Time to leave their spirits,
and venture alone into the world. You can't carry much, but
gather what little food you have and a skin of water. You have
no option but to leave your parents to their fate. With your
husband by your side, your infant in your arms, and the other
children dragging behind, you join the stream of people on the
path—to where?*

When you arrive at a village and beg for help, you meet
stony stares. Custom dictates that strangers and their livestock
can stay for three days, grazing what few plants remain, and
drinking the scarce water. But after that you must move on.

It's hard going. You need help, but the stronger are looking
out for themselves now. Food and water are sometimes stolen
from the weak, so you and your family join up with others for
security. But the leader is an aggressive man, stronger than
most, and willing to use force, even to kill if necessary to get
what he wants in order to survive.

You've been hungry so long now that you feel numb,
apathetic, emotionally shut down, unable to care any more
about your family. All you can think of is food. You feel little
when one of your children drops by the wayside and is left to
die. You have no milk for your daughter, who's growing weaker
by the day. If she survives, her brain will be damaged by
malnutrition, and she will be emotionally stunted by lack of
loving care. If she survives, she probably will be a cold,
remote, unloving adult who traumatizes her own children. And
so the cycle will be repeated.

Imagine ...
*You're an infant, too young to walk with the rest. To help her
keep up with the group and to search for food along the way,
your mother has strapped you to a board on her back. For hours
on end, you can't move to relieve your discomfort. You pee and*

defecate in your clothes. You aren't fed or comforted. But you don't cry much despite the pain. Being tied down makes you passive, and sleepy. But inside, you're raging. Your head is strapped like the rest of you to stop it wobbling around. The pressure against the board distorts your skull, and over time it becomes permanently misshapen.

The constant severe pain turns you into a vicious, aggressive, violent child, filled with rage and hatred against your mother, who caused your trauma. Later, as an adult, you turn your hatred on all women, and your sexuality is perverted. These are ideal qualities for leadership in the battle to survive in this desiccated world. You, and your equally traumatized followers, attack towns and villages, stealing livestock and food, and slaughtering or enslaving the inhabitants.

As the years pass, and the drought deepens, a deformed head becomes the mark of a successful leader. And so the heads of succeeding generations are deliberately deformed to show that they are members of the ruling class, and incidentally to turn them into sadistic monsters through suffering. Some tribes tied a second board over the face to force the skull into a high, pointed shape. Special devices collected urine and feces. The child was fed infrequently, and washed only once a week. The pain was constant and intense. The infant's face sometimes turned black with pus oozing from nose and ears. Many died. Mothers who had themselves been deformed inflicted this torment on their children, just as many Islamic women today continue to inflict genital mutilation on their daughters because it is the done thing.[11]

As part of this elite, you justify and legitimize your behavior and status with new beliefs, myths, norms, laws and institutions that reflect your damaged psyche. The strongest, most aggressive and ambitious amongst you are transformed into autocratic god-kings of new empires. And the Semitic hordes that invaded Palestine are transformed into the Children of

God, sent to punish the unbelievers.

Imagine ...

You've survived a long, long journey, you and your few companions. Your flocks of sheep and goats slowly dwindled along the way as you were forced by hunger to eat some, and others succumbed to starvation. You've been constantly hungry and thirsty for weeks; never welcomed by any community along the way. At last you've arrived where the land's green, nourished by quiet waters flowing along canals from the river. You've never seen such a beautiful sight in your life.

The workers you meet in the outlying fields aren't friendly, but at least they don't turn you away. As you draw nearer the town, you're greeted by a band of armed men. They bid you welcome, and escort you within the walls, to a large building. Once safely inside, their behavior turns rough. They search you and your friends for any valuables you have left, and take any clothes worth having. It soon becomes clear that you're not welcome strangers in a hospitable town, but new slaves to swell the workforce.

The next morning you're part of a large group taken by slave-masters wielding long whips to where they're building a new temple. There, you're forced to labor under the burning sun until you're ready to drop. You are fed, but only a small amount of the roughest food—scarcely better than the cows get. You have water to drink, but it's dirty and smelly. From now on, you realize, this is your life until you drop dead like that man just over there ...

In case these accounts seem over-dramatized, here are a few extracts from James DeMeo's detailed study of *Saharasia*.

(In the mid-twentieth century, the Ik of East Africa) remained a happy, lively culture ... before a resettlement program and drought

forced them into a semiarid highland region ... And as they starved, their social structure broke down entirely. A passive indifference to the needs or pain of others manifested itself, and hunger ... became their all consuming passion. They ... (lost) interest in the pleasures of life ... The very old and young were abandoned to die. Brothers stole food from sisters, and husbands left wives and babies to fend for themselves. While the maternal-infant bond endured the longest, eventually mothers abandoned their weakened infants and children. Older children gathered into gangs dedicated to stealing food, even from their own younger siblings, or older, weakened kinfolk. ...

The end result of (famine) is similar to armed invasion by a merciless, brutal enemy, who kills the majority of the population, scatters the survivors and steals all resources and property of value.[12]

Psychological effects (of starvation) are less obvious ... a general apathy and lethargy prevails, with loss of interest in normal concerns except for finding food. Interpersonal relationships may be broken down so completely that parents devour their own children; cannibalism has been reported during famine times in almost every part of the world ... Infants, children and the elderly suffer first; young and middle-aged adults are usually able to travel to food sources, leaving the young and the old to fend for themselves and possibly die. ... Social chaos is evident everywhere, as refugees flock to the cities or roads seeking food.[13]

During the early 1970's (in Turkey) water sources had become dry and the villages depending upon them had to be abandoned. The people—easily 1000—with all their livestock had to move and by the time we saw them they had been on the road for several months. To keep alive they would approach water sources and grazing land owned by more fortunate villagers along their way and negotiate. ... Often they were told to move on after three days of traditionally free grazing. The flocks would survive by passing from place to place and eating enough at each to stay alive until the next confrontation, which could end in violence.[14]

Reflection

With contemporary climate change, we may see the great drying repeated in many places, as John Vidal's report from Kenya in September 2009 illustrates:[15]

After three years of disastrous rains, the families from the Borana tribe, who by custom travel thousands of miles a year in search of water and pasture, have unanimously decided to settle down. Back in April, they packed up their pots, pans and meager belongings, deserted their mud and thatch homes at Bute and set off on their last trek, to Yaeblo, a village of near-destitute charcoal makers that has sprung up on the side of a dirt road near Moyale. Now they live in temporary "benders" – shelters made from branches covered with plastic sheeting. They look like survivors from an earthquake or a flood, but in fact these are some of the world's first climate-change refugees.

They are not alone. Droughts have affected millions in a vast area stretching across Kenya, Somalia, Ethiopia, Eritrea, Sudan, Chad, and into Burkina Faso and Mali, and tens of thousands of nomadic herders have had to give up their animals. "[This recent drought] was the worst thing that had ever happened to us," said Alima, 24. "The whole land is drying up. We had nothing, not even drinking water. All our cattle died and we became hopeless. It had never happened before. So we have decided to live in one place, to change our lives and to educate our children."

13. Agricultural versus State Civilizations

The cultural transformation triggered by the Great Drying has been variously called The Fall, the transition from partnership to dominator cultures, or the switch from matrism to patrism. Riane Eisler's focus in *The Chalice and the Blade* was primarily on gender and hierarchy in west Asia and southeast Europe. She described the agricultural partnership civilization as democratic, equitable and empowering, with little fear, violence, or gender discrimination. By contrast, the dominator civilizations that replaced them were authoritarian, inequitable, male-dominated and hierarchical, with a high degree of fear, abuse and violence.

James DeMeo's study of *Saharasia* covered a wider area, and focused mainly on family and sexual life, including child-rearing. From anthropological data on 1200 cultures around the world and extensive archaeological evidence, he devised a spectrum of cultural characteristics between the poles of matrism and patrism. Matrist cultures are democratic, egalitarian and peaceful, with little adult violence, and gentle, pleasure-oriented child-rearing and sexual relationships. By contrast, patrist cultures are violent, sadistic and male-dominated. They traumatize their infants and children, punish youthful sexuality, and greatly restrict the freedoms of women and youth. DeMeo found little evidence that patrist cultures existed anywhere on Earth before 6,000 years ago. He concluded that patrism arose amongst nomadic peoples from harsh desert environments during The Fall, and spread around the world by invasion and cultural diffusion.

As we have seen, hunter-gatherers, early farmers, and the agricultural civilization that followed were based mainly on the principles of partnership and matrism. By contrast, the civilizations that arose after The Fall, and most civilizations from then until the present, have been more oriented to domination and patrism. We have called these 'state civilizations', and this chapter contrasts them with agricultural civilization on a range of criteria. The summary tables are deliberately polarized, and most cultures in practice fall between the two extremes. Early state civilizations became literate soon after their establishment, and recorded many aspects of life. However, relatively little is known about many social practices in agricultural civilization, and we have assumed that they were similar to the matrist cultures described by James DeMeo.

The Emergence of Cities and States

Agricultural civilization was comprised of a network of loosely connected towns and villages separated by farmland, woods and wild country. The Fall heralded the first true cities, which were more than just large towns. Their layout was generally planned to some extent, and they included large public buildings such as temples, elite residences, food stores and army barracks. Cities also were normally fortified against attack. (See Table 7)

Table 7: Settlement Patterns in State and Agricultural Civilizations

State Civilization	Agricultural Civilization
Planned cities at the centre of an organized network of towns and villages	Informal, self-organized network of towns and villages
Monumental graves, temples, large dwellings	Few large buildings; uniform dwellings
Fortifications	No fortifications

The key difference between a city and a state was the existence of a powerful elite. This was usually headed by a hereditary king or queen who was supported by bureaucrats, the military, and the priesthood. The bureaucrats ran the economy, operating centralized irrigation systems, storing and distributing food, controlling trade, levying taxes and keeping accounts. The military raised the army, and used it to control the populace as well as to defend the state against invaders, or to conquer neighboring cities. The priesthood promulgated an ideology or religion that justified and supported the hierarchical social structure and unequal distribution of wealth. Slavery was common, but Bruce Lerro argues that the peasants were often worse off than the slaves, being severely exploited, heavily taxed, forced to feed the city's population, and conscripted to fight wars and build public works.[1] (See Table 8)

Warfare

War was rare before The Fall. With the rise of state civilizations, however, war became common and institutionalized. Bruce Lerro and Douglas Fry both list criteria that distinguish warfare from feuding or raiding.[2] War is a collective activity, planned in advance, and undertaken by a political entity, such as a state or kingdom. It is not waged for its own sake, but serves economic, social or political objectives such as defense, revenge, or appropriation of land and resources. War uses lethal weapons and indiscriminately targets anyone from the enemy side. Unlike murder, killing in war is socially approved. Warfare was lifted to a new level by state civilizations which raised standing armies under hierarchical commands of military specialists. This made it possible to wage long and complex campaigns to invade and control subject territories. Throughout history, advances in technology have made war progressively more deadly.

The Economy

A city or state must control enough land and labor to feed its population, including non-agricultural crafts-people, trades and professions. After The Fall, agriculture continued to be the largest sector of the economy, but was less dominant than in the agricul-

Table 8: Power and Authority in State and Agricultural Civilizations

State Civilization	Agricultural Civilization
Authoritarian: domination based on fear of pain and/or force	Democratic: leadership is empowering and varies with situation
Hierarchies of status and power: king, priests, bureaucrats, military, merchants, artisans, peasants, slaves	Egalitarian; relatively equal status and power
Men dominant	Neither gender dominant
Accountants, scribes, tax collectors and other administrative professions	No administrators
Professional military specialists or caste	No full-time military
Conscription for wars	Members fight voluntarily as necessary
Violent, sadistic	Little violence or sadism

tural civilization. The construction of public works, including food stores, temples, city walls and irrigation systems led to an increase in building specialists ranging from masons to engineers and architects. Metal-workers were increasingly in demand to produce bronze tools, weapons, jewelry and other artifacts. The number of scribes and accountants rose along with the need to record laws and religious precepts, and keep accounts of economic activity. Merchants and traders flourished as demand boomed for luxury goods, and essential resources.

Advances in agriculture, particularly in irrigation, created larger surpluses to feed the growing population. But farmers gained little if anything. All but the bare minimum of their production was appropriated by the authorities, and stored for later redistribution to non-farmers. And peasants were often pressed into service as laborers or soldiers as well as having to produce food. Work conditions were generally harsh, and laborers were driven with whips to the point of exhaustion or even death.

The upper echelons of society—nobles, priests and merchants—were free to accumulate wealth and possessions. But ownership meant little to the lower rungs. They were taxed heavily to pay for the elite's luxuries, armies, and grandiose tombs and public works. And to prevent pilfering, merchants not only introduced strict accounting procedures, but also invented sealed containers to protect their trade goods. (See Table 9)

Accounting and Writing

Elementary symbols, particularly for accounting, were invented before The Fall. But complex written languages became one of the defining features of state civilizations. Writing transforms oral agreements, stories, and even thoughts into enduring facts which can be accessed by many people.[3] It thus turns both secular and religious traditions and customs into laws and regulations, and displaces memory and emotion in favor of written evidence. This facilitates the management of larger, more complex organizations and societies. It also enables students to learn faster, and the literate to start thinking about things in a new way. For the first time, it became possible to study the work of their predecessors, and build new ideas and theories on the foundations they had laid.

On the debit side, writing separated knowledge from the storyteller or bard. This made it more abstract, and accessible only to those who could read, or the elite who could employ scribes. It also helped to separate people from nature. Oral languages mimicked natural sounds, and pictograms still resembled the animals and objects to which they referred. But once the alphabet had been invented, around 3,500 years ago, the symbols became purely abstract.[4] The apparent authority of the written word, which is still a powerful force today, makes it

Table 9: The Economies of State and Agricultural Civilizations

State Civilization	Agricultural Civilization
Based on agriculture, artisans, crafts, and trade	Based on horticulture and agriculture, with more limited crafts and trade
Hierarchy of wealth	Egalitarian; relatively equal wealth
Surplus production that can be seized by elite	Limited surplus
Centralized food storage	None, or household food storage
Centralized control of production and distribution of food and artifacts	Individual and household control of production and distribution
More highly specialized, including soldiers, engineers, architects, merchants, priests, bureaucrats, accountants, tax collectors, slave-masters, laborers	Some specialization between farming, crafts, trading, etc
Elite controls work of slaves, peasants and artisans through coercion	Individual freedom of work
Individual ownership of resources and possessions	Limited individual ownership of resources and possessions
Competitive accumulation of wealth	Limited competition or accumulation of wealth; more cooperation and sharing
Trade controlled by merchants	Informal trade networks
Formal accounting, and sealed trade goods	No formal accounting or sealing of goods
Writing develops to serve trade and bureaucratic control	Elementary symbolic systems developing
Taxation	No taxation

possible to subvert the truth into propaganda, and manipulate documents into powerful weapons for social change. Literacy, too, can be another step in social stratification and gender discrimination.

Technology

Pre-Fall peoples developed beautiful pottery and basic metallurgy. They trained animals to pull wheeled carts and ploughs. They built sophisticated water-harvesting systems to channel rainfall to their crops. They constructed rectangular stone buildings with decorated plaster walls. They planned some towns, and paved and drained the streets. They invented simple accounting methods and early scripts. And so the list continues.

All these were developed to a higher degree, and became more widespread after The Fall. In particular, key technologies were adapted to larger scales that required central organization and control. Experts disagree about which came first—centralized power and organization, or the need for large-scale technologies. Be that as it may, the most important innovations were extensive irrigation schemes, large buildings, monumental and defensive structures, and centralized food storage and distribution.

The only technologies used by early state civilizations which appear to be genuinely new are weapons of war, and even these were developed from earlier hunting weapons and farm tools. Weapons became far more lethal with the introduction of bronze. This alloy of copper and tin is harder than pure copper, and breaks less easily than stone. However, even the relatively sophisticated metallurgy required by bronze originated much earlier, probably in the Caucasus. Riane Eisler notes that the beauty of the crafts declined with the transition from agricultural to state civilization.[5] (See Table 10)

Religion and the Relationship to Nature

Little is known about religious beliefs and practices before The

Table 10: Technological Differences between State and Agricultural Civilizations

State Civilization	Agricultural Civilization
Plentiful weapons of war	Few or no weapons of war
More advanced writing and accounting	Elementary writing and accounting
Centralized irrigation systems	Local water harvesting
Centralized food storage and distribution	Household food storage
Large buildings and other structures	Mostly domestic-scale buildings
Extensive use of copper-tin bronze	Metallurgy confined to copper and lead

Fall, and interpretation of archaeological remains is tricky. It is generally assumed that ancient hunter-gatherers were animists like their counterparts today, revering and worshiping the natural world and the spirits that imbue it with life. However, the beliefs of later farming communities are more enigmatic. As discussed earlier, we can only speculate what motivated the carving of giant stone pillars at Göbekli, or the worship of the bulls and 'goddess' figures of Catal Huyuk. Steven Mithen sees them as intimations of an emerging separation from and fear of wild nature.[6] But there are other, very different interpretations. What is clear is that well before The Fall, religious beliefs and practices had already moved far beyond simple animism.

With the emergence of state civilizations, religion started to take on more recognizable forms. Nature spirits gave way to human-like gods and relatively weak goddesses that wielded power over humanity. These divine hierarchies reflected the emerging stratification and gender discrimination of society. Powerful rituals that were believed to influence the natural

135

world gave way to public ceremonies as faith in magic faded along with the influence of the feminine. Out of this melting pot emerged belief in a single supreme God, the Father, represented here on Earth by divinely appointed kings. State-mandated religions also developed, with codified beliefs, laws and practices, and divinely ordained male priests who officiated in rich temples and pulled the strings of power behind the scenes— a more subtle way of keeping the populace in order than naked force. (See Table 11)

Sexuality

Sexuality is arguably the most potent of all human drives after survival. Yet it has been strongly repressed in most societies since The Fall. The result is a build-up of inner tensions that may explode in anger, frustration and violence as well as sexual exploitation, rape and perversions. One consequence is the deep-seated belief in many cultures that women's sexuality is dangerous and must be controlled by genital mutilation to eliminate sexual pleasure, arranged marriages, confinement to the home, domestic violence, and other oppressive customs. Even today in many Islamic cultures, women must go veiled and avoid contact with men other than their husbands because it is feared that the sight of any part of a woman will ignite male lust. Adultery is severely punished. Women are often blamed for rape, and killed for besmirching their family's honor. According to James DeMeo, the most extreme of these cultures continue to exist in the patrist heartlands of Saharasia from which the dominator culture spread around the world.[7]

Before The Fall, there was a far more open and permissive attitude to sexuality, with a greater focus on pleasure. Extra-marital relationships were tolerated. Adolescents were often allowed to experiment freely. There were few taboos on homosexuality, incest or pedophilia, but neither were these common practices. (See Table 12)

Table 11: Religion and the Relationship to Nature in State and Agricultural Civilizations

State Civilization	Agricultural Civilization
Fear of nature	Love and worship of nature, but possible signs of emerging fear
Separated from nature	Deeply part of nature, but relationship changing with adoption of agriculture
Nature seen as a source of resources to dominate and exploit	Awe and reverence for nature
Nature created and controlled by anthropomorphic gods	Nature probably still co-created by humans and the spirits that exist in all things
Male/father oriented	Gender balanced, or female/mother oriented
Asceticism, avoidance of pleasure, pain-seeking	Pleasure welcomed and institutionalized
Full-time religious specialists; male priests and lesser female priestesses	No full-time religious specialists
Male shamans and healers	Male and female shamans and healers
Strictly codified rules of behavior and religious laws	Norms of behavior and practice informal, uncodified
Ceremonies entertain the masses, but lack power	Rituals have magic power to influence the world
Beliefs and stories justify domination and violence as inevitable, normal, moral and desirable	Empathy, cooperation, sharing, and caring relationships are normal, moral and desirable

Gender Relationships

Given the changed attitudes to sexuality, it is hardly surprising that the role and status of women declined sharply after The Fall. They lost their equality with men in public life, and became

Table 12: Sexuality in State and Agricultural Civilizations

State Civilization	*Agricultural Civilization*
Restrictive, anxious attitude	More permissive, pleasurable attitude
Genital mutilation of women	Genital mutilation of women rare
Taboos relating to female virginity	Virginity taboos rare
Adolescent lovemaking severely censured	Adolescent lovemaking often freely permitted
Homosexual tendency with severe taboos	Homosexual tendency or taboos rare
Incest tendency and severe taboos	Incest tendency and taboos rare
Concubines and/or prostitutes common	Few concubines or prostitutes
Rape common	Rape rare
Pedophilia exists	Pedophilia rare

subservient to their husbands who controlled the household. Their work was devalued, and they were more and more confined to the domestic scene, and the role of breeding and raising children. At the same time that reproduction became the main female role, the reproductive function was denigrated. Vaginal blood due to menstruation and childbirth came to be seen as contaminating and somehow dangerous, and taboos about intercourse, cleanliness and segregation at these times came into force.

Most women became little more than chattels. Wives were bought from their fathers for a 'bride price', and women had no right to choose their husbands or divorce them no matter how violent or oppressive they were. Similarly, the victors in war generally killed the men and children but spared the women— particularly virgins—who became concubines, prostitutes or slaves who might be sold. At the top of the hierarchy, the few ruling queens owned and managed property, and could represent their households in many ways. They could learn crafts, and could become scribes, musicians and singers. But they remained subordinate to their husbands, and pawns in male politics.[8] (See Table 13)

Family Structure and Relationships

Before The Fall it was common for ancestry to be traced through the female line, and for men to move to their wife's community on marriage. Afterwards, descent became patrilineal, and women had to join their husband's family. Male dominance and the inability of women to divorce their husbands led to a rise in domestic fear, and child and wife abuse. Infants were more often traumatized, and children were less indulged and received less physical affection. (See Table 14)

Reflection

This catalogue of differences indicates clearly that the emergence of the early state civilizations was far more than an evolutionary progression. It represents a deep and broad cultural revolution, the influence of which still echoes through the world today. It signaled the start of civilization as we know it, but also the loss of many characteristics of civilized life. To call it 'The Fall' seems appropriate.

Table 13: Gender Relationships in State and Agricultural Civilizations

State Civilization	Agricultural Civilization
Women had limited freedom	Women had more freedom
Women inferior to men	Women had equal status to men
'Masculine' traits and activities such as aggression and control valued above 'feminine' ones.	'Feminine' traits and activities such as empathy, non-violence and care-giving valued in men, women and society.
Woman could not choose partner	Women could choose partner
High bride price (man has to pay for bride)	No or low bride price
Compulsory lifelong monogamy, at least for women; some societies allow men to have more than one wife.	Non-compulsory monogamy
Adultery, particularly by women, severely punished	Adultery accepted
Women often blamed and punished for rape	Women not blamed for rape
Ritual widow murder on death of husband	Little or no ritual widow murder
Polygamy common	Little or no polygamy
Wife could not divorce husband	Wife could divorce husband
Males controlled fertility	Females controlled fertility
Taboos surrounding blood from the vagina (Hymenal, menstrual & childbirth)	Few vaginal blood taboos
Female reproductive functions denigrated	Reproductive functions celebrated

Table 14: Family Structure and Relationships in State and Agricultural Civilizations

State Civilization	Agricultural Civilization
Patrilineal descent	Matrilineal descent
Patrilocal residence (i.e. wife lives in husband's community)	Matrilocal residence
High degree of fear; child and wife abuse	Mutual respect and trust with low degree of fear and social violence
Less indulgence of children	More indulgence of children
Less physical affection	More physical affection
Infants often traumatized	Infants less often traumatized
Authoritarian	Children had more freedom

14. Causes of The Fall

The transition from agricultural to state civilization was a step backwards when measured by the modern values of peace and justice, human rights and dignity, democracy and equality of opportunity. And, although some of the hard edges have been knocked off state civilization over the centuries, modern civilization is still primarily a dominator culture. This leaves us with two questions. Why did partnership cultures collapse after surviving for thousands of years? And why has there not been a return to partnership during the last few thousand years? There is little doubt that the immediate trigger for The Fall was drying of the climate, exacerbated by the rise of violent conflict. But The Fall probably would have been far less dramatic if there had not been a cultural and ecological readiness for the change. From another perspective, The Fall was also a deep psychological transformation, variously ascribed to an explosion of ego, or to the trauma of aridity and war.

Climate Change

Over the last two million years, the Earth has swung in and out of ice ages every 100,000 years or so, and humanity's African womb has fluctuated between warm wet and cool dry conditions. At times, the forests shrank to a quarter of their present size, only to spread back across the grasslands when the rains returned. Our forebears faced even bigger challenges as they headed north into Europe and Asia. The Earth was cooling, and they had to adapt to the frozen tundra and cold, dry steppes of the last ice age. Then, they had to change again as the planet warmed, forests advanced north across Europe, and well-watered woodlands spread across North Africa and the Middle East. As a species, we have always faced the necessity to adapt to climate change.

From this point of view, if the transition from partnership to dominator civilizations was a response to aridity, why did it happen when it did, 6,000 years ago? In particular, why did it not happen during the Younger-Dryas, just a few millennia before the great drying? This period brought Arctic conditions back to northern Europe and drought further south between 12,800 and 11,600 BP. It ended the Natufian culture in the Middle East, as described in Chapter 10, and undoubtedly brought widespread social dislocation elsewhere. Nevertheless, the partnership way of life survived, while similar climatic events a few thousand years later coincided with The Fall. This could mean either that climate is not a significant driver of cultural change, or that other factors made agricultural civilization more vulnerable to climatic influences than earlier cultures.

Invasion

One obvious difference between the Younger-Dryas and The Fall was the advent of warfare. We have described how tribes from the steppes and Ethiopia invaded better-watered regions. Cruel, sadistic and insensitive to pain and suffering, these nomads left a trail of bloody destruction wherever they went. The traumatized survivors either learned to be violent in defense, or were slaughtered and enslaved. Together with drying of the climate, these invasions were undoubtedly a potent cause of The Fall. But why did the nomads become so violent? They came from some of the most severely drought-stricken regions, and needed to migrate to areas of higher rainfall in order to survive. Migration inevitably brought them into competition with other communities, but this would not necessarily turn a peaceful people into brutal killers. In the extreme, they could have chosen to die rather than break the taboo on killing humans, as some peoples probably did. One possible explanation suggested by James DeMeo is that harsh desert environments foster harsh, psychologically armored inhabitants.[1] More recently, Evelin Lindner drew similar conclusions. "Somalia, ... which offers extremely difficult living circumstances to wandering nomads, developed unforgiving "warriorhood." This harsh and proud culture fed years of civil unrest, hunger, and death."[2]

This predisposition to aggressive violence would have been reinforced by the nature of the great drying which continued and recurred with increasing ferocity for generation after generation. Starving mothers were unable to feed or comfort their infants who were traumatized by being strapped to backboards as they traveled in search of food and water. Those that survived into adulthood would have been boiling with rage at the callousness of the world, and unable to form intimate relationships or care for their own children. Successive generations exposed to such traumatic experiences would have been likely to lose both the ability to empathize with others, and their cultural inhibitions against killing. They would have been willing to follow strong, aggressive leaders who could fill their bellies, and give them the opportunity to release their rage in violent action.

Cultural Readiness

Millennia of benign climate had enabled some communities to become sedentary before the Younger-Dryas struck. However, agriculture was not well-established, and hunting and gathering still predominated. Hence, it was possible for most groups to return to their old nomadic ways when cold and drought returned. Population was still low, and sufficient space was generally available. But by the time of the great drying, the situation had changed. Agricultural civilization had emerged, and the population had grown significantly. It was no longer possible to return to hunting and gathering because the skills had been lost, and there were too many mouths to feed. The culture had changed greatly, too. The ethic of cooperation and sharing had been weakened by the rise of households, and families had become attached to their land and possessions.

Just how strong this sense of belonging can be is illustrated by contemporary responses to volcanoes, earthquakes, tsunamis and hurricanes.[3] Despite the devastation and risk of recurrence, people generally return home within a few years—even when new settlements are created for them elsewhere—and such disasters seldom cause significant cultural change in the long run. At first sight, this seems to indicate that climate change is not a significant stimulus for cultural evolution. But the great drying was not a brief, one-off event like an earthquake. People living in Saharasia would have experienced prolonged, repeated, widespread droughts of increasing severity for generation after generation. These would have caused recurring traumas due to famine, migration and competition for food with neighboring groups. Even when the droughts were separated by wetter periods of several decades, memories of the events would have remained in the myths and oral history of the society. Traumatized parents also would have unwittingly passed the trauma to following generations.

Compared to the Younger-Dryas, communities at the onset of the great drying would have been more inclined to stay put, less willing to share (particularly with strangers), and more likely to defend their territory. They would have intensified their farming with water harvesting, the plough and draught animals until finally forced to leave by famine. Then, they would have become refugees or pastoralists rather than hunter-gatherers. Another key difference was the incidence of violence. The cooperative spirit never broke during the Younger-Dryas, and hence the main sources of trauma were famine and displacement. But during The Fall, some tribes became aggressive, sparking a self-reinforcing spiral of violence as other tribes followed their lead, and settlements tried to defend themselves. In this way, mass killing, rape, pillage and slavery were added to the traumas of famine and displacement.

Co-evolution of Culture and Environment

The natural environment provides opportunities for social, economic and technological innovation, imposes constraints on what is possible, and creates challenges to survival. But how societies respond to their environment depends on their social and cultural systems. Great riverine civilizations arose on the flood plains of Mesopotamia and Egypt, but not along the Murray-Darling river in Australia, or the Mississippi in North America.[4] Similarly, state civilization was not the only possible outcome of desiccation. As we have seen, nomadic herding proved to be a more sustainable response. Also, humans do not simply inhabit a given environment, but actively modify it to meet their needs. Sometimes this results in long-term sustainability, but many civilizations failed because they degraded the natural resources on which they depended.

Agricultural civilization probably arose in southwest Asia because it was better endowed than other regions with plants and animals suitable for domestication.[5] Similarly, the emergence of state civilizations in Mesopotamia and Egypt was not due to inevitable cultural and technological progress. Rather, it resulted from the interaction of many social and geographical factors. These included the location and flow regimes of the Tigris, Euphrates and Nile rivers, desertification of the lands surrounding the rivers, increasing density of population, the need to grow more food, the availability of cheap labor, social trends arising from the transition to agriculture, and so on. In other words, the natural environment and human culture co-evolved in a complex, interactive process.

The Ego Explosion

Steve Taylor argues that, at The Fall, a "giant can of psychological worms seems to have opened within the human mind."[6] This left us alienated from our bodies, emotions, each other and nature. We scramble to fill this void with possessions, entertainment, success, and power; and we reveal our suffering in depression, drug abuse, eating disorders, self-mutilation, anxiety, guilt, jealousy, and more. Since The Fall, we have suffered from a collective insanity in which it seems natural to kill, torture and exploit each other, to destroy nature, to seek ever more wealth, status and power, but to remain forever discontented and unfulfilled.

Taylor attributes this madness to a shift in consciousness that he calls the ego explosion. Unable to return to hunting and gathering, we had to invent new survival strategies, and to plan and organize new ways of being. In our efforts to solve problems, we held inner debates, and reasoned with ourselves. But to do this, we needed a strong sense of individual identity, ego, or 'I'. Hence, Taylor concluded, "The Fall was, and is, the intensification of the human sense of "I" or individuality."[7] Bruce Lerro followed a similar line of reasoning, claiming that individualists are more self-reflective, more objective, less influenced by external social forces, and better at abstract thinking.[8] In consequence, they handle rapid change better, and are more likely to transform society in a crisis.

Conditions at The Fall favored strengthening of the ego in other ways, too. Hardship encouraged selfishness, and separation of the individual from the community. Pain and discomfort led to dissociation from our suffering bodies, and identification with our minds instead. And nature came to be seen as a harsh enemy to be conquered. In time, this sharpened sense of individuality became the normal pattern of human development, leading, Taylor claims, to an era of striking intellectual advances including the invention of writing, mathematics and astronomy, many technological advances, and ultimately to great literature, music, and science.

Taylor suggests that this ego explosion became a source of insanity and suffering when we lost control of our inner voices, and our minds became filled with an endless stream of thoughts, images and memories. Normally, we do not notice this chatter amongst the activities of life, but whenever we stop we may be flooded with a confusion of 'voices' expressing fears for the future, guilt and regret over the past, and dissatisfaction because of what might have been. As the personal 'I' grew stronger, we not only suffered from mind chatter, but also lost our sense of unity with others and nature. This left us with a sense of isolation, incompleteness, and existential loneliness. Similarly, we stopped fully sensing our surroundings when mental energy was diverted to focused thought. Instead of experiencing the world ablaze with life, color and depth, we encounter it as dull, flat, and uninteresting except when it is enlivened by new experiences. We sacrificed rich perception to the ego and survival, entering what Taylor calls "perceptual sleep."

In our efforts to escape this inner "psychic disharmony" we fill our lives with distractions—entertainment and hobbies, the transient joys of material possessions, and the continuous effort to be someone special. Taylor argues that the ego is responsible for other characteristics of the post-Fall psyche as well. We are made warlike by our desire for wealth and status, our loss of empathy, and our longing for excitement. The ego's craving for power gave rise to the religious idea that the mind is pure, and the body sinful. This, in turn, resulted in male domination because women are more closely associated with the body through menstruation and giving birth. Social inequality and the harsh treatment of children similarly emerged from the ego's drive for status and power.

The ego explosion hypothesis is one of very few attempts to explain The Fall, and is significant because it points to the importance of psychological rather than social, economic, technological or environmental factors. However, as Steve Taylor acknowledges, the ego explosion may represent a sudden increase in strength of the ego, not its birth. In discussing the great leap forward in Chapter 8, we argued that the ego may have emerged

100,000 years ago.[9] If this is the case, it would have had tens of millennia to develop before The Fall. Its presence and strength in agricultural civilization is indicated by the decline of cooperation and sharing, the appearance of family households, and the rise of ownership of land and possessions. It seems likely that the ego would have continued to develop steadily even if the great drying and The Fall had not happened.

Trauma

Ego can take different forms. A truly strong ego does not need to be special, or to be seen to be powerful. Rather than seeking to control others, it facilitates and empowers, allowing them to take the credit. It is empathic, compassionate and loving. By contrast, the ego that emerged at The Fall only appears strong. It is aggressive, domineering, violent and competitive; hungry for success, power and status. But behind this façade is often weakness, a lack of self-esteem and self-confidence. It is a defense mechanism arising from trauma. We believe the trauma of drought and war sparked by The Fall underlies the ego explosion.

This conclusion is supported by James DeMeo who argues that the shift from matrist to patrist cultures was triggered by trauma. He bases his theory on Wilhelm Reich's concept of psychological armoring which we described in Chapter 4. In brief, Reich held that a child learns to repress its basic drives if its needs are not met. This results in unexpressed fear, anger and resentment which either corrode the individual from within, or explode later in violent, sadistic, antisocial behavior. An infant that becomes armored does not develop the capacity for intimate, loving relationships with others. As an adult, it will experience dysfunctional relationships, and will be cold and harsh towards its own offspring. In this way, it passes the trauma to the next generation. However, DeMeo argues that for a whole society to become violent and patrist requires a trauma that is not only powerful, but also prolonged, widespread, and from an external source. The famine caused by the great drying, and invasion by aggressive nomads provided that stimulus.

Reflection

We search for a single cause of The Fall in vain. It arose from a concatenation of environmental, social, cultural, psychological, economic and technological factors. However, it seems that trauma, particularly due to climate change and growing violence, played a major role.

15. Reactions to The Fall

Steve Taylor identified two historical waves of reaction to the Fall.[1] These have ameliorated many of the harshest features of dominator civilization, and continue to have a moderating effect. But the stark reality is that, 5,000 years on, the world has still not returned to a peaceful, cooperative and caring partnership way of being. Why is that?

The First Wave

The first wave began with Indian sages more than 2,500 years ago, and can be traced through the mystical traditions within all major religions. These teachings stress that we cannot escape the psychic disharmony wrought by the ego explosion by accumulating wealth, status or power. We can find contentment and inner peace only by transcending the ego and the mental suffering it brings. In order to do this, we must recognize that we are not actually isolated egos, separate from each other, nature and the rest of material existence. Rather, we are expressions in physical form of an underlying spiritual essence or life force which is variously called Brahman, God, Consciousness and many other names. Another way of expressing this is that we are creations of the spirit of evolution which drives the cosmos towards ever-greater complexity and consciousness. When we truly understand this, we realize that the ego, or 'I', with which we identify so strongly is not our true identity. We are actually manifestations of cosmic Consciousness, the source of all existence. This realization brings awareness of the unity and interdependence of all life, and the perception that our personal identity is a mirage. We exist only as integral parts of one dynamic, interactive whole. This awareness brings empathy, love and compassion in its wake.[2]

History shows that this fundamental insight failed to have

more than a minor impact on dominator cultures. In many cases, states and hierarchies successfully co-opted the spiritual teachings, turning them into institutional religions that supported the status quo. Mainstream Christianity clearly falls into this category with its close connection to rulers, political ideologies and war. A key reason why the first wave failed may be that most spiritual teachings focus on escape from the sufferings of life to Nirvana or Heaven, rather than on reform of civilization and the creation of heaven on earth. Exceptions include engaged Buddhism and the Religious Society of Friends, or Quakers.

Another possible reason is that spiritual enlightenment threatens the survival of the individual ego which defends itself by blocking awakening with all the psychological weapons at its disposal. As a result, most people find the message and practices of the sages unattractive compared to the glittering distractions of the world, and the lure of wealth, status and power. According to Grant McFetridge, this ability of the ego to block access to higher states of consciousness may be a result of trauma.[3] If this is the case, the trauma of The Fall not only caused the transition to dominator ways of being, but also explains the failure of the first wave to have more impact.

Despite this history, there are signs that spirituality may yet play an important role in the transition to a partnership culture. For the last few decades, traditional, institutional religions have been declining in the western world. But simultaneously there has been an upsurge of interest in spirituality, and the emergence of many new teachers with powerful messages, including The Dalai Lama, Thich Nhat Hanh and Eckhart Tolle. Whole libraries of books have been published, and thousands of workshops are given each year, that teach ways to understand and transcend the ego. It seems that the first wave may yet have a major impact.

The Second Wave

The second wave of reaction to The Fall began in the eighteenth century. Over the years since, there has been a swelling flood of social reforms in relation to corporal and capital punishment, prison conditions, child labor, education, slavery, democracy, rules of warfare, peacekeeping, women's rights, human rights, animal rights, social security, and so on. Steve Taylor claims that this softening of the hard edges of the dominator culture is due to an upsurge of empathy and compassion. Unlike the first wave, he suggests that this is not due to a weakening of the ego so much as the evolution of humanity to a higher level of consciousness.[4] However, the continued strength of the ego undermines the power and energy of the second wave, limiting its potential. Even when we are empathic and compassionate, we may be motivated subconsciously by ego, and use the reform movement to boost our own self-importance, and to meet our emotional needs for recognition and power. This desire to be someone special may be why the myriad non-governmental organizations with similar aims and programs do not unite into a stronger, more coherent reform movement.

Evelin Lindner brings a slightly different perspective.[5] For thousands of years, civilizations were based on the belief that there is a natural order in which some are born to rule, and others to be ruled. However, during the last 250 years this ideology has slowly been giving way to a perception that every person is of equal value. Early expressions of this new perspective were the American Declaration of Independence of 1776, and the French Revolution of 1789. Vital to the rise of this movement was a weakening of conflict between European nations over resources. Colonialism greatly expanded available supplies at the expense of non-European peoples who were not included within the ambit of human rights.

The emergence of the human rights ideology, and the rise of empathy and compassion, coincided with the advent of science and objective reason as a source of mastery over the material world. This heralded a further lifting of resource constraints as knowledge began to replace physical resources as the key to economic success. Unlike natural resources, knowledge is not depleted by use and can grow without limit. Unfortunately, science and reason have cast aside traditional intuitive wisdom, and the ethical restraints that values bring. Arguing that knowledge is neutral and value free, they are equally at home serving violence, war, tyranny and hate as they are compassion, peace, liberty, and love. Reason has become an instrument of power, blind to the ends it serves, thus undermining the ability of the second wave to end the dominator culture.

Richard Rhodes proposed yet another explanation for the reforms of the last few centuries.[6] Violence was the normal way of settling disputes at all levels of medieval European society. However, Rhodes noted that this pattern began to shift during the renaissance when monarchs sought to control the use of military weapons in order to protect their tax income. By the nineteenth century, this monopoly of violence was generally exercised by national police forces. Concurrently, access to law courts improved, and the rising middle class began to settle disputes by litigation. Also during this period, child-rearing practices slowly became less brutal, and education spread. From this viewpoint, violence was constrained and trauma reduced by strengthening power at the top of the hierarchy, thereby opening the way to other social reforms.

All these explanations probably contain elements of the truth. But, whatever the reasons, signs of this historical progress towards partnership are all around us today. It is developing into a global grassroots movement which links those working for peace, justice, human rights, an end to poverty, community development, action on climate change, environmental conservation, and other causes. This is well illustrated by WiserEarth whose website helps people and organizations around the world to connect, collaborate, share knowledge, and build alliances.[7] In June 2009, its database listed over 110,000 organizations in 243 countries, out of an estimated 1 million worldwide. In her book *The Power of Partnership*, Riane Eisler noted that we do not hear about this movement in the media because it is decentralized and uncoordinated, and lacks a defining name.[8] As already noted, this fragmentation may be a weakness arising from the ego-driven agendas of many of the movement's leaders as a result of trauma. It also may be a strength that makes it hard for the power hierarchy to control.

Despite this progress, the dominator culture is still strong, and the second wave seems to be making slow and uncertain progress. Eisler points out that "there are regressive forces pushing us back toward ... patterns of domination. Some are terrorists ... Others are in our own nation. And most of us carry inside us the dominator habits that get in the way of the good life we yearn for."[9] The twentieth century and the beginning of the twenty-first were marked by constant warfare, unprecedented mass slaughter, genocide, torture, poverty, famine, exploitation, renewed slavery, centralization of power, greed, environmental destruction, climate change, depletion of resources, and other typical dominator activities. Meanwhile, the 'wars' on terror, drugs and crime are eroding civil liberties painfully gained in earlier times. In mid-2009, corrupt state and corporate power hierarchies appeared to have survived the financial meltdown of 2008 at the expense of the mass of the population. They were intent on patching up the old system rather than reinventing it as many people had hoped.

This discussion reveals that two ideologies currently coexist. One is cooperative, compassionate and egalitarian, seeking to live in peace and harmony with the each other and the Earth. The other is mired in greed, violence, corruption and environmental destruction. A civilization based on partnership ideals is struggling to be born despite the backlash of the dominator system that has ruled since The Fall. Fighting for its survival, the power hierarchy is seeking to entrench its position by absorbing and institutionalizing reforms that do not threaten its core values and structures, resisting those that do, subverting grassroots movements to its own ends, and pacifying the masses with propaganda, promises and a return to escalating consumerism. It seems as if the future of civilization and humanity is balanced on a knife's edge, and could tip either way. Given enough time, the first and second waves may yet prevail. But we do not have much time. The challenges facing us are urgent. We need to develop a new strategy, and look for ways to promote a third wave.

The Dynamics of Power

The dynamics of power help to explain why the first and second waves have not succeeded in reforming the dominator culture, and re-establishing partnership. Consider the options available to a tribe threatened by an aggressive neighbor. If they choose not to resist, they will be conquered and destroyed, or simply absorbed into the victorious culture. Passive resistance along Gandhian lines will not work if the enemy is ruthless enough to slaughter or enslave resistors. Withdrawal to a new place is possible, but any unoccupied area is likely to be inhospitable, and the tribe can move to an area that is already occupied only by conquering or displacing its inhabitants. Finally, the tribe could choose armed defense. Whichever way the tribe responds, it either uses power itself, or rewards and reinforces the use of power by others. Thus, aggressive power is like a disease that spreads until it is universal, and the course of history is dictated by the most warlike.

This is what international relations theory calls the security dilemma. In Evelin Lindner's words: "I have to amass power, because I am scared. When I amass weapons, you get scared. You amass weapons, I get more scared."[10] Even if nobody wants war, arms races and bloodshed emerge from mutual distrust. As

Andrew Schmookler expressed it: "no one is free to choose peace, but anyone can impose upon all the necessity for power."[11]

A similar dynamic exists within nations and societies, where the most aggressive, power-hungry individuals become dominant unless there are strong traditions and norms to prevent it. As we described in Chapter 9, such conditions existed in many hunter-gatherer bands which emphasized alternating leadership and democratic decision-making, and distrusted those who sought power. Following The Fall, however, civilization came to be equated with a hierarchical social structure in which more powerful and higher-ranked individuals ruled and exploited those of lower rank. Fellow humans came to be seen as resources to be exploited. The mass of the people were forced to serve systems of power rather than cooperative networks.

Today, globalization and interdependence are changing the instruments of power. Imperial wars are giving way to economic competition, but the power hierarchy remains firmly in place. The vast majority of humanity is enslaved by the capitalist machine that exploits us in the service of the rich and powerful. This became abundantly clear after the financial crash of 2008, when ordinary taxpayers footed astronomical bills for bailing out the super-rich who continued shamelessly to award themselves huge bonuses for failure, and to profiteer from market speculation.

For several thousand years after The Fall, the rigid ranking of society was accepted as divinely ordained. Every person was expected to know their place in the order of things, and all strata of society obeyed a moral duty to keep inferiors in their place. But the rise of the human rights movement in the last few centuries has changed this belief system. Respect for the innate value of every individual is now the ideal, enshrined in the UN's Universal Declaration of Human Rights. In theory at least, a lowly street-sweeper is as worthy of human dignity as the highest official. Wounding a person's dignity now means wounding their core self—as profound a violation as injuring their body. Humiliation has become the ultimate act of aggression, and is now commonly inflicted on victims before they are killed. An old Somali proverb states: "Humiliation is worse than death; in times of war, words of humiliation hurt more than bullets."[12] In Rwanda, before being killed, grandmothers were forced to parade naked in the streets, daughters were raped in front of their families, and tall Tutsis had their legs cut off to lower their arrogance. Victims were willing to pay for bullets and begged to be shot rather than be slowly humiliated to death.[13] Evelin Lindner argues that it is humiliation that transforms simple deprivation into unbearable suffering and triggers extremism and terrorism. Humiliation, she claims, is the catalyst that turns grievances into "nuclear bombs of emotions."[14] The ideology of human dignity and humiliation gave birth to an era of popular, often bloody, revolutions. But these did not end the dominator cultures as many of their supporters hoped. Instead, they served only to shuffle the hierarchy and put new despots at the top.

The Potential for Partnership or Domination

We humans embody the potential for both domination and partnership. There is our selfish, greedy, power-hungry side. And there is our cooperative, peaceful, caring side. The balance between these characteristics depends less on our genes than on the environment in which we grow up. If we are surrounded with cooperation, caring and empathy, these traits will develop. And if we are treated with violence, aggression and humiliation, we will learn to behave that way ourselves. The lust for power and status that we see all around us does not reflect human nature so much as the post-Fall culture that develops psychopathology through systematic trauma, as Andrew Schmookler explains:[15]

By systematically traumatizing its members, especially in their most impressionable and formative years, a society can recast the image of man (sic) to achieve its own ends. ... A fulfilled person at peace with the world is an instrument of limited utility (to power). But frustrate him enough, and his energies turn to rage which can be channeled for his society's power. ... What hurts the individual human being may therefore be helpful to the power-maximizing system, helpful not necessarily despite the human injury but sometimes even because of it. ... It is not just that the struggle for power grinds people up, or that the selection for power is indifferent to human needs. Beyond that, the evolving systems of power-maximization utilize human suffering as a major fuel to energize their operation. ... the pent-up rage of society's members can fuel the engine of social power, by strengthening the ruling part and by fortifying the aggressive drive of the whole.

If we are to reverse The Fall and create a new civilization based on partnership, we must find ways to constrain the dynamics of power so that a culture of cooperation and caring can grow and flourish without being crushed or co-opted by the existing power system.

Closure to Part IV

For tens of thousands of years, prehistory was a story mostly of cooperation, sharing and equality as humanity progressed from hunting and gathering to agricultural civilization. Then, in the space of just one or two millennia, a new culture appeared in Saharasia which was hierarchical, aggressive, warlike and greedy. So great was this transformation that it seems there was hardly a belief, value, attitude, social structure or behavioral norm that was unaffected. At first restricted to Mesopotamia and Egypt, these societies set a pattern which spread like a disease around the world through conquest, colonization and cultural influence. So dominant has this way of being become that its characteristics have become synonymous with civilization.

Almost certainly there was no single cause of The Fall, but a key trigger was severe and enduring desiccation of the climate. As a species, we had survived similar environmental challenges many times, but never before had cooperation and sharing been displaced by violent and ruthless competition. Clearly, a new combination of factors must have been at work. These included a culture that was already evolving in this direction, a new sense of belonging to a particular place and owning possessions, a higher population density, the loss of hunting and gathering skills, the harshness of the central Asian steppes, and the existence of the fertile flood-plains of Egypt and Mesopotamia. But running like a dark, unifying thread throughout the history of The Fall is trauma, and the response to it. The trauma of famine and migration. The trauma of being a refugee. The trauma of seeing your family and community brutally slaughtered before your eyes. The trauma of pack rape and enslavement. The trauma of hungry infants, in pain and lacking tender maternal care. The collective trauma of generation after generation who not only experienced worsening aridity and violence, but also were raised by cold, harsh, traumatized parents.

Down the centuries, there have been many attempts to revert to a partnership culture. The Buddha, Lao Tsu, Jesus and other great spiritual teachers pointed towards a more loving, compassionate way. But their words have been perverted and ignored. More recently, reformers from the eighteenth century onwards have slowly chipped away at the dominator edifice. But the dominator culture has proved to be powerful and resilient. Like a hydra, as soon as one head is lopped off, another raises itself to ensure that male power, aggression and violence remain in charge.

The main reason for this is the self-perpetuating cycle of trauma. But there is still hope. Prehistory demonstrates clearly that humans are not innately violent, aggressive, and selfish. We are not inevitably doomed by our genes to destroy ourselves. There is another side to our nature that is cooperative, peaceful, compassionate and generous; a side that we can foster and bring to the fore once again as we learn to heal our existing wounds, and minimize the creation of fresh trauma.

Part V. Trauma Today

If we provide enriched, nurturing, predictable, and safe environments for our children, they will create an enriched, safe, and humane society. If we keep raising our children with ignorance, unpredictability, and fear, we will have a rigid and reactionary society. It is our choice—our responsibility—our opportunity.
Bruce Perry[1]

Following The Fall, a self-perpetuating cycle of trauma became a defining feature of civilization. Despite some softening of dominator cultures in the last few centuries, trauma remains a central characteristic of modern society, and one of the most powerful drivers of cultural evolution. It may also have become a key driver of biological evolution. Modern civilization favors the most aggressive and dominant individuals, thus creating a selection pressure for genes that promote these characteristics.

In the last few decades, sophisticated and sensitive scientific techniques have enabled the workings of the human brain and body to be explored in exquisite detail. For the first time, we are beginning to understand how trauma works at the genetic, molecular and neurological levels. Simultaneously, research in psychology, epidemiology, sociology and other social sciences, is revealing just how widespread and severe trauma is today, and how large an impact it has on all our lives.

Part V provides an overview of trauma today, and seeks to answer several questions:

- What is known about the biological mechanisms of trauma?
- How and where are the memories of traumatic experiences stored?
- How is trauma transmitted from one generation to the

next?

- How common is trauma today?
- How does trauma affect the development of the individual?
- How do the effects of trauma vary with age?
- What impacts does trauma have on modern society?
- How is trauma related to the problems we are facing as a civilization and a species?

16. The Memory of Trauma

Trauma is a function of memory. If we did not remember past events, there would be no trauma. But memory is not just a database of information stored in the brain. Memory happens at many levels, and takes many forms. Our genes encode mutations that have survived the rigors of natural selection over evolutionary time, and thus record a memory of our ancestors. The activity of these genes is switched on and off by molecules that record our experiences—memories that we may pass to our offspring. The unique balance of hormones that controls many of our functions also reflects our past lives, as does the complex inner chemistry of our cells. Similarly, the way our organs work, the patterns of muscular tension throughout our bodies, our emotional responses to events, and the electrical and chemical traces laid down in our brains are all elements of memory. In order to comprehend the impact of trauma on our mental, emotional and physical lives, and on society as a whole, we must first understand how these various strands of memory work, and how they are woven into a coherent story of who we are. Science has not yet revealed all the details and subtleties, but an extraordinary, fascinating picture is emerging.[1]

Nature and Nurture

There is a strong belief today that we are the product of our genes. Regularly, there are triumphant announcements of the discovery of 'the gene for' this or that disorder ranging from autism to schizophrenia, alcoholism to violence. But few conditions are caused by single genes. In most cases, there is a complex web of interactions amongst many genes, each of which affects many characteristics. Also, the potential encoded in the genes is sculpted by our experiences between conception and death. These experiences have a significant influence on the size and structure of the brain, the balance of intellect and emotion, personality, and even which genes are active. In other words, we are products of both nature and nurture, genes and environment. Without the physical systems built from genetic blueprints there would be nothing for experience to work on. But it is experience which shapes what the genes create, and adapts it to the environment. Trauma is a critical part of the experiences which make us who we are.

We have argued that humans embody the potential to be loving, peaceful and cooperative, or savagely aggressive and violent, or anywhere in between. Where each of us is positioned on this spectrum depends on both our genetic inheritance and our life experiences. The genetic component is illustrated clearly by animal breeding experiments. By selecting the tamest or most aggressive young in each litter, it proved possible to transform the behavior of rats within about 20 generations. Two lines were produced this way. The tame ones are friendly and can be handled with ease, but the aggressive rats are vicious and must be approached with chain-mail gloves. These traits did not change when tame offspring were raised by aggressive mothers, and aggressive offspring were raised by tame mothers.[2] This demonstrates that nurture cannot override such a strongly-selected genetic predisposition, but does not mean that it has no effect. In other studies, the development of rat pups has been shown to be significantly affected by maternal care, diet and other environmental factors.[3] The scope for such environmental influence also would be greater in a more genetically diverse population.

In an article about research on domestication of wild animals, Henry Nicholls suggests that the need for cooperation in order to survive may have led humans to weed out the more aggressive individuals over millions of years. In other words, we may have domesticated ourselves! This hypothesis fits well with the partnership phase of prehistory, but the evolutionary pressure has been reversed since The Fall. In dominator cultures, it seems likely that we are selecting primarily for dominance and aggression rather than cooperation. Given that animals can be domesticated in 20 or 30 generations, this process may already have had a significant impact on our personalities.

Of Genes and Membranes

Another common belief is that the genes control the inner workings of the cells they inhabit, but this exaggerates their role. Each gene is simply a recipe for making a specific protein—one of the building blocks of life. Every cell in our bodies has the same genes, and hence the same database of recipes. But different selections of recipes are used to create over 100 types of cell, from neurons to muscles. How this selection process works is still far from fully understood, but in most cases gene activity, or gene expression as it is often called, is controlled by the combination of several regulatory molecules. Each of these molecules may affect many genes, and the same molecules may occur in a variety of cell types in different parts of the body at different stages of development. Thus, it seems that the regulatory molecules are like words whose meaning changes with their context. It is the combination of words into a meaningful command that matters. This means that the effect of adding a regulatory molecule to a cell depends on the cell's history, and which molecules are already present. One new molecule may appear to do nothing, whereas another may be the last piece of the jigsaw that triggers a major process, such as development of the eye.[4]

Some regulatory molecules are produced by genes within the cell itself. But for the body to develop correctly, each cell must coordinate what it becomes with the rest of the organism. To do this, it must communicate with its environment via the cell membrane, which does far more than hold the cell together. The membrane controls what goes into the cell, and what comes out, and many of the chemical reactions that take place within it. The source of this power lies in hundreds of thousands of 'integral membrane proteins' or IMPs embedded in the membrane.[5] There are thousands of different IMPs, but they can be divided into two basic types. 'Receptor' molecules receive signals in the form of molecules or energy such as sound, light or radio waves. Each receptor responds to a particular signal, such as a molecule of a particular shape, or an energy pattern with which it resonates. When it receives a signal, the IMP changes shape, thus sparking a cascade of chemical reactions within the cell. The second type of IMP is known as an 'effector', and works like a valve. When it detects an ion or molecule of the right type, the effector opens to let it into or out of the cell, and then closes again.

Collectively, the IMPs perform several functions including gene regulation. Some of the molecules admitted to the cell are gene regulators themselves, and others may initiate chemical reactions that produce regulators. Similarly, a regulator may be made in response to a signal received by a receptor. Another function of the membrane is to control basic cell operations such as nutrition, excretion and energy production. It also monitors the cell's environment, and adjusts the cell's biochemistry in response. Part of this monitoring is an exchange of signals with surrounding cells by which they tell each other about their health and activity. In this way, the cells cooperatively coordinate their activities to form a functioning organism without needing a hierarchical control system. As part of this process, each cell must 'remember' its particular mix of regulatory molecules and pattern of activated genes so that it can pass on its characteristics when it replaces itself as it ages.

Not only does the internal chemistry of the cell change in response to external conditions, but also the sensitivity and number of receptors are adjusted according to the concentration of specific messenger molecules in the surrounding fluid.[6] In other words, the pattern of IMPs represents a memory of past conditions. For example, when we fail to release the energy of arousal following a traumatic event, our cells adjust to elevated levels of stress hormones, thus 'remembering' the experience. The cell membrane also plays a vital part in personal identity. The IMPs include unique 'self-receptors' that enable the immune system to distinguish what is part of us from what is not. Bruce Lipton points out that it is not the receptors nor the cell that contains the 'self'. Rather, it is implicit in the signals from the environment that activate the self-receptors. He concludes that our unique identity does not lie within us, but in our response to our surroundings.[7]

The relative importance of the genes and membrane to the cell as a whole is illustrated by experiments in which part of the cell is removed. If the nucleus is removed, together with its genes, the cell cannot replace damaged proteins or reproduce. But it can sustain all the complex processes of life until lack of repair causes a lethal breakdown. By contrast, if the IMPs are destroyed, the cell immediately becomes comatose even though its genes are undamaged.

Epigenetics

Bruce Lipton points out that there are around 100,000 different proteins in the human body, but only 25,000 genes. Hence, many genes must be able to produce several proteins depending on environmental conditions. In some cases, over 2,000 protein variants can be created by a single gene.[8] Such variation in gene expression not only enables many different cell types to be produced from the same blueprint, but also means that development after conception is quite malleable and not determined by a rigid genetic blueprint. It can be modified by nutrition, stress, trauma, emotions, learning, environmental changes, and other factors.

The significance of such 'epigenetic' variation is illustrated by laboratory studies of mice. A single faulty gene can create obese, yellow mice. However, when a yellow pregnant mother was fed a diet rich in methyl groups, her offspring were normal. In other words, the modified diet silenced the faulty gene by a process known as 'methylation'.[9] By late 2009, the human epigenome had been deciphered, revealing that there are an astonishing 50 million methylation sites that control the expression of just 25,000 genes.[10]

In another experiment on rodents, it proved possible to compensate for an inactivated memory gene by providing a mentally stimulating environment in adolescence. More surprisingly, this improved memory was passed to the mother's pups when she was stimulated before becoming pregnant even though she still had the faulty gene.[11] The first direct evidence that such epigenetic inheritance occurs in humans was published in 2008. This was based on a study of methylation patterns on the IGF2 gene in Dutch people whose mothers had been severely malnourished during pregnancy in World War II. The researchers found that famine in the first 10 weeks after conception resulted in much less methylation than in siblings of the same sex whose gestation had not been affected by famine. In other words, environmental conditions early in pregnancy influenced gene expression for life, and there is a possibility that these patterns have been passed on to their children.[12]

Other research has shown that the level of the hormone testosterone to which the fetus is exposed in the womb has a significant effect on mental and behavioral development—presumably by influencing the expression of certain genes.[13] Such epigenetic control of gene expression represents another form of memory of our experiences, including trauma. In some cases, this memory may be transmitted to the next generation, and possibly beyond.

The Chemical and Electrical Brains

Many of the molecules which bind to receptor IMPs have been emitted by other cells in the organism, and distributed in the blood, cerebrospinal fluid, and the liquid around the cells. These molecules are variously called hormones, steroids, neurotransmitters, peptides and other names. But they are all 'information molecules' that are made and 'read' in most parts of the body. Seldom are these molecules limited to a single function and part of the body, which is why it is so difficult to develop drugs with no side-effects.[14] As Candace Pert expressed it, these information molecules "are the sheet music containing the notes, phrases, and rhythms that allow the orchestra—your body—to play as an integrated entity. And the music that results is the tone or feeling that you experience subjectively as your emotions."[15]

This complex communication system coordinates the nervous, immune, endocrine and other systems, as well as the many organs, and trillions of individual cells in the body. In order to do this, it is necessary for every organ and system to remember and learn from past experience. The immune system, for example, keeps copies of antibodies it has developed to particular pathogens. But its memory is more sophisticated than this. In one experiment, researchers took mice with an overactive immune system, and fed them with sweet water laced with a drug to suppress the immune system. After a learning period, the immune system responded to sweet water alone. In other words, it remembered that sweet water coincided with loss of immunity and suppressed itself! Similar results have been obtained in humans.[16] Bruce Perry states that the muscles, nervous system and glands also have memories.

The chemical brain was the first coordination system to evolve, and works well in organisms with only a few cells. However, it is too slow for animals with billions of cells, and so evolution invented the faster electro-chemical brain and nervous system to work alongside it. The human brain is the most complex system known, with over a trillion cells linked in intricate, ever-changing networks. There are two main types of brain cell: neurons and glial cells. The vast majority are glial cells which support and guide the growth of the neurons, and build an insulating sheath around them to increase their efficiency. Of more interest here are the 100 billion neurons which communicate with each other, and store information. There are hundreds of types of neuron with different functions, but typically they are long and divided into many branches. Those branches that receive information are called dendrites, and those that send information are called axons. Where an axon from one neuron comes close to a dendrite from another, an interface is formed called a synapse. Synapses link neurons into chains and networks, which perform specific functions, such as contracting a muscle or recalling an image.

About 100 different messenger molecules, or neuro-transmitters, flow across the synapses in response to electrical signals. When a neurotransmitter binds to a receptor, it sets off reactions within the neuron. These may include switching certain genes on or off, with long-lasting effects on the way the neuron grows and responds to signals. For instance, high levels of a particular neurotransmitter may induce the neuron to reduce the number of receptors for it, and too little may have the opposite effect. As they cascade through the network, such processes can regulate whole chains of neurons.

Most research has focused on the operation of the synapses, but Candace Pert points out that as much as 98% of the brain's communications may actually occur through receptors elsewhere on the neurons' membranes. These include receptors for most of the messenger molecules produced in other parts of the body, many of which are not neurotransmitters.[17] This means that the older chemical information system is closely integrated with the brain's operation, and the two should be considered as a single system. Their joint task is to coordinate the activity of the trillions of cells in the body to produce a coherent response by the whole organism to external events. In order to achieve this, the brain may hover on the border between order and chaos. For much of the time, information input to the brain may accumulate in an orderly way, like grains added to a pile of sand. But occasionally there is a sudden and unpredictable avalanche that reorganizes the sand pile, or the state of the brain.[18] It is possible that trauma results from such a chaotic avalanche, and that another avalanche sometimes may be needed for healing.

Emotions

The emotions illustrate how the chemical 'brain' cooperates with the electrical brain and conscious mind. Like memory, emotions are central to the experience of trauma—especially anger, fear and shame. Candace Pert argues that they are produced by 'molecules of emotion' that bind with specific receptors at major nerve junctions, and activate relevant brain circuits.[19] The mind in turn can modify the emotions by ordering the nervous system to release appropriate regulatory signals. Each emotion is probably associated with a specific molecule, but each type of molecule may have more than one function. For instance, the molecule that causes a feeling of thirst may also stimulate the kidneys to conserve water. Bruce Lipton argues that these emotional signals evolved as a way to communicate the overall state of the organism to all its cells simultaneously.[20]

Each molecule of emotion induces a specific pattern of muscle tension, and corresponding body sensations. The mind then interprets these sensations as anger, fear, shame or some other emotion, thus bringing it to conscious awareness. The basic emotions are probably genetically determined. They produce universally-recognized facial expressions, and are reflected in body postures and movements, as well as everyday language (Table 15). This interaction between body and emotions also works in reverse. The emotional feeling of a past event often can be evoked by adopting the appropriate expression or posture, or by an associated smell, color or other stimulus. This is frequently how flashbacks to past traumatic experiences are triggered.

Table 15: Some Indicators of Emotion

(Adapted from Rothschild 2000)

	Anger	*Fear*	*Shame*
Language	A pain in the neck	Butterflies in the stomach	Can't look you in the eye
Body sensation	Tension, particularly jaw and shoulders	Racing heart, trembling, nausea, stomach pain	Heat, especially face
Behavior	Yelling, fighting	Flight, shaking	Hiding
Body cues	Clamped jaw, red neck	Wide eyes, lifted brows, trembling, blanching	Blushing, averted gaze

The emotions play other vital roles as well. The senses send far more information to the nervous system than the mind can process and store. Hence, most of these data are filtered out before they reach the brain. The filters are receptors and associated signal molecules at major nodes in the nervous system which have been programmed by our past experiences—yet another instance of memory. This means that the stimuli to which we pay conscious attention are selected by our emotions.[21] This conclusion is consistent with other research which shows that people who cannot feel emotions find it very difficult to make decisions. Indeed, neurologist Antonio Damasio claims that we need to feel the consequences of alternatives emotionally in order to make a rational choice.[22] Similarly, intuition and 'gut feelings' have been shown to be a better guide to action than rationality in complex situations.

Development of the Electrical Brain

The brain is too complex to be encoded in a genetic blueprint. Instead, the genes provide a rough sketch of the brain's form and how it should work, and set up ways by which it can be refined through experience. This gives our offspring exceptional flexibility to match the brain's development to their social and material environment.[23] The process is self-organizing, influenced by many factors but controlled by none. Factors include the active genes in each cell, the molecules and ions in the cell fluid, interactions with the physical environment, relationships with parents and other humans, and the current stage of development. As an example, vision does not work at birth, but as soon as light hits the retina a cascade of reactions completes the system. In similar, if less dramatic, ways we learn throughout life as new experiences trigger fresh development.

The brain starts to develop soon after conception, and most neurons are formed before birth. Some are large and long, others short; some have many dendrites for inputs from hundreds of other neurons, and some have only one. This differentiation is triggered by signals from the cell's environment that tell it which genes to turn on or off. Each type of neuron is then guided to where it is needed by signals from genes, glial cells and chemical markers. This process is mostly completed before birth, and can be adversely affected by infection, lack of oxygen, exposure to alcohol, and some psychoactive drugs.[24] Many areas of the brain end up with more neurons than they need. Any that are unused die, while those that are heavily used grow more dendrites which form synapses with nearby axons. A steady flow of neurotransmitters through a synapse stimulates it to become more efficient, but it dissolves if activity is low. During the first 8 months of infancy, there is a remarkable 8-fold increase in the number of synapses. These connections are then pruned and refined over the next few years.

The main structural features of the triune brain develop in

sequence, starting with the reptilian brain, i.e. the brain-stem and mid-brain. These parts are fully operational at birth, ready to regulate breathing, heartbeat and other essential functions. At this stage, the infant also has basic sensory systems and reflexes which only need stimulation after birth to mature. Experiences in the womb are vital for this development. In the third trimester of pregnancy, the infant uses the rhythm of its mother's heartbeat as a template for organizing its own brain. Similarly, the mother's movements during her daily activities provide stimulation. The sounds of speech and singing by its mother and others may be important for developing hearing and language. And the father's voice, touch, and gentle lovemaking that emotionally includes the baby may start to build a loving relationship that can blossom in infancy.[25]

As higher brain levels mature, they gain the ability to regulate lower areas. Thus, a three-year-old child's behavior is still governed by the mid-brain, and she cannot control a tantrum. Later, however, she learns to use higher parts of the brain to moderate her behavior when angry. Development of the brain's structure is not automatic, but depends on appropriate experiences at critical times. These windows of opportunity are often narrow, and the early ones are the most important because the stages of development build upon each other. If the right experiences do not happen at the right time, the limbic system and cortex may remain permanently under-developed. For example, lack of nurturing and exposure to violence compromise the development of empathy, sympathy, remorse and attachment, predisposing the child to impulsive, reactive, aggressive and violent behaviors. Conversely, given plenty of positive social interaction, the infant's cortex develops emotional intelligence, empathy, and the ability to control inappropriate instinctive and emotional impulses from lower levels of the brain.[26]

Maturation of the cortex is significantly influenced by sex hormones which modify the expression of genes controlling the growth of dendrites and the formation of synapses. By 18 months, the psychological gender of the child is fixed, including differences in emotional regulation, aggression, and cognitive talents.[27] The most important determinant of orientation is the gender in which the infant is raised, including genital play and parental attitudes to it. Research on rats has shown that the more licking a pup is given, the more brain development is pushed towards the male end of the spectrum. It is possible that differences in nurturing similarly underlie some gender-related diseases in humans, including the prevalence of depression, and Parkinson's and Alzheimer's diseases.[28]

Many key developmental events are irreversible, so that inappropriate infant experiences produce lifelong effects. The adult brain is less adaptable than the infant brain, and lower levels are less flexible than higher levels. By three years old, most of the brain is already organized. Only the cortex remains significantly plastic, and able to learn new skills. As a result, our ability to heal childhood trauma is limited. Reflecting on this development process, Bruce Perry argues that neglect may be the most destructive and least understood aspect of child maltreatment.[29] He believes it is easier to heal abuse by changing a traumatized part of the brain than it is to develop a missing part after the window of opportunity has passed. However, others believe the brain remains more plastic than is generally thought, and that it is possible to compensate partially for some missed stages.[30]

All these processes are regulated by the experiences of the fetus and infant, so that the brain develops to match the demands of the world into which it is born—whether that be a hunter-gatherer group or a modern urban family. The down-side of this process is that the brain also adapts irreversibly to neglect, abuse, starvation and other traumas. Here again is a remarkable example of memory. The very structure and wiring of our brains and nervous systems hold a record of our early lives.

Varieties of Memory

The brain operates several different types of memory, all of which involve patterns of activity in networks of neurons. Short-term, or working, memory only lasts for seconds before the information fades or is transferred to long-term memory as part of a pattern. The more often a pattern of stimuli occurs, the stronger and more permanent the memory becomes. Patterns that occur infrequently generally decay from lack of use. But a rare traumatic experience may be powerful enough to create a long-term memory of fear even if it is not repeated.

Long-term memories fall into two main categories: explicit and implicit. Explicit memory is conscious, cognitive, and can be expressed in language. It is comprised of facts, stories, and instructions for doing things such as recipes or mathematical operations. It also keeps track of when experiences happened, and in what sequence. Storing explicit memories is the responsibility of the hippocampus, which is part of the limbic system. The hippocampus does not mature until the age of about three, and its development may be impaired by repeated stress in infancy. This may account for the fact that children suffering from PTSD often experience memory and learning difficulties. The hippocampus is also suppressed during traumatic stress in adults, sometimes resulting in amnesia.[31] This happens because explicit memory is too slow in life-threatening situations. What is needed in emergencies is a gestalt—a holistic, total picture of past experience with which to compare the current situation.[32] This is provided by implicit memory.

Implicit memory is unconscious, and cannot be expressed in words. It consists of recorded body sensations and emotions, and also includes automatic skills such as riding a bicycle. Implicit memories are mediated by the amygdala, which is another part of the limbic system. Unlike the hippocampus, however, the amygdala is active from birth. It also remains active during traumatic events and flashbacks, when the hippocampus is switched off. This highlights yet another role of the emotions. What we consciously remember are things that have some emotional significance. We forget those that do not. Early childhood memories from before explicit memory developed are often random images with no particular significance that happen to be associated with certain feelings. But later in life, memories are more likely to be of events that were emotionally meaningful. Some researchers have concluded that events must have some emotional significance in order to be remembered.[33]

This division of memory helps to explain why we do not consciously remember infancy experiences, but nevertheless may be disturbed by emotional triggers associated with them. Before the hippocampus becomes active, memories of our emotions and physical sensations are stored in implicit memory, but we lack the factual and temporal context that explicit memory normally provides. The inactivation of the hippocampus during traumatic experiences also explains how it is possible to have disturbing memories of emotions and body sensations, and strange behavioral impulses in adulthood without any awareness of how, why and when they were formed.

Ivan Pavlov is famous for training dogs to associate the ringing of a bell with food. As a result, they would salivate when they heard the bell even when no food was available. Babette Rothschild suggests that such classical conditioning may explain triggers for flashbacks.[34] During a traumatic experience, specific cues may become associated with the trauma, and elicit a similar response in the future. When this happens, repressed memories spontaneously surface in response to a triggering event that is similar to some aspect of the original experience. Possible triggers include body posture, heart rate, mood and sexual arousal as well as color, sight, taste, touch or smell. Usually, flashbacks are triggered accidentally, but they may be activated deliberately in some forms of therapy. In severe cases, the response can escalate over time. Rothschild gives the example of a woman who was raped by a man wearing a red shirt. Later, she might panic when walking past a shop with red fabric in the window. Not understanding why this happened, she might then avoid that street. Later still, this might develop into agoraphobia—a panic attack in any street.

Repeated traumatic experiences can mold, or condition, behavior. Imagine a child is punished every time she speaks assertively. As a result, she suppresses this natural impulse, and in adulthood experiences panic at the thought of giving a speech. Similarly, repeated violence may extinguish the urge to protect oneself, leading to vulnerability later in life. Such conditioned patterns of behavior and beliefs can persist throughout life, even when there is plenty of objective evidence that they are not valid. On a more positive note, the power of conditioning also can be used to heal trauma.

Reflection

There is yet another, more speculative, form of memory arising from relativity and quantum physics. Many scientists believe the material reality we experience emerges from a universal field in which time and space form a timeless, spaceless unity. Some scientists have suggested that this field may hold a memory of everything that has ever happened, and everything that ever will happen in the cosmos. It is possible that the human mind can connect with this field, modifying it through our experiences and memories, and drawing information from it. In this way, we may remember and resonate with events that are distant in time and space. This could give rise to paranormal phenomena as well as the transmission of generational and collective trauma. Similar concepts are found in some ancient spiritual traditions and underlie some alternative therapies. This is not the place for in depth discussion of these ideas, but if you would like to know more, Malcolm Hollick discussed them in detail in his earlier book *The Science of Oneness*.

17. Before and at Birth

In the Beginning

The idea that we might be influenced by trauma before we are conceived may seem ridiculous at first. But imagine if a traumatic experience by one of our parents altered the expression of one of their genes, including in the egg or sperm that became us. According to traditional genetic theory, this is impossible. But recent research has shown that it does happen, at least to some extent.

The germ cells that eventually become eggs or sperm in adulthood are actually formed in the embryo. They then become dormant until they are needed after puberty. During these years, their genes are isolated from the changes going on in the developing child, including any due to trauma. But these protected germ cells are immature, and must complete their development before they can be used in reproduction. This process takes 10 weeks for sperm, and 28 days for the egg. During this maturation period, the germ cells are more sensitive to environmental influences, and the expression of some of their genes is changed in a process called genomic imprinting.[1]

At conception, we receive two copies of each gene, one from our mother and one from our father. Usually, both copies are active, but in some cases only the paternal or maternal version is expressed. Which one is active is determined by genomic imprinting in a tug-of-war between the genders. By mid-2008, 63 imprinted genes had been identified, and it was thought that several hundred of the 20,000 human genes may be imprinted. They have far-reaching effects on growth and development, including that of the brain, and they probably affect behavior, cognition and personality as well. Indeed, Christopher Badcock and Bernard Crespi developed a hypothesis that strong maternal bias in imprinting of certain genes leads to psychosis, and strong paternal bias leads to autism. They foresaw the possibility of developing a unified theory of psychiatric disorders based on genomic imprinting.[2] This would complement Dorothy Rowe's theory outlined in Chapter 1 that such disorders are different responses to fear, since fear could be a causal factor in the pattern of imprinting. Biologist Bruce Lipton draws equally far-reaching conclusions:[3]

Research reveals that parents act as genetic engineers for their children in the months before conception. In the final stages of egg and sperm maturation, a process called genomic imprinting *adjusts the activity of specific groups of genes that will shape the character of the child yet to be conceived. ... Research suggests that what is going on in the lives of the parents during the process of genomic imprinting has a profound influence on the mind and body of their child ... Interestingly, aboriginal cultures have recognized the influence of the conception environment for millennia. Prior to conceiving a child, couples ceremonially purify their minds and bodies.*

From this point of view, it matters whether a baby is conceived in love, tenderness, and out of a desire for a child, or in the violence, anger and hatred of rape. It matters whether the baby is wanted by its mother, or the pregnancy is a disaster for her. It matters whether its parents' lives are filled with stress, anxiety and loneliness, or are calm, secure and supported by friends and family. Amazing though it may seem, our genetic blueprint may contain a record of our parents' physical, emotional and mental state at the time we were conceived, and this may have significantly affected our development.

So much for the period before and at conception. But what about earlier still? About a month after your mother (or father) was conceived, their germ cells were formed and migrated to the budding genital region. There, as already noted, they were inactivated until they were needed to create the egg (and sperm) that became you. In this way, so the theory goes, their precious cargo of familial genes was protected from all the processes of gene activation and silencing that occur during the life of the fetus and child. But just how pristine are these genes? When each of your parents was conceived, the genes from their parents, your grandparents, fused in the embryo. The resulting package of genes included imprinted ones that may have carried a memory of *your grandparents'* traumas. These same genes would have been passed to the germ cells when they formed. In other words, the genes that you inherited from your parents may have been influenced by the experiences of your grandparents' lives. These imprints were carefully protected in the germ cells until a few weeks before you were conceived. Here, then, is a possible mechanism by which traumatic experiences could be passed genetically from ancestors to descendants down through the generations.

Conception and Implantation

The traditional image of conception is a race between millions of sperm, with the first to get there crashing into the egg and taking the prize. But the picture revealed by modern science is very different.[4] The process from ovulation or ejaculation through to implantation of the fertilized embryo in the wall of the uterus is complex, providing many opportunities for things to go wrong, and for memories of traumatic experiences to be recorded in cell membranes and gene expression.

The first sperm may reach the egg in as little as 30 minutes, but is unlikely to be successful. Laggards may take up to six days, and still may win. This is because sperm cannot penetrate the egg's membrane until they have been 'capacitated' by spending five hours or more stuck to the wall of the reproductive tract. This process also spreads the time at which the sperm arrive, thus helping to ensure that some are around when ovulation takes place. When the egg is ready to be fertilized, it emits chemicals to attract the sperm. Capacitated sperm bind to the egg, and release a chemical to dissolve its outer coat. The successful sperm then binds to the egg's inner membrane, which sends out little protuberances to draw it inside. Once one sperm has entered, the egg prevents further break-ins. Inside the egg, the nuclei of the sperm and egg move towards each other, and fuse to form the new genome just before the egg divides for the first time.

In reflecting on this process, it seems likely that the successful sperm may be given preferential treatment. Perhaps the timing of its release from the reproductive tract is synchronized with ovulation? Perhaps during capacitation it is given extra power to penetrate the outer membrane? Perhaps the egg chemically recognizes compatible sperm, and actively chooses the one it draws inside?

The fertilized egg divides rapidly as it drifts down towards the uterus. Along the way, chemicals make a hole in the egg's outer coat, and the embryo squeezes through. According to Professor Helen Martin of Oxford University, once the embryo reaches the uterus they "talk to each other, molecularly speaking, which allows them to interact. When the embryo lands on the surface of the uterus wall, it triggers a cascade of signals in both the embryo and uterus. The resulting changes allow the embryo to invade the lining. This invasion process has to be tightly regulated for a placenta to form correctly and hook up with the maternal blood supply."[5] Once the embryo is implanted in the wall, the placenta starts to form, and the embryo begins to exchange nutrients and wastes with its mother. However, a 'placental barrier' remains between the two blood supplies to protect the embryo from attack by its mother's immune system, and from many harmful substances in the mother's body.

Things can go wrong at both conception and implantation. In most cases, the woman's monthly egg is not fertilized at all, and many that are fertilized are faulty and die. Many others fail to implant properly, resulting in miscarriage. Some that complete implantation may have been damaged along the way from maturation of the germ cells. Little is known about this, but it is possible that traumatic 'memories' from this journey are encoded in patterns of cell membrane receptors, or changes in gene expression.[6]

Life in the Womb

We tend to think of the fetus as unconscious until birth. The idea that we may be able to recall fetal experiences runs counter to our scientific beliefs. But psychiatrist Stanislav Grof found that clients using 'holotropic breathing' often remember their life in the womb. His own experience, which he described in the third person, convinced him that this is not a fantasy.[7]

He had the odd sensation of shrinking in size, his head considerably larger than the rest of his body and extremities ... He felt himself suspended in a liquid that contained some harmful substances that were coming into his body through the umbilical cord ... He could taste the offending substances, a strange combination of iodine and decomposing blood or stale bouillon.

As all this was happening, the adult part of him, the part that had been medically trained and had always prided itself on its disciplined scientific perspective, observed the fetus from an objective distance. ...

The idea that a functioning consciousness could exist in a fetus was in conflict with everything he had been taught in medical school. ... Still, he could not deny the concrete nature of these experiences. ... After a period of considerable struggle, he gave up his analytical thinking and accepted all that was happening to him. ... It seemed now that he was connecting with the memories of the undisturbed periods of his intrauterine life. ...

On one level, he was still a fetus experiencing the ultimate perfection and bliss of a good womb ... On another level, he became the entire universe. ...

This rich and complex experience lasted for what seemed an eternity. He found himself vacillating between experiencing himself in the state of a distressed, sickened fetus and the state of blissful and serene intrauterine existence.

The existence of consciousness before birth is beginning to be supported by more objective research. Bruce Lipton describes a video of parents having a violent argument in which the response of the fetus is visualized by ultrasound. It jumped when the argument started, and arched its body and jumped again when a glass shattered.[8] In their book on early childhood development, J. Shonkoff and D. Phillips state that: "The prenatal period is when damaging environmental conditions may have some of the most devastating effects on development ..."[9] More specifically, Thomas Verney claims that: "Awake or asleep ... (unborn children) are constantly tuned in to their mother's every action, thought and feeling. From the moment of conception, the experience in the womb shapes the brain and lays the groundwork for personality, emotional temperament, and the power of higher thought."[10] The quality of our experience in the womb also programs our susceptibility to many adult diseases including coronary artery disease, stroke, diabetes, obesity, osteoporosis, mood disorders and psychoses.[11] Anything that distresses the fetus may cause trauma that affects the development of the unborn child by changing the patterns of membrane receptors and gene expression. Table 16 outlines some relevant physical and emotional factors.[12]

The focus of this chapter is on the traumatic aspects of life in the womb, but we should not forget Grof's insight that "During the periods of undisturbed intrauterine life, the conditions for the baby are close to ideal. ... There is security, protection, and instant, effortless gratification of all needs."[13] Nor should we forget that providing this blissful experience is not the mother's responsibility alone. Bruce Lipton stresses that: "Mothers and fathers are in the conception and pregnancy business together, even though it is the mother who carries the child in her womb. What the father does profoundly affects the mother, which in turn affects the developing child."[14]

Alcohol and Other Toxic Chemicals

The world is awash with chemicals of unknown toxicity, many of which can cross the placental barrier to affect the fetus. Over 280 chemicals have been found in umbilical cords in both North

Table 16: Experiences that can damage and traumatize the fetus
(Sources: Shonkoff 2000, Gilbert 2000, Ellwood, 2008)

Pregnancy complications, e.g. morning sickness, pre-eclampsia/toxemia, placenta previa, multiple fetuses

Mechanical injury, e.g. pressure during intercourse, maternal accidents, domestic violence

Other fetal disturbances, e.g. loud noises, arguments

Maternal physical health, e.g. malnutrition, anemia, high blood pressure, autoimmune disease, diabetes, phenylketonuria

Maternal mental health, e.g. chronic stress, anxiety/fear, depression, loneliness

Maternal infections, e.g. fever, German measles, herpes simplex, parvovirus, syphilis, toxoplasmosis (Note: HIV and hepatitis B are transmitted at birth)

Pharmaceutical drugs, e.g. streptomycin, tetracycline, warfarin, cortisone

Lifestyle drugs, e.g. alcohol, tobacco smoke, cocaine, heroin

Organic chemicals, e.g. methyl mercury, PCBs, food additives, and possibly thousands of other agricultural and industrial chemicals

Inorganic chemicals, e.g. lead, aluminum

Ionizing radiation, including x-rays

America and Europe. Five families in Canada yielded 46 substances, of which 38 were known to affect reproduction and impair child development.[15] Particularly sensitive periods are 15-60 days after conception when major organs are forming, and the second half of gestation when the brain is developing.[16]

Alcohol is one of the commonest toxins. It is unclear if there is any safe level of consumption, but both the US and UK governments advise pregnant women to abstain. Nevertheless, many women continue to drink during pregnancy. Some studies suggest that light drinking may benefit the fetus by relaxing the mother,[17] but others claim that blood alcohol levels below the legal limit for driving can cause measurable loss of brain cells.[18] For example, a study of mice revealed that 0.07% blood alcohol content for one hour caused four times the normal number of neurons to die.[19] However, it is agreed that binge drinking is more harmful than the same amount spread over a longer period.

Statistics on the incidence of fetal damage due to alcohol are sparse and unreliable. A report by the British Medical Association in 2007 reported that on average 9 infants per 1,000 live births in western countries may be affected by alcohol, but estimates ranged up to 20-40 in Italy. Of these, 10-15% had full-blown Fetal Alcohol Syndrome (FAS), described below, and 30-40% had Partial FAS. Around half had alcohol-related brain damage.[20] This is equivalent to 6,000 babies a year born with FAS in the UK alone.[21]

The symptoms of FAS are many and long-lived. They include facial deformities, retarded growth (including low birth weight), and brain damage. Infants and toddlers are often hyperactive and impulsive, have difficulty relating to others, are late developers and mentally retarded. Affected children have a mean IQ of 68.[22] As adolescents, they may be aggressive and unable to understand social cues. They also are more likely than their peers to drink heavily and use drugs. Affected adults may find it hard to lead independent lives, suffer from mental disorders such as depression, or get into trouble with the law.[23] Lifelong effects include poor physical coordination, and problems with attention, memory, problem-solving and abstract thinking. There also may be a link to the development of freaks such as people with one eye or two heads.[24]

Maternal Stress

The stress hormone cortisol crosses the placental barrier and is detectable as early as 17 weeks into gestation. Levels are far lower than in the mother, but sufficient to affect fetal development.[25] In rats, it may produce hyperactivity, anxiety (reflected in lack of exploration), and impairment of both mental development and social behavior. However, these symptoms may also be produced by differences in maternal care after birth. If the mother is stressed in the last week of pregnancy, she licks and grooms her pups less than normal.[26] It is possible that stress also reduces nurturing of their newborn infants by human mothers.

The mother's stress level primes the fetus for life after birth. In effect, the fetus assumes its mother's stress is a good indicator of what life will be like outside the womb, and adjusts its arousal accordingly. Moderate maternal stress is beneficial, but severe stress can induce a permanent state of arousal which retards development and affects health in adulthood. According to Professor Vivette Glover, emotional cruelty, arguments, and domestic violence are particularly damaging stresses in the UK. In other words, the father has an important role to play in caring for the fetus during gestation.[27]

Professor Glover leads the Fetal and Neonatal Stress Research Group at Imperial College, London. They have found that stress during pregnancy can result in:

- Low birth weight;
- A reduction in IQ of about 10 points at 18 months old;
- An increased incidence of anxiety;

- A doubling of the risk of Attention Deficit Hyperactivity Disorder (ADHD) in four-year-old boys; and
- A greater likelihood of emotional problems in both genders.

The group concluded: "It suggests that there is a direct effect of maternal mood on fetal brain development, which affects the behavioral development of the child."[28] There are about a million children in the UK with impaired development of the brain and nervous system, 15% of whom may be the result of maternal stress in pregnancy. Hence, Prof Glover argues that action to reduce stress could help 150,000 children.[29]

More dramatically, a study of the long-term effects of the Six Day War between Israel and Arab nations in 1967 found that acute stress had the greatest effect in the second month of pregnancy. Amongst female offspring, there was a fourfold increase in schizophrenia in adulthood, but only a slight increase in men. These results are probably applicable to any acute stress including being in a war zone, a terrorist attack, a sudden bereavement, or a natural disaster such as an earthquake, hurricane, or famine.[30]

Famine and Malnutrition

Maternal malnutrition is common due to famine, poverty, food allergies, the popularity of fast and processed foods, and eating conditions such as anorexia. Poor maternal nutrition not only reduces birth weight and stunts fetal brain development, but also has numerous effects on adult health. These include increased incidence of:[31]

- Diabetes
- Cardiovascular disease
- Lung disease
- Cholesterol ratios

- Obesity in women
- High blood pressure
- Breast cancer
- Schizophrenia and
- Antisocial personality disorder.

The quality of the maternal diet is as important as the caloric intake. For example, 20-25% of babies worldwide suffer iron deficiency anemia, and many more are less severely affected. Lack of iron in the developing brain impairs memory and motor development, and increases fearfulness, wariness and fatigue.[32] Another important micronutrient is vitamin B9 which is associated with spina bifida, and also may be linked to schizophrenia.[33]

Most information on the effects of famine comes from studies of Dutch people whose mothers were pregnant when the Nazis cut off food supplies towards the end of World War II. The Dutch mothers were well-nourished before and after the famine, and the chronic malnutrition in many third world countries can be expected to have more severe effects that may extend across generations. For example, it is important for the mother to recuperate after she stops breastfeeding before becoming pregnant again. If she does not, the growth of the new fetus is retarded. Further, a study in Bangladesh showed that women who had been small at birth were 2.5 times more likely to have an abnormal pregnancy. Clearly, reductions in infant mortality, still births and fetal retardation depend on a sustained, long-term improvement in nutrition.[34]

The Birth Experience
Birth is a traumatic and painful experience for the fetus even when it goes well, and it has lasting consequences for adult behavior and mental health. At birth, implicit memory of emotions and sensations is fully functional, but not the explicit

memory of images or cognitive facts. Nevertheless, in rebirthing therapies people often recall aspects of the process, such as the umbilical cord wrapped around their neck or the use of forceps. They may also remember specific details of the delivery room and people present. Some of these reports are undoubtedly due to forgotten stories told by their mothers, but psychiatrist Stanislav Grof has been able to verify a number of cases in which there was no prior intellectual knowledge.[35] Powerful archetypal themes also frequently emerge in rebirthing. Again, some of these may be due to projection of adult knowledge onto implicit emotional and bodily memories. But the universality of the themes suggests that there is a common consciousness underlying them all that may be significant in collective trauma.

Based on his work with thousands of clients, Grof described the birth experience in detail. Life in the womb is relatively serene until interrupted by chemical changes that herald birth. These are followed by intense pressure due to uterine contractions that floods the fetus with pain and anxiety. This pressure restricts its blood supply, thus reducing the flow of nutrients and oxygen, and restricting the comforting emotional connection to its mother. As the cervix is still closed, there seems to be no escape from this intolerable situation which lasts anything from minutes to many hours. In Grof's words, the dominant feeling at this stage "is that of an apocalyptic event that destroys the peaceful intrauterine world and changes the oceanic and cosmic freedom of the fetus into agonizing entrapment and a sense of being overwhelmed by unknown external forces. ... the general atmosphere is that of unbearable emotional and physical torture. ... whatever is happening seems eternal, as if it will never end."[36] In rebirthing, "The cellular memory of birth can emerge into present consciousness with such a force that the person believes beyond any doubt that real biological death is possible and actually imminent."[37]

The pressure continues even after the cervix opens. The head is now wedged into the pelvic opening, squeezed and deformed. The oxygen supply may be reduced further because the cord is wound around the neck, or pinched between the head and the pelvic wall. All this time the fetus may be bathed in the fear and confusion of an inexperienced mother, or her negative feelings towards her baby if it is unwanted. But at least now there is a way out, and hope of liberation even though it may be delayed by the infant's position, a narrow pelvic opening, weak contractions, the placenta blocking the exit, or the mother's fearful tension. At some point in this struggle, there comes an upsurge of rage and aggression, the primal fury of an organism whose survival is threatened. Often, too, the fetus experiences a strange sexual arousal that mirrors the intense sexual feelings stirred in many women when giving birth. Indeed, some radical midwives encourage partners to stimulate sexual feelings during the birth process to help the mother relax.[38]

Grof noted that this stage of the birth process "represents an enormous pool of problematic emotions and difficult sensations that can, in combination with later events in infancy and childhood, contribute to the development of a variety of disorders. Among them are certain forms of depression and conditions that involve aggression and violent self-destructive behaviors. Also sexual disorders and aberrations, obsessive-compulsive neuroses, phobias, and hysterical manifestations seem to have important roots in this matrix."[39] Paradoxically, when the fetal distress reaches its peak, "the situation oddly ceases to have the quality of suffering and agony. Instead, the very intensity of the experience is transformed into wild, ecstatic rapture ..."[40] There is a marked similarity here with the 'freezing' dissociative response to traumatic stress in which pain and fear disappear as natural opiates are released.[41]

In normal births, there is a sudden, explosive release as the infant breaks free from the pelvic opening, and is expelled into an alien world. As it takes its first breath, its lungs expand and start to supply oxygen. Other organs begin to process its wastes, and, shortly, to digest food. This is a big improvement on the birth trauma, but is far from the utopian womb. The infant's biological needs are no longer automatically satisfied, and it is no longer shielded from temperature changes, loud noises, bright lights, and harsh touch. It may be overwhelmed by the confusion of sound, light and activity around it, and experience panic, terror and horror. Its distress may have been increased by forceps delivery—or perhaps reduced by caesarean birth.[42]

At this vulnerable moment, the infant needs, above all, the comfort of its mother's body with its familiar heartbeat, warmth, smell and emotional energy. It needs to be held, stroked, gazed at lovingly, and given the breast. But this is the time when modern medicine all too often intervenes with further traumatic experiences. The umbilical cord may be cut within a minute, depriving the infant of vital iron and oxygen in the blood. Delaying cutting for three minutes is recommended by some experts, and many alternative birth practitioners wait for five minutes, by which time the blood flow ceases naturally.[43]

Modern birth practices are often rightly criticized, but we should not lose sight of the fact that medical care, particularly by trained midwives, has greatly reduced infant and maternal deaths and illness.[44] On balance, the benefits from reduced trauma probably far outweigh the increases in trauma. However, there is little doubt that birth trauma could be reduced further. Practices to consider changing include:

- Induction, particularly when it is for the convenience of medical practitioners;
- Forceps delivery;
- Painkilling drugs, especially ones that may affect the fetus;[45]
- The timing of cord-cutting;

- Bottom-smacking;
- The use of stinging antiseptic eye drops;
- Circumcision, particularly without anesthetic;
- Separation from the mother;
- Isolation without touch or the sight of faces;
- Being left to cry unheeded;
- Schedule feeding; and
- Bottle feeding unless medically necessary, and accompanied by loving holding.

A challenge for such reform agendas is that doctors, parents and other caregivers who were traumatized themselves at birth have difficulty understanding or sympathizing with the traumas and needs of infants.[46]

Reflection

Spiritual teacher Eckhart Tolle notes that some babies seem to come into the world already burdened by trauma, or a heavy emotional pain-body as he calls it. Some cry a lot for no apparent reason, as if they have a big share of human unhappiness and pain. This may be a consequence of experiences in the womb or at birth. But it also may result from an inheritance of collective trauma, passed down the generations or even between lives.[47]

There is a tribe in East Africa in which the age of the child is counted from the first time it is a thought in its mother's mind. Aware of her intention, the mother sits alone under a tree and listens until she can hear the song of the child she hopes to conceive. Then she returns to her village, and teaches the song to the child's father-to-be so that they can sing it as they make love, inviting the child to join them. After conception, she sings to the fetus in her womb. And she teaches the song to the old women and midwives so that the baby hears it during the pain of labor and is greeted by it at the moment of birth. After it is born, all the villagers learn the song too, and sing it when the child is hurt or triumphant, at rituals and initiations. It is sung at his or her marriage, and around the deathbed.[48]

18. Infancy

The first few months after birth are sometimes referred to as the fourth trimester of pregnancy because the newborn baby is so helpless. He or she is totally dependent on caregivers for food, cleanliness, temperature regulation, management of emotions, and brain development. During infancy, patterns are set which permanently affect the adult's body, mind, emotions, relationships and social life. If all goes well, by three years old the baby develops into a healthy, energetic, confident, curious, playful toddler with sound basic language skills, and a secure relationship with his or her primary caregiver. By that time, too, they will be able to regulate their bodily functions and emotions, and empathize with other children and adults. If all does not go so well, the infant may become insecure, passive, sickly, emotionally volatile, angry, aggressive, lacking in empathy, and/or be physically and/or mentally impaired. Some of these deficits can be reduced by later positive experiences, but others are fixed for life. Whilst there is a genetic component to some developmental problems, the great majority of cases seem to be due to poor parenting, maltreatment, or traumatic experiences.

Secure Attachment

The newborn's survival depends on quickly forming a relationship with its primary caregiver, usually its mother. The bonding process is almost certainly innate. Cross-cultural studies indicate that the infant's most important need is for consistent, prompt attention to its demands, but nurturing, warmth and affection are also beneficial.[1] Emotionally and physically healthy mothers are drawn to their infants, wanting to smell, cuddle, rock, coo, sing and gaze at them. In response, the infants snuggle, babble, smile, suck and cling. The result is mutual pleasure, calmness and satisfaction. Successful bonding depends on having time together in which to weave enduring physical, emotional and mental patterns from face-to-face interactions, eye contact, physical proximity, touch, smell, sound and taste.[2]

A secure attachment relationship protects the infant, regulates her immature bodily functions, modulates her emotional responses, and stimulates her mental activity. It soothes her distress, and brings a lasting sense of trust and security. The relationship works well when the mother is attuned to her baby, can read his emotional cues, and responds appropriately and lovingly. Time and again, she comes to the hungry, scared or cold infant, bringing food, cleanliness, warmth, comfort and safety. However, infants do not need to be looked after by their parents all the time. Indeed it is better if the responsibility is shared with an extended family or community. In our hunter-gatherer past, children grew up in close contact with people of all ages, thus stimulating their capacity for a rich diversity of relationships.[3] Even highly-skilled professional child-care is less good because the larger number of children per caregiver means relationships are less intimate. Infants also become distressed when personnel change.

Secure attachment helps infants handle stress, and makes it easier for toddlers and young children to form relationships with friends, teachers and others. It fosters a balanced sense of self, good memory, an understanding of emotions and friendship, and a robust conscience. Securely attached children are more responsive than others to parental instruction and guidance, thus reinforcing the parents' sensitivity to the child, and further strengthening attachment. In sum, secure attachment produces a happy, confident child who shows trust and delight in the caregiver's presence.[4]

In the USA, 60-70% of one-year-olds are thought to be securely attached. When their mother is in the room, they explore actively, checking in with her periodically for reassurance. However, they become upset when she leaves, and explore little. On her return, they greet her warmly, seeking comfort and physical contact.[5] Once secure infants can walk, they become exhilarated and excited, with boundless energy and joy. Increasing independence means that they must learn to regulate their own emotions, helped by appropriate responses from their mothers. But their development will be inhibited if she fails to interpret their feelings accurately. These interactions are critical, since they fix the expression of specific genes, thus setting the way we respond to stress throughout life.[6]

In effect, the primary attachment relationship creates persistent beliefs and expectations about trust, comfort, love, security and other issues. It provides a model of relationships, and a template for behavior. Failure to achieve a secure attachment affects intimate relationships later in life in ways that are very difficult to change. For example, one study showed that three-quarters of secure, autonomous pregnant women later had securely attached infants. By contrast, three-quarters of preoccupied and dismissive women had insecurely attached babies. In this way, patterns of relationships are passed down the generations by learning.[7]

Achieving secure attachment can be challenging, particularly if the temperaments of mother and child are poorly matched. Some infants bond easily, are adaptable, and have mild, mainly positive moods. At the other extreme, 15% of babies have difficulty forming a secure attachment. They cry a lot, are timid, fearful, unresponsive, irritable, hard to soothe, and slow to adapt to change. They need frequent comforting, holding and feeding, and are often stressed and emotionally insecure because their parents cannot meet their demands. An infant may be difficult for many reasons, including genetic factors, bad experiences in the womb, prematurity, birth injuries or trauma, pain, illness, domestic or community violence, or being in a refugee family or war zone.[8] Attachment is also affected by parental behavior.

Carrying an infant in close contact with its mother's body increases the likelihood of secure attachment, as does responding quickly to crying. Even very irritable babies may do well if their parents are emotionally available and able to regulate the baby's arousal. Animal studies show that good parenting can even offset genetic predispositions. In one study, offspring of genetically fearful rats were easily stressed when reared by their biological mothers. But, when reared by non-fearful mothers, they developed normal fear responses.[9] Most parenting problems are due to ignorance or an unconscious replay of the parent's own upbringing, and can be overcome with training.

Insecure Attachment

Lack of secure attachment is traumatic for infants. Without appropriate nurturing and stimulation their physical and mental development may be impaired, and their ability to form healthy relationships later in life affected. In general, the earlier the deprivation, the more difficult it is to heal later. Insecure infants may exhibit a wide range of symptoms, both at the time and later, including:[10]

- Muscle tension and shallow breathing;
- Disturbance of the immune and hormonal systems;
- Delayed development of motor, language, social and cognitive areas of the brain;
- Inappropriate attachment to any adult, such as hugging virtual strangers;
- Lack of empathy and ability to control impulses;[11]
- Strange food habits, such as hoarding or hiding it, gobbling, difficulties with swallowing, and vomiting;
- Repetitive or self-harming activities in severe cases, such as rocking, banging their heads, or biting or scratching themselves; and
- Increased risk of psychopathology later in life, including

dissociative disorders, aggression, conduct disorder and self-abuse.[12]

One in three infants in the USA is thought to be insecurely attached, and similar levels are found elsewhere. It generally arises because the mother is unable to respond adequately to her baby, often because she experienced inadequate care from *her* parents. In this way, the problem is passed down the generations through learning, and it may also be inherited epigenetically through changes in gene expression.[13] This has been shown to occur in rats, and this mechanism may well apply to humans too.[14]

Another common cause of insecure attachment is maternal depression, which is experienced by 10% of new mothers in the USA. Many depressed mothers are good parents, and problems tend to arise only when it is associated with other stresses such as poverty, marital discord, domestic violence, or substance abuse. Some depressed mothers withdraw, and find it hard to respond to their babies. Others actively engage, but are insensitive and intrusive, misinterpreting their infant's signals, and handling them roughly. Not surprisingly, children of depressed mothers tend to be unhappy, withdrawn, inactive, and slow to develop. They tend to avoid intimacy, lack self-control, be aggressive and become depressed themselves.[15] Infants of intrusive mothers are at risk of developing depression, antisocial personality traits, anxiety disorders, attention deficit disorder, and elevated stress hormones.[16]

There are three types of insecure attachment: avoidant, resistant (or ambivalent), and disorganized. Interestingly, the incidence of the different forms varies markedly between cultures, reflecting different styles of parenting.[17] Avoidant toddlers show few emotions, ignore their mothers, show little distress when separated from her, and turn away on reunion. This pattern tends to arise when the infant's mother cannot cope with its anger, resulting in mild emotional abuse and neglect, or critical, intrusive parenting. Such infants learn to suppress their anger, and avoid their feelings by withdrawing, becoming emotionally dissociated and numb. As Sue Gerhardt put it, they slam on the emotional brakes to avoid feelings they cannot handle. The child represses its own feelings to protect its mother instead of being helped by her to manage them.

In contrast, resistant toddlers explore little, stay close to their mother, and are very distressed by separation. On reunion, they are ambivalent or angry, and resist physical contact. They are 'drama queens' who express their feelings without regard for others. Resistant insecurity is produced by inconsistent parents who are sometimes concerned and available, but at other times are switched off, absent or rejecting. The child becomes fearful and needy, watching for good moments to seek attention.[18]

5-10% of children are more severely damaged, and exhibit disorganized attachment. They are confused, not knowing if they can trust a caregiver who sometimes hurts and frightens them. When their mother appears, they may bang their head on the wall, or eagerly approach and then shy away, or simply sit on the floor making a high-pitched sound. Sue Gerhardt suggests that their parents may be so traumatized by abuse or major loss themselves that they are unable to provide protection and a safe base for exploring the world. As a result, the infant does not learn how to respond to events or manage her feelings, and small stresses escalate into major distress.[19]

Sensory Stimulation and Visual Interaction

The newborn baby's senses need stimulation in order to complete their development. This stimulation also provides important cues for development of the brain, nervous and hormone systems, and for regulation of social and emotional behavior. Without it, the relevant brain circuits atrophy, with consequences not only for the adult but also for future generations through both learning and epigenetics.[20]

In the first two months, the most important senses are smell and taste, after which touch becomes more important. Visual stimuli predominate at 10-12 months, with sound gaining importance later still. During this process, information from the earlier-maturing senses such as smell and touch is used to help organize developing senses, such as vision. The mother's role is to provide novel stimuli that focus her baby's attention long enough to coordinate its senses into a coherent experience. Thus touching a playful mother's face, seeing her smile, and hearing her laugh helps development as well as bringing joy.[21]

Even though vision does not predominate until the infant is almost a year old, the newborn is able to focus on faces, and rapidly learns to read their expressions. This innate ability facilitates bonding as mother and child gaze at each other just minutes after birth—a process that is all-too-often disrupted by masked faces and separation following hospital births. The baby scans her mother's face, particularly the eyes, and is aroused by dilated pupils indicating interest and pleasure. Hormones are released in the infant's brain that not only bring pleasure and excitement, but also stimulate development. Correspondingly, the sight of the infant, especially the movement of his eyes, induces maternal feelings and actions. As they gaze at each other with joy, they enter deep communication. This interaction is controlled by the infant who turns his gaze away when he has had enough, signaling to an attuned mother to moderate her input accordingly.[22] Babies are primed to respond to other faces, too, as Dorothy Rowe's delightful story of Ethan's birth illustrates.[23]

One minute later he is comfortable and relaxed as he is held by his mother, Julie. He opens his eyes and looks directly at her. He watches her intently, his eyes scanning the details of her face. As Julie talks to him, his face becomes more mobile and expressive. A few minutes later, Ethan is handed to his father, John. He gazes intently at his father and is totally absorbed. Then John slowly and clearly protrudes his tongue, and Ethan attends closely. He appears to be concentrating completely on his mouth as he frowns and shuts his eyes, then he looks back at John and protrudes his own tongue. He is fifteen minutes old.

Continued visual interaction with her mother is essential for development of the infant's brain. When she sees that her mother is pleased, endorphins and dopamine are released in her brain that not only make her feel good, but also stimulate growth of neurons and the cortex. Conversely, a disapproving face sets off stress reactions that block the endorphins. In other words, plenty of doting looks and pleasure early in life are the best ways to create rich brain networks. This visual relationship changes when the infant turns into a mobile toddler. As he explores his world, the toddler needs frequent reassurance. Often, a few seconds of eye contact is enough to check that what he is doing is OK with his mother. Similarly, the toddler's gaze tells his mother how he is feeling, and enables her to adjust her response accordingly. Such close attunement results in resonance, shared experiences, and the firing of the same neurons in each brain. These visual reunions may permanently affect the infant's future emotional life.[24]

As language develops, verbal communication becomes more important. But facial expressions remain one of our most significant means of social communication. We each create a catalogue of face templates which reflect emotions such as pain, joy, anger, fear, doubt, confidence and threat. And we use facial expressions such as a smile, frown or glare to elicit specific emotional and behavioral responses.[25] The expressions corresponding to basic emotions are universal across many cultures, suggesting that they are important enough to have been genetically hard-wired by evolution.[26]

The Importance of Touch

The importance of touch was first demonstrated in experiments on monkeys in the 1950's.[27] Infant monkeys became emotionally disturbed when raised with dummy mothers made from warm, soft cloth. Those given metal wire surrogates were more severely disturbed. Without real mothers to hold, stroke and play with them, these monkeys grew up to be aggressive and violent, unable to tolerate affection or touch, and sexually disturbed. They became cold mothers, unmoved by their infant's cries and unwilling to pick them up. Thus their trauma was passed to future generations. Similar patterns are seen in human children raised in orphanages.

In later experiments, monkeys were raised for the first six months within sight, hearing and smell of others, but with no physical contact. They became fearful, hugged themselves, sucked their digits, made noises to themselves, and engaged in repetitive activities. When united with other monkeys as adolescents or adults, they were very aggressive, avoided social contact, and were unable to perform normal sex. Females failed to care for their infants, and over a third physically abused them. However, there were few abnormalities other than aggression when they were raised normally for the first six months, and then isolated for the next six months. When raised by their mothers, but without peers, the infants were timid, and became aggressive and antisocial. Similarly, when raised with peers and no mothers, they clung to each other, explored and played little, and were easily frightened. They grew up to be socially, sexually and maternally deficient.[28]

Similar findings emerge from studies of rats. During the first week, mothers stimulate their pups by licking them. Pups who are licked less than normal are more stressed, explore less, and suffer impaired spatial learning and memory. Adults who were not licked much as pups develop into mothers who lick their offspring little. Like monkeys, rat pups also react to separation from their mothers. They grow into fearful, hyperactive adults with impaired mental abilities and social behavior. However, tactile stimulation with a paint brush can partially offset the effects of maternal deprivation. Frances Champagne attributed these results to epigenetic changes in gene expression, and thinks similar effects are likely to be found in humans.[29]

The message from these animal studies is clear: physical contact with both parents and peers is essential for normal development. Similar experiments on humans are not possible, but there is ample evidence that the same conclusions apply. Breastfeeding brings a sense of tranquility to both the mother and her baby. By her presence, touch and nourishment, she protects him from stress and coincidentally provides him with antibodies to disease. Without this maternal regulation, the baby's stress response may be over-aroused, creating an anxious adult vulnerable to depression.[30] Premature babies provide further evidence. Left alone most of the time in a harsh, noisy ward, they may collapse due to the uncontrollable stimulation. When they are attended to, they are often face down and their carer is masked, thus reducing tactile and visual interaction. Not surprisingly, studies have shown that touch increases weight gain and improves development, provided the infant is not overwhelmed.[31] Gentle stroking and flexing of limbs improve feeding and digestion, but infants treated this way tend to collapse later—perhaps because they are returned to the deprived situation.[32]

Many other observations have been made on the importance of touch. In early infancy, it helps shape development of the cortex and the growth of dendrites in the brain. It modulates stress, helping infants learn to regulate their emotions, and giving them a sense of being attractive. More generally, cultures which maintain close physical contact with their babies and do not repress sexuality are mostly peaceful, whereas low-touch societies tend to be violent.[33]

Learning Physical Independence

Young infants are still effectively part of their mother's body, dependent on her for nutrition, regulation of heart rate and blood pressure, immunity to disease, and warmth. In the first three months after birth, they learn to regulate their own bodily functions, and during this period they need love as well as physical care.[34] Beyond these basic requirements, however, infants are remarkably flexible, learning to cope in many cultural settings. The !Kung infant, for instance, is in constant skin contact with its mother day and night, and fed every 15 minutes. When the baby fusses, it is usually attended to before it cries, and no effort is made to get it to sleep through the night. By contrast, in the USA and Europe, babies are isolated for long periods, feeds are larger and more widely spread, and establishing a day-night rhythm is a priority.[35]

Shonkoff and Phillips claim that infants cry in all cultures, and found scant evidence that crying in the first three months leads to physical or behavioral problems later. Nevertheless, they noted that babies move more smoothly into non-crying communication when their needs are met promptly. If their cries are ignored, infants quickly learn not to bother, but this is an indication of despair and trauma rather than progress, and has long-term consequences. In between these extremes, inconsistent caregivers produce the fussiest, most whiny babies who never quite give up hope of the love they crave. Inadequate care raises stress levels, and leads to permanently elevated levels of stress hormones. These suppress the immune system, predisposing the future adult to autoimmune diseases such as rheumatoid arthritis and multiple sclerosis. Infant stress also can lead to coronary artery disease, peptic ulcers, ulcerative colitis, anorexia and bulimia later in life.[36]

Learning Emotional Independence

Besides regulating their bodily functions, babies must learn to handle their emotions. At first they tune in to their mother's emotions, experiencing them as if they were their own, and relying on her to regulate potentially overwhelming stimuli. Gradually, these interactions mould the infant's ability to regulate her own feelings. This process sets emotional patterns for life, and shortcomings can lead to psychiatric disorders later.[37] Of particular importance is the 'set point' for stress arousal, which is established by the age of 6 months. This is the normal level of arousal the person experiences when there are no unusual threats or challenges.

The mother's task is to find a balance between too much and too little stress, which can also be harmful. The infant needs to be encouraged to bear increasingly strong challenges and feelings before she is comforted so that she can learn to handle stress and her own emotions.[38] However, too much stress results in permanent hyper-arousal which stunts brain development and the ability to manage emotions. It leads to fear, irritability and withdrawal; and impairment of the ability to interpret social cues and adapt to social norms. Later in life it is also associated with:

- Increased risk of depression, anxiety, suicidal tendencies, eating disorders, alcoholism, obesity, sexual abuse and osteoporosis;
- Impairment of memory, thinking, behavior management, the immune system, wound healing, and muscle mass.

It is possibly a factor in diabetes and hypertension as well.

Paradoxically, too low a level of stress hormones is also a common problem. In infancy, it is associated with avoidant attachment, and it is present in most aggressive young boys. Later in life, low levels are associated with PTSD, chronic fatigue (or ME), asthma, allergies, arthritis, seasonal affective disorder, and flattened emotions.[39]

The toddler's emotional life is shaped by many factors besides stress arousal. These include the security of attachment, discussion of emotional events, parental coaching, and peer interactions. Daniel Goleman argues that the frequent moments of attunement, or misattunement, between parent and child are far more important influences on her emotional life than less frequent but dramatic events. Infants catch emotions from their caregivers, and are distressed by misattunement. If this is frequent or prolonged, the child may begin to avoid expressing, or even feeling, her emotions, thus obliterating them from her repertoire as an adult.[40]

Discussing feelings and emotional experiences is like holding up a mirror to the child. In this way, he learns to distinguish between emotions, and to express his feelings in words. Secure attachment brings confidence that she will not only be heard, but also supported when necessary to control her emotions. It also leads to greater self-reliance, confidence and self-esteem. By contrast, people who repress and do not understand their own feelings often find it difficult to talk about them.[41] As parents, they may feel hostile towards their baby, and be insensitive to their infant's cues. They may be unable to give emotional guidance, particularly with regard to issues on which they are still carrying unhealed pain from childhood. Mother and infant may wind each other up until the baby is stressed, and the mother feels rejected. As a result, she may avoid her child, or become verbally or physically abusive, resulting in disorganized attachment.[42]

Even young babies are capable of empathy. They smile in response to a smile, and cry in response to a cry. But within a year, they begin to realize that not all emotions are theirs. If all goes well, by two years old they understand that others have feelings like theirs, and try to comfort them when distressed. Empathy lies at the heart of morality in later life, and failure to develop it is a root cause of violent crime and child abuse. Perpetrators are simply unable to feel or understand the emotions of others.[43]

A child who does not learn to regulate her emotions may become self-centered, inflexible, and lacking in empathy. She may either try not to need others, or seek endlessly to get others to satisfy her unmet infant needs. As an adult, she may constantly fall in and out of love, be addicted to food or drugs, or become a workaholic. In extreme cases, he may develop borderline personality disorder. This is characterized by:

- Rampaging emotions;
- Impulsive and self-destructive behaviors;
- A tendency to dissociate;
- Hostility;
- Shame; and
- Ineffectiveness.

Emotional immaturity may also lead to an insecure sense of self—that is, no coherent story of who he or she is. Self-identity requires good communication between the left and right halves of the brain, which is shaped by the child's significant relationships in its second and third years.[44]

Learning Social Independence

When the infant starts to toddle, he becomes more willful, and comes into conflict with his parents, peers and siblings. By one year old, infants like to control the action, and do not like interference or instructions. At this stage, the mother's primary role changes from caregiver to disciplinarian and agent of socialization. She faces the challenge of knowing when to say 'no'. It is important to teach the child to consider others with support and not humiliation. Cooperation increases if the parent follows the child's interests whenever possible, and makes sure that he both understands the situation, and agrees to go along with the decision. However, one study of 11-17 month-olds counted an average of one prohibition every 9 minutes. Such battles of will can be counter-productive. Children can be encouraged to internalize their parents' standards of behavior by clear, consistent limits, emotional calmness, ample affection, and little use of power, threats or criticism. If handled well, the process forms the basis for developing empathy, caring, sharing and conflict management.[45]

Allan Schore argues that emotions are the key to socialization, particularly judicious use of shame. He describes how mothers inhibit over-excitement by disapproving or embarrassed facial expressions. In response, the toddler may feel exposed, and want to hide. He blushes, stops smiling, and becomes motionless with hanging head and averted eyes. Unable to regulate this emotional pain, pre-verbal toddlers seek reunion with, and comfort from, their mothers. This process of moving from positive to negative feelings and back again helps to develop self-regulation and emotional resilience. It builds a positive self-image, and confidence that negative experiences can be endured. It also helps set the level of stress response, and maturation of the limbic system. However, if her mother does not respond positively, the toddler may get stuck in feelings of humiliation, rejection, abandonment, helplessness and hopelessness. In this context, shamed infants often feel isolated and humiliated, and later have difficulty controlling their rage.[46]

Making friends is an important life skill. By the time they are toddling, children form simple friendships, and play happily with those they know who are at a similar stage of development and like the same activities. Securely-attached preschoolers tend to be popular and have supportive friendships. They generally work things out by negotiation and compromise, and continue to play together. By contrast, insecure, angry, aggressive or whiny kids who feel unloved and unlovable make poor playmates. Those who are rejected by their peers tend to be aggressive and domineering, with high levels of stress hormones. They often come from homes with physical abuse, conflict and violence between partners, and hostile, inconsistent caregiving. Many of their families have a history of psychiatric disorders, criminality and substance abuse. Later in life, they often do poorly at school, get in trouble with the law, and develop psychiatric problems.[47]

Reflection

It is clear that our early relationships and experiences have more influence than our genes on how we turn out as adults. If we do not receive the right care at the right time in the right environment, we may miss vital developmental windows of opportunity. No matter how good our genetic heritage, the result may be lifelong impairment of physical, mental and emotional health, relationships, and social behavior. Any maltreatment is then passed to future generations through epigenetics and learning.

It is also clear that some western childrearing practices, let alone the prevalence of maltreatment, encourage aggression, violence, and the creation of fresh trauma. Early life is often traumatic for the infant, and suboptimal and dysfunctional from society's perspective. We may conclude that many of the problems we face as a civilization can be traced to inadequate care in the first three years.

Given the range of developmental tasks and windows of opportunity to be negotiated in infancy, it seems amazing that any of us turn out more or less physically, mentally, emotionally and socially functional! That so many of us do speaks volumes for the resilience of the human infant, and the dedicated care of most parents. But we believe that the damage is far more extensive than is apparent, and that most of us are impaired to some extent. What we regard as 'normal' health and behavior is the average outcome from flawed child-rearing practices applied by untrained and often traumatized parents. It seems highly likely that what we take to be 'normal' is actually far below our potential.

Many studies point towards a future in which:

- Infants cry little because their needs are met quickly;
- Infants are in constant physical contact with their primary caregivers, whose warmth, love and empathy demonstrate that the world is a benevolent, safe place;
- Gentle touch, affection and encouragement stimulate brain development and the control of aggression, as well as the release of feel-good hormones; and
- Children develop independence, confidence, caring, and a feeling of safety in reaching out to others.

19. Childhood

Childhood raises much the same issues as infancy. The body and brain continue to grow and develop. The mind becomes ever-more sophisticated. The regulation of emotions improves. And social skills increase. Sensitive and loving caregiving remains vitally important, and there are more windows of opportunity that may be missed with lifelong consequences. In other ways, however, childhood is quite different to infancy. Individuality increases, and the child learns to cope with imperfect parents, the challenges of school, and the stresses and traumas of growing independence.

A Historical Perspective

The Fall and the rise of state civilization ushered in an era of harsh, domineering child-rearing practices. As historian Lloyd deMause put it, the history of childhood "is a nightmare from which we have only recently begun to awaken. The further back in history one goes, the lower the level of child care, and the more likely children are to be killed, abandoned, beaten, terrorized and sexually abused."[1] Similarly, psychoanalyst Boris Cyrulnik notes that for most of history there was no concept of child abuse.[2]

The Bible makes many references to children, but deMause points out that none of them is concerned with their needs. Rather, they cover issues such as child sacrifice, stoning, beating, obedience, love for their parents, and honoring the family name. He argues that even Jesus' command to "suffer little children ... to come unto me" relates to the customary practice of exorcising innate evil. In Roman times, fathers were entitled to whip, imprison, exile, enslave or even execute their children. Malformed or unwanted infants might be thrown in the street, smothered, or starved. In the Middle Ages, a more profitable alternative was to sell them as slaves to rich neighbors or

Saracens.[3] Children in medieval Europe were regarded as inherently sinful, and in need of discipline. Even kings grew up receiving and witnessing violence as a normal part of life. Most advice on child-rearing before the eighteenth century approved of severe, regular beating starting early in life. Such treatment was legal, and death of the child was not regarded as homicide provided the punishment was not excessive![4]

It was not until the Renaissance and the second wave of reaction to The Fall that practices began to change, with the degree of violence decreasing from the eighteenth century onwards. But as beatings became less severe, other ways were found to terrorize and subjugate children, such as shutting them in dark cupboards, or taking them to see executions and rotting corpses. Nightmares and hallucinations were common, and children were punished for having them. The idea that children are evil and need to have their will broken was still strong in the nineteenth century, with medical advice prescribing punishments such as holding stress positions and immersion in cold water, as well as beatings.[5] The main effect according to Evelin Lindner was to produce people who blindly followed orders regardless of ethics.[6]

Similar beliefs and practices are still prevalent among fundamentalist Christians. But, on the whole, childhood today is relatively benign. Since the nineteenth century the idea has grown that children are not perverse animals, but developing humans. The first laws to punish abusive parents were passed in France in 1889, but it was not until 1962 that a paper was published on the battered child syndrome, and as recently as the 1970's that the idea of abuse became widespread.[7] However, despite more enlightened attitudes, the prevalence of childhood neglect, abuse and trauma may actually be increasing again in the last few decades.[8]

Child Maltreatment in High-income Nations

In 2009, Professor Ruth Gilbert and colleagues published a major review of research on child maltreatment in the high-income countries of North America, Europe, Australia and New Zealand. Also included was information on newly-independent countries that were previously part of the Soviet bloc. They defined maltreatment as "any act of commission or omission by a parent or other caregiver that results in harm, potential for harm, or threat of harm to a child (usually interpreted as up to 18 years of age), even if harm is not the intended result." They found that 80% of maltreatment is by parents or guardians, with the exception of sexual abuse which is more commonly by acquaintances or other relatives.[9]

This definition covers physical, sexual, psychological and emotional abuse and neglect, and witnessing violence between intimate partners. This is broad enough to encompass most parental shortcomings, but the study confined neglect to tangible things such as lack of food, medical care and a safe place to stay. It did not cover the significant developmental effects of emotional neglect, particularly in infancy. The inclusion of witnessing violence is important, as it can have a profound effect on infant development, leading to disorganized insecure attachment, and fear of, or for, their mothers. In one study, a child experienced labored breathing, high heart rate and trembling when her parents argued.[10]

Interpretation and synthesis of data from diverse studies in many countries is challenging, but Prof. Gilbert's team published summary statistics that give a feel for the scale of the problem. Every year in high-income countries 4-16% of children are physically abused, 10% are emotionally abused, and 10% are neglected. The figures are even higher, ranging up to one third, in former eastern-bloc countries. In the course of childhood, 5-10% of girls and up to 5% of boys suffer penetrative sex, and three times this number are exposed to other forms of sexual abuse. Up to a quarter of children in the USA witness violence between intimate partners at some time in their childhood.

In the late 1990's, Bruce Perry reported that 4-5 million American children were exposed to severe abuse or neglect each year, and that a total of 16-20 million children were at risk of developing trauma-related problems. To put this in context, he pointed out that 'only' 1 million US servicemen suffered from trauma during the 10 years of the Vietnam war. As he expressed it, millions of American children are literally "incubated in terror."[11]

Even these huge figures may underestimate the problem as research is revealing that relatively mild experiences can have significant long-term effects. For example, a study in New England, USA, followed 346 children from the age of five. By the time they were 15 years old, about half of them reported increased arguments with and between parents. Fifteen years later, these individuals were more than three times as likely as the remainder of the study group to suffer major depression, or to indulge in drug or alcohol abuse. They were almost three times as likely to engage in antisocial behavior, and more than twice as likely to be unemployed.[12]

Perhaps not surprisingly given these statistics, Daniel Goleman noted in the mid-1990's that there was a downward slide in the mental health of children in the USA and many other countries. He claimed that the most common cause of disability amongst teenagers was mental illness, and that children were becoming more withdrawn, anxious, depressed, delinquent and aggressive, and less able to concentrate or think clearly. He saw this as "a new kind of toxicity seeping into and poisoning the very experience of childhood, signifying sweeping deficits in emotional competences."[13] There is little reason to believe the trend has changed.

According to Goleman, no area of society is exempt from these problems, and even strong families are disintegrating and unable to give their children appropriate care. Children are more and more often left to their own devices or poor-quality child-care as both parents go out to work. Parental substance abuse, itself a possible consequence of earlier childhood maltreatment, is a factor in four out of five cases of maltreatment in the USA. Alcohol is implicated in 10-50% of cases in European countries.[14] This lack of care and intimate family relationships undermines emotional intelligence and regulation, fuelling anger and resentment which explodes in violence and delinquency. Neglect also leads to depression, loneliness, eating disorders, drug and alcohol abuse and other problems.

Prof. Gilbert and her collaborators discussed the long-term physical, psychological and social consequences of maltreatment between birth and age 18. Their conclusions are summarized in Table 17, together with additional risk factors identified by other authors.[15] This makes it apparent that, in the words of Bruce Perry: "Abused children absorb the pain and either pass it on to others in a destructive way (e.g. violence) or keep it and let it eat at themselves like a cancer. These "social ills" rob the individual and, in the end, rob our society of the benefits these individuals could have made to us."[16]

Childhood Trauma in Poor Countries

The extent and consequences of child maltreatment in high-income countries are distressing and damaging enough, but the situation in poor countries is worse. In a companion paper to Prof Gilbert's, Richard Reading and colleagues commented that "maltreatment of children takes place in all societies and most evidence suggests that it is more common in low-income and middle-income countries." In addition, children in poor, non-western parts of the world often suffer far more extreme traumatic events. The impact of war is perhaps the worst, but there are many others. They include severe poverty, malnutrition, disease, famine, child labor, slavery, child marriage, and genital mutilation. All of these have lasting effects on physical, mental and emotional development. For instance, James DeMeo

Table 17: Long-term Consequences of Child Maltreatment
(Sources: Gilbert et al 2009, Shonkoff and Phillips 2000, Zeanah and Scheeringa 1997, Gerhardt 2004, Perry 1997, 2000, Champagne 2008)

Social Consequences

Reduced educational achievements. Lower-skilled employment; increased risk of unemployment. A link between sexual abuse and prostitution. Increased risk of teenage pregnancy. Increased risk of delinquency and crime. More likely to carry a weapon for self protection if physically or sexually abused. As adults, 20-30% abuse their own offspring.

Physical Consequences

Increased risk of obesity due to physical or sexual abuse, or neglect. Increased risk of gynecological and gastrointestinal disorders, birth difficulties, chronic pain, headaches and fatigue following sexual abuse. A factor in heart disease, cancer, chronic lung disease, skeletal fractures and liver disease. HIV probably more common.

Psychological Consequences

Impairment of emotional intelligence. Inability to give or receive affection. Egocentricity. Lack of empathy. Increased risk of:
  Anxiety and depression
  Aggression and violence
  PTSD following a traumatic experience
  Suicide
  Alcoholism in girls
  Eating disorders (bulimia, anorexia) as a result of sexual abuse
  Substance abuse including illegal drugs
  Psychopathology

Intellectual Consequences

Impairment of:
  Brain development
  IQ
  Language skills

commented that "the emotional response of a child to famine and starvation are similar to those stemming from maternal rejection or isolation-rearing, factors which are known to have powerful disturbing effects upon later adult behavior."[17] Even during times of plenty, survivors of such experiences are likely to raise their own children in ways that pass the trauma down the generations.

We cannot do justice to the sufferings of the world's children here. We can do no better than recommend the book *They Poured Fire on Us from the Sky* by three young survivors of the long-running war in Sudan which has killed millions of people, and left millions more eking out their existence in a ravaged countryside and refugee camps.[18] Along with tens of thousands of other boys, many as young as 5 years old, the trio were torn from their homes and families. Their villages were destroyed, and their families killed, often before their eyes. These youngsters walked barefoot for hundreds of miles, exhausted and starving, often wracked with thirst, sickness and injury. Constantly in danger from snakes, lions, hyenas, crocodiles, armed men, and invisible Antonov bombers, they were tortured by lice, ticks, chiggers and mosquitoes. At times, friendly adults looked out for them as best they could, but others chased them away or beat them as the social system collapsed under the strain. They saw countless people drop dead by the roadside, endless rotting corpses, and piles of human skulls—including many of children. For several more years they endured constant privation, semi-starvation and continued beatings and dangers in a Kenyan refugee camp. During that time, they focused all their energy on education—a focus that finally won them resettlement in the USA.

These three boys demonstrated almost unbelievable resilience, but their experiences left indelible shadows. Here is how their collaborating author, Judy Bernstein, summed up their epic journey:[19]

They endured and witnessed as small children things that

permanently scar mature soldiers. With death by starvation, thirst, wild animals or enemy forces constantly at their heels, they lived in a state of continuous fear that few of us ever experience. They are among the most badly war-traumatized children ever examined. ...

Bringing these stories to print required ... tremendous bravery in putting on paper experiences so painful that many veterans hide similar memories from their closest friends and family for their entire lives. ... (T)hey are voices for those still suffering in silence from the world's longest war. Although difficult to extract, relaying these events has been a valuable part of the healing process.

Untold thousands of other boys were not so lucky. Many undoubtedly have become brutalized, seeking to assuage their grief through vengeance, and vent their rage through senseless violence—an outcome that can only serve to prolong the suffering of their people. Many older boys were taken by the Sudanese People's Liberation Army and trained to fight—blank-eyed children with real guns sent to be slaughtered in the front line. How can such suffering, hatred, bitterness and terror ever be healed, and reconciliation and peace become possible? Will this war become a folk memory that erupts again in centuries to come, as happened in Kosovo? This is just one amongst many wars around the world, including Darfur (also in the Sudan), the Congo, Somalia, Afghanistan, Iraq, Israel-Palestine, Sri Lanka, and more.

PTSD and Other Disorders

The number of children with defined psychiatric disorders, particularly PTSD, provides another measure of the incidence of trauma. Not all children exposed to a specific traumatic event develop PTSD, and the severity of symptoms varies amongst those who do. Variations in resilience, or vulnerability, are due to differences in the characteristics of the child, the event, and the family and social context. For instance, young children are less resilient than older ones, children are more vulnerable than adults, and girls are more vulnerable than boys. PTSD is more likely to develop if the event is repeated, the child is physically injured, or her home is destroyed. The risk of trauma is reduced if the family has good parenting skills and is supportive.

Another key factor is helplessness. In his book on *Emotional Intelligence,* Daniel Goleman comments: "If people feel there is something they can do in a catastrophic situation, some control they can exert, no matter how minor, they fare far better emotionally than do those who feel utterly helpless. The element of helplessness is what makes a given event *subjectively* overwhelming."[20] This is particularly pertinent to children who are normally powerless within an abusive family context, in school, or with adult strangers in the community.

Bruce Perry reviewed several studies which showed that 15-90% of children exposed to defined traumatic events develop PTSD. These include:

- 93% of those who witness domestic violence;
- 34% of those who experience physical or sexual abuse; and
- 58% of those who suffer both physical and sexual abuse.

In all these studies, significant symptoms were also observed in most of those who did not meet all the criteria for PTSD.[21] More generally, Keith Oatley and his co-authors estimated the incidence of childhood psychiatric disorders in western countries as 8% of preschoolers, and 12% of pre-adolescents. They noted that these figures mask significant cultural and gender differences. For example, boys in the USA are three times more likely than girls to be diagnosed with conduct disorder, including truanting, stealing, arson, sexual assaults, fights, cruelty and use of weapons. By contrast, the rates of depression and anxiety are similar for both genders.[22]

Bruce Perry has described the challenges of accurate diagnosis in children.[23] Signs of PTSD include impulsiveness, poor concentration, unhappiness, emotional numbness, avoiding social contact, dissociation, sleep problems, aggressive play, school failure, and delayed or regressed development. However, the diagnostic criteria are so complex that two children may both meet them, and yet have very different symptoms. Also, the criteria for PTSD are very similar to those for other disorders, such as attention deficit hyperactivity disorder (ADHD) and depression. This means that many children suffering post-traumatic stress (PTS) who do not satisfy all the criteria for full-blown PTSD may be diagnosed with some other condition. Sometimes, too, their symptoms may meet the criteria for more than one disorder, leading to a primary diagnosis of PTSD, together with ADHD, depression, oppositional-defiant disorder, conduct disorder, separation anxiety, or a phobia. In some studies, most traumatized children have met the criteria for three or more disorders. Misdiagnosis also happens because the child's trauma history is not identified accurately. The psychiatrist may not be aware of traumatic stresses such as domestic violence or abuse; or the child's family may not associate a problem, such as failure at school or social withdrawal, with a past event such as a car accident, medical procedure, or death of a relative.

The confusion becomes worse when children are evaluated several times over a period of years. The assessor seldom has access to a complete history, and may rely on the opinion of one caregiver and a single interview, often at the child's school. Perry reports that it is not unusual for a child with PTSD due to chronic abuse to accumulate six or eight diagnoses over several evaluations. Each of these may be associated with a different treatment approach, to the frustration of those trying to help the child. Perry argues that these multiple labels shed little light on the causes of the child's problems, their appropriate treatment, or prognosis. Nevertheless, he concludes that childhood trauma can lead to a range of disorders in addition to PTSD.[24]

The way multiple disorders arise can be illustrated by imagining an abused child who becomes hyper-vigilant, constantly scanning her surroundings for danger. She learns to read non-verbal cues, such as facial expression, tone of voice, eye-contact, and friendly touch, which may be a prelude to sexual abuse. These 'street smarts' are vital for survival in her world, but prevent her learning cognitive, social and emotional skills. When he enters school, such a child is immediately at a disadvantage. Swamped by fear, he responds inappropriately to non-threatening social cues. He may be unable to sit still, or concentrate on cognitive learning because he is on the lookout for danger. He tries to solve problems with aggression and violence, as would be appropriate at home. His teacher may see him as bright, but unable to learn easily, leading to a diagnosis of ADHD, possibly coupled with being learning disabled.

In reality, many such children are literally 'scared out of their wits.' Not only are they unable to take in new information, but also they cannot access what they have already learned. It is like having permanent exam nerves that block achievement. Another way of looking at this is that intellectual knowledge is of little value when our survival is threatened because it becomes inaccessible. Traumatized children cannot perform in the classroom unless their fear is soothed. Action learning through role-play, song, rhyme or rap may work better than normal academic education in this situation.[25]

Even in rich countries, the majority of traumatized children get no professional help. Those who do get help often have limited access and brief sessions. This situation is partly due to the false belief that children are naturally resilient. Unfortunately, too, there is as much confusion about how to treat children with PTSD as there is about the diagnosis. There are several competing theoretical perspectives, each of which brings certain insights without providing a complete and unambiguous approach. This can be confusing for caregivers faced with conflicting recommendations. Some therapists, for example, claim that talking about the traumatic event is most important, while others recommend not talking and focus on the practical problems arising from the trauma, such as strategies for coping at school. Yet others bring a smorgasbord of methods.[26]

On the positive side, Daniel Goleman points out that children often heal themselves by creating games out of the traumatic event. This applies particularly to collective traumas such as mass shootings at a school. Through these games, the children are able to repeat the experience in an unthreatening context, thus gradually reducing the sensitivity of emotional triggers, and allowing more normal responses to develop. The children can also magically create different outcomes, and thereby replace their helplessness with a sense of control. However, in severe cases these games may need to be repeated endlessly for years,[27] and the children may still need help to deal with the most frightening parts.[28]

Reflection

Even in rich nations, the extent and depth of childhood trauma today is horrifying. Many of the stories from the poorest countries of the majority world, particularly from war zones, are harrowing and gut-wrenching. At times, we became so distressed just reading about the situation that it was hard to keep writing. Yet many traditional societies provide a wonderful childhood, despite material simplicity and the hazards of their ways of life. The stories of the three lost boys from Sudan illustrate this well. They had five years or more of nurturing home life during which they were loved, supported and protected by their parents, and an extended family of uncles, aunts, and cousins. During those years they participated fully in family and community life, caring for the goats and other responsibilities. They frequently faced real dangers in the form of snakes, lions, hyenas, and horseback raiders. But they clearly developed a deep, inner sense of confidence, security, hope, and a zest for life that gave them an unimaginable resilience when their lives were shattered by war; a resilience that ultimately brought them as young adults to a new life in the USA.

On the plane to New York, Alepho dreamed of a pile of skulls that smiled and spoke to him. They said: "How can you find peace yourself? If you answer that question, everybody will answer that question." What a profound insight—that peace starts in the heart of each one of us. But for Alepho, the answer was not simple: "*Find peace in my heart.* That wasn't something I'd been searching for. Revenge had been there so long. It would have to move aside first and I wasn't willing to let go so easily or quickly."[29] In time, Alepho moved on. But what about the untold thousands who were not so fortunate? Not so much the ones who died, and continue to die, tragic though that is. But the ones who are still living the nightmare, who have lost their humanity in the brutalizing process, and who are now bent on vengeance? And what about the brutalized children in countries that are officially at peace? Kids who grow up to pass their trauma on to their own children, who join the army and perhaps become jailers at the next Guantanamo or Abu Ghraib, or who out of their pain mow down a dozen kids in a school playground?

How can we possibly dream of a peaceful future while this situation continues? In order to create a sustainable partnership future we must take urgent action to reduce childhood trauma through parenting training, the reform of education, and the provision of healing therapy for the traumatized.

20. Adolescence

Adolescence is a time of turmoil. Hormones go on the rampage, the body matures physically and sexually, and the brain is restructured, with unused circuits being pruned while others become permanent. But from a larger perspective, the key patterns have already been set by genetic predispositions, and experiences in the womb, infancy, and childhood. These patterns may endow us with the resilience to sail easily through adolescence and adulthood, or they may leave us vulnerable to trauma. If our stress response system has been set too high, we are likely to be susceptible to a host of mental and physical diseases, and may be vulnerable to fresh traumas throughout life. There are many potential causes and consequences of trauma in adolescence and adulthood (Tables 1 & 3), a few of which are discussed in more detail in this chapter and the next.

The Incidence of Adolescent Trauma

Keith Oatley and his co-authors estimated that 15% of adolescents in western countries suffer from psychiatric disorders.[1] Most of these diagnoses do not acknowledge the role of trauma, but traumatic events frequently underlie mental illness, and are experienced by many adolescents. In the USA, over 40% of adolescents and 80% of college students reported at least one traumatic experience before the age of 18. Few of these teenagers would have had a diagnosable disorder, but sub-clinical symptoms often cause significant impairment.[2] By comparison, 2-5% of US adolescents are estimated to suffer from full-blown PTSD.[3] However, the figures are much higher for those exposed to specific events, such as an earthquake or school shooting as the following examples illustrate:[4]

- A year after Hurricane Hugo, up to 6% of exposed

adolescents had PTSD, the level depending on gender and ethnicity; 20% were still having flashbacks and 18% were hyper-aroused.

- In 1972, a dam collapsed, destroying the community of Buffalo Creek. Two years later, 32% of affected children and adolescents had symptoms of PTSD, falling to 7% after 15 years.
- 9 months after a fire killed 25 people, 20% of children and adolescents who witnessed it or who lost a friend or relative had PTSD.
- Half the adolescent survivors of Khmer concentration camps in Cambodia still had PTSD 6 years later; another study found 20% with PTSD after 12 years.
- 25% of adolescent Bosnian refugees resettled in the USA had PTSD a year later.

Further, Becker and colleagues noted that most adolescents in deprived urban areas in the USA witness violence, including killings, and exhibit stress symptoms similar to those of children in war zones.[5] Horrifying as they are, these data may underestimate the problem since adolescents are generally reluctant to admit to symptoms of trauma out of shame, and a desire not to talk about the event.[6]

The Impacts of Adolescent Trauma

It is common for trauma symptoms to appear in adolescence as a delayed response to infant or childhood experiences. Psychoanalyst Boris Cyrulnik notes that these symptoms may be amplified by a judgmental response such as: "You're finished. You were damaged during your early childhood, and science shows that the damage cannot be undone. What is more, you are the child of genetically inferior parents. Worse still, you have so many social handicaps that you have no reason to be optimistic."[7] Cyrulnik goes on to argue that, despite what the experts say, the brain remains sufficiently flexible that healing is possible provided the teenager's peers and close adults believe it is. This is an important perspective to bear in mind, given the emphasis on developmental windows of opportunity in the last few chapters. We need to be aware of the issues, but not condemn victims out of hand.

Despite so many patterns being set earlier in childhood, there are some unique features to adolescent trauma.[8] In some ways adolescents are more vulnerable than younger children or adults. They tend to take risks that expose them to potential trauma, and modern society expects them to move through major life changes with little support and no rites of passage. On the other hand, they are better able to protect themselves than younger children, and their rebelliousness, sense of invulnerability, and group loyalty help them to cope better than adults with some situations. However, these qualities may be undermined by extreme physical danger. Similarly, sexual or aggressive trauma may damage their developing sexuality and assertiveness, sparking either an aggressive, angry reaction, or a deep sense that sexuality and/or assertiveness are dangerous. Either response stunts their capacity for intimate relationships. Traumatic experiences may also challenge teenagers' ethical beliefs, particularly when their community is destroyed. For example, they may need to find ways to justify stealing food from other victims in order to survive. On the positive side, however, trauma may stimulate more mature moral reasoning.

Adolescents often blame themselves for what happened. They may feel that they deserved the abuse, that they could have done more to prevent what happened, or that they should not have survived when others died. Just as children create games in which they reconstruct the outcome, so adolescents often create fantasies in which they change events. They may also fantasize about revenge, potentially leading to rash actions when coupled with typical teenage feelings of omnipotence and invulnerability.

Conversely, adolescents often become convinced that they have no future—that their lives will be short, and they will not survive into adulthood. Such beliefs interfere with the pursuit of personal and vocational goals, and, when combined with risky behavior, can be self-fulfilling. Similarly, they may come to see themselves as helpless victims, suffering from disabling symptoms.

There are marked gender differences in the response to trauma. Females are more likely to be affected, and typically internalize the stress as anxiety and depression. By contrast, males are more likely to externalize it in disruptive behavior, including aggressive violence. In general, trauma may arouse self-doubt, guilt, shame or anxiety, thus eroding budding self-esteem and self-identity, and disrupting peer relationships and daily lives. In the long-term, trauma increases vulnerability to anxiety and depression, dissociation, and relationship difficulties.

Childhood maltreatment is strongly associated with substance abuse in adolescence, and their risky lifestyle means that addicts are more likely than others to experience trauma. One study found five times the normal rate of PTSD amongst people in drug treatment facilities. Childhood maltreatment is also linked to conduct disorders due to insecure attachment and parental modeling of violence. Half the adults who responded to a national survey in the USA reported that they had been physically punished in adolescence. This increases the risk of depression, suicide, and substance abuse as well as domestic violence later in life. Teenagers are at high risk of suicide, and this is linked to the lifetime accumulation of stress, a sense of powerlessness, and low self-esteem—all of which would be increased by maltreatment. Similarly, sexual abuse increases the risk of teenage pregnancy and later sexual offences. However, it is important to bear in mind that most abused children do not become violent, and not all violent people were abused as children. Also, secure attachment and supportive relationships with family and peers provide resilience and strong protection against trauma.

Sexuality

As noted earlier, sexuality is arguably the most potent human drive after survival. It first appears in infancy as a strong sensuality that craves skin contact and gentle holding, and relishes genital play. It explodes in adolescence as hormones surge, and the brain undergoes final reconstruction before adulthood.[9] Shaman Sandra Ingerman claims that adolescent girls in the USA are confused and overwhelmed by the onset of menstruation. Unable to understand the transition from girl to sensual, life-giving woman, and lacking a meaningful rite of passage, the adolescent is unable to embrace her female power. As a result, a part of her dissociates, and a piece of her soul is lost. In a similar way, teenage youths are often overwhelmed by the social and peer pressures of the transition from boyhood to manhood, and become confused about how to act towards girls who are turning into women. They, too, often lose part of their soul at this time.[10]

This confusion and dissociation is one reason why teenagers' intimate relationships are so fraught with problems. A deeper reason may be a lack of nurturing in infancy. We saw in Chapter 18 that monkeys raised without mothers were incapable of normal sexual activity or relationships. Similarly, psychoanalyst Wilhelm Reich believed that adult human sexuality is disturbed by childhood trauma. Thus, maltreatment may be reflected in the results of a survey in 2009 by the National Society for the Prevention of Cruelty to Children in the UK. They reported that 90% of 1400 girls between the ages of 13 and 17 had been in intimate relationships. Of these, one third suffered sexual abuse, and a quarter experienced violence from their boyfriends, including slapping, punching, beating and forced sexual touch. 17% had been pressured into intercourse, and 6% had been raped.[11]

According to Reich, the child armors herself against traumatic experiences with unconscious muscular tensions. These reduce sensitivity to sensations in general, and to sexuality in particular, thus preventing complete release of sexual energy.[12] In Reich's view, full sexual potency requires surrender to both the sensory, erotic and emotional, romantic aspects of lovemaking. Simultaneous feelings of tender love and erotic excitement are necessary for uninhibited discharge of dammed-up sexual tensions. More recently, McAnarney similarly claimed that sexual intimacy requires psychological as well as physical maturity. He argued that we need to know who we are as individuals before we can merge our identity with that of a sexual partner. From this perspective, he suggested that adolescents usually start having sex prematurely, possibly from a need for loving touch. Girls in particular often have sex simply to be cuddled.[13]

Repression of sexuality may lead to trauma and a build-up of inner tensions that surface in anger, frustration and violence, as well as in sexual exploitation, aggression and perversions. This is clearly demonstrated by James Prescott's analysis of 400 cultures around the world. He found that societies which gave their children plenty of physical affection, and allowed free expression of adolescent sexuality, had low levels of adult violence. The reverse also held, with high levels of violence in cultures that had little physical affection and body pleasure.[14] From this and his own analyses of over 1,000 cultures, James DeMeo concluded that: "Cultures which tended to inflict pain and trauma upon infants and young children, punish young people for sexual expression, manipulate them into arranged marriages, subordinate the female and otherwise greatly restrict the freedoms of young people and older females to the iron will of males also tended to possess high levels of adult violence, with various social institutions designed for expression of pent-up sadistic aggression."[15]

It seems clear that reducing sexual repression is a key factor in shifting civilization away from the dominator model towards partnership. This might be done by allowing sexual play, and open adolescent sexual relationships supported by freely-available contraception, health advice and relationship counseling. Anthropological studies indicate that fears of consequent unbridled promiscuity and the breakdown of family structures are unfounded.

An outstanding example is the Trobriand Islands society studied by Malinowski in the 1920's, and discussed at length by DeMeo. The Trobriand Islanders had a place where children could meet on their own without adult interference or supervision, and where they developed friendships and love affairs. From as early as five years old, children played sexual games, and initiated each other into the mysteries of sexual life long before they could actually carry out the sex act. In adolescence, groups travelled between villages to meet others of their age. Girls were as sexually uninhibited as boys, and virginity was seen as peculiar or pitiful. However, pregnancies among unmarried girls were rare, probably due to the use of herbal contraceptives. Out of this free experimentation grew longer-lasting love affairs in later adolescence, and stable marriages in adulthood. Marriage was not compulsory and emerged from strong emotional bonds, sexual attraction, and genital gratification. The Islanders were observed to be emotionally and psychologically healthy, and free of childhood trauma. There was no male dominance, and the fathers were fully involved in child care. Sadly, the influence of Christian missionaries radically changed this fascinating culture shortly after these studies were made.

By comparison with Trobriand Island society, even sexually liberated secular western countries continue to be inhibited, as shown by attitudes to genital and sexual play in childhood, and sexual expression in adolescence. Indeed, teenage sex is widely regarded as a problem. As a result, it is mostly indulged in secret, often without adequate protection from disease and pregnancy. In adulthood as well as adolescence, undischarged sexual tensions burst out in violence and perversions ranging from pornography and pedophilia to sadomasochism and sex slavery. The prevalence of such practices in our society highlights the continued existence of deep-seated sexual hang-ups.

Male Circumcision and Female Genital Mutilation

Perhaps it is the very potency of sexuality that makes it so feared in the many cultures that repress it through child-rearing practices, behavioral norms, social customs, and religious beliefs and taboos. Two of the commonest forms of repression are male circumcision, and female genital mutilation. We have described them in some detail because we believe they are an important source of trauma, aggression and violence in the world today.

The World Health Organization reports that as many as 30% of males worldwide may be circumcised, two-thirds of them Moslems. Historically, it appears to have been adopted as a way to curb sexual activity. Moses Maimonides, Rabbi of Cairo in the 12th century, claimed that one reason for it was "to lessen the power of passion and of too great desire."[16] Similarly, one of the claimed benefits of introducing circumcision into the USA in the 19th century was prevention of "masturbatory insanity." At that time it was advocated along with a host of painful devices and practices to thwart any vestige of genital pleasure in children.[17] Today, the practice is medically controversial, with disagreement about potential health benefits, effects on sexual function, and traumatic impact. However, in the last few years, research has confirmed that it provides partial protection from HIV infection.

Amazingly, newborn babies even in developed countries are still frequently circumcised without anesthetic despite evidence of the pain and emotional consequences. The following account of his circumcision at about five years old is by Benson Deng, a Dinka from Sudan. It clearly illustrates the traumatic and dangerous nature of many traditional practices.[18] However, it also reveals that there were social benefits. In many cultures, circumcision was, and sometimes still is, an initiation ritual and rite of passage to higher status, marriage and sexual activity.

(My father) grabbed my hand, holding it tighter than I had ever felt, and led me to the acacia tree. All the men's eyes were on me like hyenas staring at a lost goat kid. I got scared and stopped walking. My father lifted me up into the air. Now I knew there was something bad. I kicked my feet and slapped my hands on his chest. Four men grabbed me and laid me on my back, holding me down and turning my face up to the sky. A pot of water boiled on a fire. The man with the blue robe was washing the blood off a razor blade. ...

The man kneeled and leaned over me. He took hold of my penis and began cutting off the skin. I'd never felt such pain in my life. I tried to jerk away but I was held so strongly that I couldn't move a muscle. The pain felt like he was tearing my skin off with only his fingers, not cutting it with a sharp blade. I cried but it was going so slowly my voice began wearing out. My mother came and tears were flowing down her cheeks.

"The blade is blunt," said the man who was cutting off the skin.

"Ma, please help me," I cried. "They are killing me."

"Be calm, son," my father said. "It will be over soon and then you will be a strong and brave son of mine."

When the man finished they washed me with very hot water and my father carried me home on his shoulder while I dripped blood all down his shirt. After a few weeks, I was playing and wrestling with the boys again. When girls sang this song: "Uncircumcised, he is like a cow with an untrimmed tail. When he farts, it smells like broth." I was happy to have passed the uncircumcised stage, but it wasn't worth the pain I went through.

The belief is still widespread that female sexuality is dangerous and must be controlled. In many Islamic countries, women still must be veiled and are isolated from men other than their husbands to avoid stirring male lust—a response that the very practice may encourage. Arranged marriages, often before puberty, also constrain the expression of female sexuality. But the most pernicious practice is female genital mutilation This generally has two objectives. One is to ensure that the girl remains a virgin until marriage. The other is to remove any possibility that she will experience sexual pleasure in order to reduce the risk of adultery.[19] The practice involves the partial or total removal of the external female genitalia, the most extreme form of which is infibulation, described by J. Lantier below.[20] It is even more painful, and more life-threatening, than male circumcision, and seldom brings any social benefits. But failure to be mutilated may lead to insults, ostracism, and being considered unclean.

The child, completely naked, is made to sit on a low stool. Several women take hold of her and open her legs wide. ... (T)he operator, usually a woman experienced in this procedure, who sits facing her, with her kitchen knife pierces and slices open the hood of the clitoris. Then she begins to cut it out. While another woman wipes off the blood with a rag, the operator digs with her fingernail a hole the length of the clitoris to detach and pull out the organ entirely. The little girl, held down by the helpers, screams in extreme pain; but no one pays the slightest attention.

The operator finishes this job by entirely pulling out the clitoris ... The neighbor women are then invited to plunge their fingers into the bloody hole to verify that every piece of the clitoris is removed. ... After a short moment, the woman takes the knife again and cuts off the inner lips ... Then the woman, with a swift motion, begins to scrape the skin from the inside of the large lips ... without the slightest concern for the extreme pain she inflicts (and the girl's screams). When the wound is large enough, she adds some lengthwise cuts and several more incisions. ... At this stage of the operation, the child is so spent and exhausted that she stops crying, but often has convulsions.

Lantier goes on to describe how the wound was closed with long acacia thorns, and the girl's thighs were tied together. She was then swathed in a bandage from her knees to her waist for about two weeks. During this time she remained lying on her mat, with her excrement collecting in the bandage. The aim of the whole process was to leave as small an opening as possible—just enough to allow urine and menstrual flow to pass—because the smaller the hole the higher the bride price. Death, amazingly, is not common, but "There are, of course, various complications which frequently leave the girl crippled and disabled for the rest of her life." These include accidental piercing of the urethra or opening of the rectum, and biting off her own tongue. On their wedding night, infibulated women are cut open just enough to allow intercourse. The extensive scar tissue makes childbirth difficult, and further cutting may be needed. The difficult birth traumatizes the baby as well as the mother, and maternal mortality is common.

Many countries have now banned the practice, but a recent study of female genital mutilation in Egypt revealed that it was still commonplace six years after it was prohibited. Nearly four thousand Egyptian girls between 10 and 14 years old were interviewed. 85% had been mutilated since the practice was outlawed, two-thirds by non-medical personnel. The girls' parents explained that they disobeyed the law to comply with religious and traditional beliefs, and curb the sexual drive of their daughters. Also, mothers may be unconsciously motivated by revenge, wanting their daughters to suffer as they did.[21] In 2008, the World Health Organization estimated that three million girls a year undergo mutilation in Africa.[22] When multiplied by an average post-circumcision lifetime of around 40 years, this translates to well over 100 million women who have been subjected to this extreme trauma. Even in the UK, 20,000 girls under the age of 15 are thought to be at risk of female genital mutilation, and 250 forced marriages are reported every year.[23]

It is easy to single out Islamic practices for criticism today, but, from the time of St Paul, Christianity has also exhibited strong anti-feminism. Fear of women's power underlay the horrors of the Inquisition and medieval witch hunts that killed millions of innocent victims. And it still underlies the practice in some churches of priestly celibacy—often leading to sexual abuse, the refusal to allow women to control their reproduction, and the rejection of women for the priesthood.

Crime and Violence

Official statistics in both the USA and UK show that teenagers commit more crimes than other age groups. These are mainly minor offenses fuelled by adolescent rebellion, peer pressure, and the search for excitement. Most outgrow this phase by their early twenties. More problematic are adolescents who showed signs of antisocial behavior in kindergarten, and often go on to become lifelong violent criminals.[24] A long-term study of more than 500 males born in 1972-3 in New Zealand found that just 10% fell into this category, but they were responsible for almost half the convictions for violent crime by age 26. Earlier in childhood, they typically had a low IQ, poor language skills, and were diagnosed as having ADHD. Research indicates that this outcome is mainly due to maternal rejection early in life, a lack of nurturing, and exposure to traumatic violence in infancy.[25]

An interesting genetic contribution has been traced to variations in a gene called MAO-A. The gene alone is not associated with criminal behavior, but when combined with childhood abuse, the low-activity variant is strongly linked to violence. In the New Zealand study, abused boys with this variant were three times more likely than others to have conduct disorder in adolescence, and ten times more likely to have been convicted of a violent crime in adulthood. By contrast, those with the high-activity gene seemed to be impervious to abuse. Brain scans revealed that people with the low-activity gene have a more active amygdala and less active prefrontal cortex.[26] In other words, they have a higher level of stress arousal, and weaker cognitive regulation of emotions. This is consistent with Bruce Perry's argument that anything, including alcohol, that increases the power of the lower brain relative to the cortex raises the risk of violence and aggression. The fact that many traumatized people resort to alcohol or other drugs to relieve their pain is one reason why so many of them behave violently. "It is often the intoxicating agents that allow expression of the neurodevelopmentally determined predisposition for violence."[27]

About a third of children with early antisocial behavior show a different pattern. These children have an under-active amygdala. They appear to be fearless because they do not interpret threat signals correctly. They are cruel, callous and unemotional because they lack empathy and guilt, and cannot understand others' pain. In this case, research indicates a strong genetic predisposition, with only weak links to abuse and poor parenting. Treatment is difficult because these adolescents are indifferent to their own pain, and unresponsive to punishment. Perhaps surprisingly, however, they are highly responsive to rewards and praise for good behavior.[28]

Reflection

We have seen the vital role of parenting from birth to adolescence in the development of the structural balance between the emotional lower brain and the controlling cortex, in setting the baseline stress response, and in learning to regulate emotions. We also have seen how symptoms of trauma are often confused with those for other mental disorders such as ADHD and depression. All these factors point towards the possibility that the role of genes in violent behavior has been overestimated. In particular, observed differences may turn out to be epigenetic responses to early maltreatment rather than being inherited.

Similarly, family traits may be due to a combination of learning and gene imprinting, rather than genetic inheritance.

21. Adulthood

The biggest causes of trauma in adulthood today are violence and aggression, particularly by males. Their most obvious expression is in child abuse, domestic violence, rape, murder, robbery with violence, terrorism and war. But they also arise in a personal context as self-harm and suicide. Non-physical, emotional and psychological violence and aggression are common in the workplace, social hierarchies, and many relationships. In most cases, the origins can be traced to trauma in family and cultural history, or in the womb, infancy or childhood. In this chapter, we explore some of the connections between trauma, violence and mental health.

The Need to Belong

Humans evolved as social beings. As a result, one of our deepest needs is to belong, to be accepted and to be respected. In the distant past, infants were born into a band to which they naturally belonged. Later, in more complex cultures, they would have been born into a caste which gave them an identity and role in life. Today, it is not so easy. There is no longer any group to which we belong automatically. We face the challenge of relating to many groups, and playing many overlapping and possibly conflicting roles in our family, workplace, sports team and church. As we move into adulthood, we have to choose amongst alternative careers, employers and social groups, and assume new roles as partner and parent. This is a stressful situation, full of fear and uncertainty, which leaves many people suffering a deep existential loneliness. As a result, we are vulnerable to being drawn into any group that offers us a place to belong, and peers who accept and respect us. In most cases, this is beneficial for both us and society, but it also can lead to the evils of Nazi death camps, Rwandan genocide, Guantanamo prison, or suicide bombers.

Psychologist Philip Zimbardo argues that people who commit violent, sadistic or other 'bad' actions are not brain damaged, mentally ill, or genetically evil.[1] Rather, their behavior is determined by the situations in which they find themselves. Our burning desire to belong, to cooperate and to seem normal can easily lead us to conform to group ideas and actions that we would otherwise reject. From this perspective, 'peer pressure' actually comes from within ourselves. However, it can be strengthened by activities that enhance group solidarity, such as marching, dancing, singing, and propaganda.[2] Our willingness to act wrongly can be boosted further if we know we will not be held accountable. The sense of accountability can be weakened by anonymity, disguise (e.g. masks or uniforms), a well-established role (e.g. jailer), a set of rules to follow, a contract to fulfill, orders from a higher authority, or threats by an authority figure. Often, we also try to justify behavior we know to be wrong by redefining it as morally justifiable, or portraying it as less damaging than it really is.

Another way to encourage bad behavior is to dehumanize the victims by making them appear to be 'animals' or vicious enemies. This is why suspected terrorists in Guantanamo and other prisons are portrayed as inhuman monsters who deserve torture and gross humiliation. In fact, most suicide bombers are not monsters, but decent, middle-class people from caring families, many of whom have been to college and are married with children. Their need to belong and their desire to do something about injustice in the world is manipulated by recruiters. They are invited to join a small secret cell of trainees where they learn the trade. They are assured not only that they will go straight to paradise, but also that their families will receive money on earth and rewards in heaven. A key point comes when he or she makes a commitment on video that is sent to their family. After that, the loss of face from backing out becomes unthinkable for most would-be bombers.

When we fall into line with the group, our brains release more dopamine—a reward chemical. Correspondingly, an 'error signal' is sent when we differ from our peers. So powerful are these effects that we tend to adjust our perception of reality rather than face conflict.[3] This is an indication of just how traumatic it can be for many people to oppose their group. In our view, most of us can be led astray easily because we suffered some degree of trauma in infancy. For instance, maternal deprivation may lead to an intense need to be loved, and harsh caregivers may scare the infant into fearful obedience to all authority figures. Zimbardo did not investigate the trauma histories of his research participants, but he argues that people who are willing to stand against bad situations are heroes. Sometimes physical bravery is needed, but more often it is the courage to risk ridicule, humiliation, rejection and other psychological injuries. We believe heroic figures such as Mahatma Gandhi and Nelson Mandela may have been able to assert their individuality because their early experiences built strong self-esteem and resilience.

From interviews in Germany and Rwanda, Evelin Lindner concluded that "the most painful form of humiliation is being forced to become a perpetrator because you are too weak to resist, too much of a coward to say no and face death."[4] In Rwanda, many Hutus were forced to kill their Tutsi spouses and Tutsi-looking children to demonstrate their allegiance to the Hutu cause. Often, they later became insane, wishing they were dead instead of their loved ones, and loathing themselves for their weakness. Lindner concluded: "As important as it is to hold perpetrators of atrocities responsible, all those who are spared such moral dilemmas ought to be thankful and refrain from arrogantly stigmatizing as "evil" those who were caught."[5] None of us knows how we would react if pushed into an inescapable dilemma.

Violentization

Trauma not only can make us conform to group norms, but also can shape our characters in deeper ways. Criminologist Lonnie Athens set out to discover what makes dangerously-violent criminals.[6] From in-depth interviews with many brutal murderers and rapists, he identified a four stage 'violentization' (or violent socialization) process. In essence, the individual progresses from experiencing severe personal trauma, usually in childhood, to inflicting it on others with little provocation. The first stage is brutalization, usually by members of the victim's family or gang. It takes anything from weeks to years, but is normally complete in males by adolescence. It includes violent subjugation by physical battering, or the threat of it; witnessing someone he is close to, such as his mother, a sibling or friend, being violently subjugated; and coaching in violence by a member of his family or gang. Next comes belligerency, when the victim suddenly realizes that violence is sometimes necessary, and resolves to use it if he is seriously provoked and has a chance of success.

The third stage is the performance of violence. If he loses, he may give up or look for a way to do better next time. If he wins, others start to treat him with caution and fear—a power most victims welcome. Success discharges the energy of arousal of that particular event, but leaves him still with the trapped energy of past brutalizing episodes. He remains hyper-vigilant, on the look-out for danger, and ready to respond to perceived new threats. Each success briefly relieves his arousal and fear, leaving him feeling omnipotent, like superman. This feels so good that he becomes addicted to violence.

The final stage is virulency. Stimulated by his new status, he starts to attack people with the intention of doing serious harm, or even killing them, with little or no provocation. He moves from defense to offence; from victim to brutal oppressor. Athens argues that people who reach this stage are incurable, and should be segregated in jail. But the vast majority of criminals have not gone so far, and can be healed. It would make sense to provide therapy and training for them within supervised programs of community service rather than complete their violentization by sending them to jail.

Bruce Perry agrees with the core of Athens' theory:[7]

The most dangerous among us have come to be this way because of a malignant combination of experiences—lack of critical early life nurturing, chaotic and cognitively impoverished environments, pervasive physical threat, persisting fear, and, finally, watching the strongest, most violent in the home get what he wants, and seeing the same aggressive, violent use of power idealized on television and at the movies. These violent offenders have been incubated in terror, waiting to be old enough to get "one of those guns," waiting to be the one who controls, the one who takes, the one who hits, the one who can "make the fear, not take the fear." Nowhere is this predatory food chain more evident than in juvenile justice settings where, too often, the youth is either a victim or predator, with no third option.

However, Perry emphasizes that the majority of neglected and traumatized children never become violent or remorseless predators. He argues that such behavior develops only when it is supported by an appropriate belief system such as racism, sexism, idealization of violent heroes, cultural tolerance of child maltreatment, tribalism, or nationalism. Elsewhere, Perry also argues that abused children who do not become violent always have some element of hope in their lives.[8]

The Brutalization of War

There is considerable disagreement about the psychological impacts of war on service personnel. A national survey of US Vietnam veterans conducted in the mid-1980's found that nearly a third of men and over a quarter of women were suffering from PTSD.[9] More recently, 12-20% of US veterans of the Iraq war are thought to have PTSD, with as many as 30% suffering mental disorders. By contrast, the UK Ministry of Defence (MoD) puts the number of British veterans from Iraq and Afghanistan with PTSD at only 4-6%. Further confusion is created by the emergence of a new disorder labeled Post-Concussion Syndrome (PCS) which may surface weeks or even years after being blown up. Some specialists believe it is a form of PTSD, and is not due to brain injury.[10]

Piers Bishop suggests that this stark difference between the two nations may be due to MoD doctors being reluctant to diagnose PTSD.[11] Another reason may be that the US routinely screens returning servicemen, and the UK does not.[12] Without screening, soldiers may be reluctant to seek help for fear that 'cracking up' could end their military careers. Evidence is accumulating that the UK statistics may underestimate the problem. In 2008, the UK charity Combat Stress reported rising numbers of ex-servicemen seeking help.[13] Further, a study by prison probation officers released in September 2009 revealed that nearly 10% of UK prisoners were war veterans—a percentage that had risen by one-third in five years. Nearly half of a sample of convicted veterans were suffering from PTSD, and most had chronic drug or alcohol problems. The majority of convictions were for violent offences, particularly domestic violence.[14]

Part of the reason for the high level of PTSD, according to Paula Caplan, is a change of US combat policy. In World War II, when a soldier broke down he was sent far from combat and given time to recover. Now, the emphasis is on keeping him close to the combat zone, telling him he will be fine soon, and returning him to combat as soon as possible. Antidepressants may be given to relieve his symptoms.[15] By contrast, the British army has adopted a preventive approach called Trauma Risk Management. All units include a person who has been trained to identify those at risk after potentially traumatic incidents, and to ensure that no-one is left to struggle alone. It is said to work well because it provides peer support by trusted friends.[16] Nevertheless, it seems that soldiers returning home are often severely damaged.[17]

A key reason why so many servicemen suffer psychological problems is that humans are reluctant killers, with a strong inhibition against taking life. At the battle of Gettysburg during the American Civil War, thousands of soldiers on both sides avoided shooting at the enemy by repeatedly loading their muskets without firing them. Similarly, extensive interviews with US soldiers during the second world war revealed that an astonishing 75-85% of them did not fire their guns when the opportunity arose. Indeed, fear of killing was a bigger cause of 'battle fatigue' than the fear of being killed.[18] This reluctance to kill is well illustrated by a case study recounted by Paula Caplan:[19]

> *On September 11, 2001, Drew went straight from high school to enlist in the military, consumed with avenging all those deaths and defending his country. What he had not counted on was the part of basic training when they order you to run around a field aiming a gun, yelling "Kill! Kill!" Horrified, he became obsessed with images of suicide. Compared to the thought of killing "the enemy" he found it easier to think of killing himself. One night, the pull toward suicide became so powerful that he panicked, went AWOL, and flew home.*

When the low rate of firing was revealed, the US military revised its training methods. This lifted the rate to 55% in the Korean war, but many men may have deliberately fired into the air. This possibility is supported by the fact that 50,000 bullets were fired in Vietnam for each enemy killed. Modern weaponry turns killing into a remote, impersonal action. By contrast, as former

US military officer Dave Grossman put it: "Looking another human being in the eye, making an independent decision to kill him, and watching as he dies due to your action combine to form the single most basic, important, primal and potentially traumatic occurrence of war. If we understand this, then we understand the magnitude of the horror of killing in combat."[20] One reason for the high rate of PTSD in Iraq may be that much of the action has been up close and personal.

For war to be possible, ordinary, decent men and women must be transformed into killers. Lonnie Athens noted that the violentization process he identified can be used to produce soldiers as well as brutal criminals.[21] Indeed, many features of modern military training could have been designed by Athens. Violent subjugation comes early in basic training to fragment the recruit's sense of self by harsh discipline, isolation from his past life, disorientation and overwhelm. While in this vulnerable space, he is encouraged to bond with fellow recruits and instructors in order to build the trust, comradeship, unquestioning allegiance and mutual responsibility required in battle. Aggression is developed through boxing or other forms of combat, and the recruits are immersed in violent language and imagery. Group dynamics are exploited to manipulate people into treating outsiders violently and sadistically, and soldiers are taught to stereotype the enemy as sub-human and evil. In some specialist courses, they are trained to harness their rage, visualizing the enemy as an object of pure hatred.[22]

This focus on brutalization rather than honor, courage and other old-fashioned values may make soldiers more efficient killing machines, but it creates another problem. Somehow, a dividing line must be drawn between the use of violence against enemy soldiers, and its use against civilians or in private life. All-too-often that dividing line is breached. As Philip Zimbardo put it:[23]

Under the extreme stresses of combat conditions, with fatigue, fear, anger, hatred and revenge at full throttle, men can lose their moral compass and go beyond killing enemy combatants. Unless military discipline is strictly maintained and every soldier knows he bears personal responsibility for his actions, which are under surveillance by senior officers, then the furies are released in unimaginable orgies of rape and murder of civilians.

Richard Rhodes emphasized the role of betrayal in such failures. This can take many forms: officers who do not share the risks, lax discipline, blunders that bring death by friendly fire, equipment that does not work properly, encouragement to seek revenge for the death of comrades, mistaken or illegal policies such as approval of torture, or lack of political support at the highest level. Such failures can spark the rage that tips soldiers into the final stage of violentization that Athens called virulency. The result is massacres such as at My Lai in Vietnam, or atrocities such as the Abu Ghraib prison in Iraq.

Intimate Relationships

Given the prevalence of insecure attachment and child maltreatment, it should come as no surprise that intimate adult relationships are in trouble. Many children learn to suppress their emotions, and fail to learn how to regulate them; many learn that aggression and violence in the home are normal and acceptable; many learn sadistic and perverted forms of sexuality; and many learn that adults cannot be trusted. The devastating results are revealed in the statistics.

According to Amnesty International, at least one in three women in the world is beaten, coerced into sex, or otherwise abused in her lifetime. 70% of murdered women are killed by their male partners. In the UK, an incident of domestic violence is reported to police every minute, and one in nine women is severely beaten by her partner every year. Yet on average, a woman is assaulted 35 times before she calls for help. There are 167 rapes every day, 45% of them by their partners, and nearly half of murdered women are killed by their partner, or ex-partner.[24] The picture is similarly bleak for marriage. In 2008, half of all marriages in the UK ended in divorce.[25] Similarly, Daniel Goleman lamented that in the mid-90's two-thirds of marriage partnerships in the USA eventually broke up.[26] Sometimes, divorce is a positive step that ends the trauma of a toxic relationship. But all too often it involves fresh trauma for the partners and their children. And all too often the patterns that caused one partnership to snap are carried over into later ones.

Goleman sees upbringing as the source of these problems. In most of the world, boys and girls mix little and play different games. Boys play in large, competitive groups, and are proud of being autonomous and tough. By contrast, girls form small, cooperative groups, and webs of caring relationships. Parents display more emotions with their daughters, and talk more about emotional things with them than with their sons. Hence, girls develop high emotional intelligence, while boys learn to repress fear, guilt and vulnerability. In adulthood, intimacy for a woman means talking things over, whereas men tend to avoid emotional issues and want to do things together. Often, the result is a relationship in which the man retreats behind a wall of silence in response to contempt and harsh criticism. The consequence is a growing sense of hopelessness, loneliness and parallel lives going nowhere but divorce.[27] The absence of a supportive, intimate partner in the stresses of life, and the suppression of emotions leads to many diseases including allergies, asthma, arthritis, ulcerative colitis, chronic fatigue and cancer.[28]

Mental Health

Violence is generally regarded as normal, but may also be seen as one type of mental illness amongst many. The seeds of mental health are sown in the womb, infancy and childhood, and the prevalence of psychiatric disorders today is due in large part to growing up in a traumatized world. In 1994, it was estimated that almost half the population of the USA suffers a psychiatric disorder, including alcohol or drug abuse, at some time in their lives.[29] More recently, the US National Institute of Mental Health estimated that more than a quarter of those over 18—or 60 million people—suffer a diagnosable mental disorder every year, *excluding* the large numbers with alcohol or drug problems. Of that quarter, nearly half meet the criteria for two or more disorders. Mental illness is the top cause of disability for those between 15 and 44 years old in the USA and Canada,[30] and the situation is similar in the UK.[31]

The commonest problems are mood and anxiety disorders, including depression, bipolar disorder, panic attacks, various phobias, and generalized anxiety. With regard to these, Oatley and colleagues wrote: "It is clear that most episodes of major depression and some types of anxiety occur when things go severely wrong in people's lives ... most emotional disorders are responses to events and circumstances."[32] They noted that three types of childhood experience frequently precede adult depression: parental divorce, physical abuse by a relative or friend, or an event so frightening that it was thought about for years afterwards. Sue Gerhardt also stated that a root cause of depression is growing up in a negative, critical atmosphere that generates a sense of rejection, not being good enough, and being unlovable.[33] In summary, childhood trauma is a major cause of mood and anxiety disorders.

The picture is similar with alcoholism, drug abuse and eating disorders. These often are ways to cope with, or block out, emotional and psychological distress. Alcoholism, for example, is associated with stress, anxiety, emotional pain, low self-esteem, impulsiveness, aggressiveness, depression, and other psychiatric disorders. All of these, in turn, are linked to childhood trauma. Many people who suffer such symptoms do not consult a psychiatrist, or may not be severely enough affected to be diagnosed with a disorder. Anything that temporarily relieves their distress, or makes them feel good, has the potential to become an addiction. As well as alcohol, legal substances often used in this way include sugar, tea, coffee, chocolate, tobacco, aspirin, paracetamol (Tylenol or acetaminophen), and valium (diazepam). There is a growing list of illegal highs from cannabis, heroin and cocaine, to amphetamines, ecstasy, and more. Gambling, shopping, computer games, hard exercise, sex and other behavior patterns can also be addictive ways of dealing with unwanted emotions.

Eating disorders such as anorexia, bulimia, binge-eating and compulsive overeating are yet another way of coping with difficult emotions and stress. There are over 1m sufferers in the UK and 8-10m in the USA—mostly women. The numbers explode if obesity is counted as an eating disorder. The World Health Organization estimated that there were 400m obese people in the world in 2005, and the number was growing rapidly. At that time, one-third of adults in the USA were obese, and a quarter in the UK.[34] As the Eating Disorders Association explains it: "Problems with food can begin when it is used to cope with those times when you are bored, anxious, angry, lonely, ashamed or sad. Food becomes a problem when it is used to help you to cope with painful situations or feelings, or to relieve stress perhaps without you even realizing it."[35] Factors involved can include low self-esteem, lack of confidence, family relationships, death of a loved one, poverty, anxiety, depression, sadness, anger, and sexual, physical or emotional abuse.[36] This analysis is confirmed by ex-anorexic Jane Grieg:[37]

When I was anorexic, the constant mental agony was so intense that the only relief from it was physical pain. I was almost constantly suicidal. The low recovery rates for anorexia are due to the way it is treated. ... Anorexia is nothing to do with not eating; it is about having self-esteem so low that you feel like you are taking up too much space in the world. What people with anorexia need is reassurance that their lives are worth living and to find other things that they are good at, apart from not eating.

Another significant factor is the social pressure to be thin. Psychotherapist Susie Orbach suggests that the sense we have of our body, our physical self, may develop in a similar way to our mental and emotional selves. Its genetic potential is shaped in childhood not only by nutrition and physical activities, but also by the values and beliefs we absorb from our family and culture. She laments that we strive for a uniform ideal rather than celebrating bodily diversity. And she claims that a hidden public health emergency is revealed in the statistics on self harm, obesity and anorexia.[38]

Patterns of mental illness often run in families, and it is easy to assume that this is due to genetic inheritance. For example, children of depressed parents have six times the normal risk of becoming depressed themselves, and almost a third of them develop an emotional disorder. However, many studies have shown that a genetic predisposition is not sufficient on its own to cause psychiatric disorder. There needs to be an environmental trigger as well.[39] For instance, the best predictor of maternal depression is the relationship the woman had with her own mother in childhood. This is probably due to a lack of emotional support, and a consequent failure to learn how to regulate her negative feelings.[40] Even when there is strong evidence of a genetic component, this may turn out to be an epigenetic response to in utero or childhood experiences.

Reflection

Life is full of potentially traumatic experiences. How we respond to them depends on our emotional, psychological and physical resilience. If we are lucky, we have good genes, had wonderful parents, grew up in a peaceful and harmonious community, and will come through whatever life throws at us relatively unscathed psychologically. But if we are unlucky, we may have inherited a predisposition to some disorder that is triggered into action by poor parenting, difficult social conditions, or bad luck in infancy or childhood. As a result we may be vulnerable to trauma from relatively mild experiences that can tip us into physical ill health, social isolation, and mental disorders.

Currently, scientific and public attention is focused on genetic causes of individual and social ills. Links between particular genes and recognized diseases, disorders and behaviors are being discovered at an unprecedented rate. Yet it is rare for there to be a single genetic cause. Normally, many genes interact to produce an effect, and it is often the expression of a gene rather than a mutation that is important. As the study of epigenetics is demonstrating, genetic predispositions generally come into effect only with an appropriate environmental trigger. In other words, our unformed genetic potential is shaped and developed by our life experiences from before conception until death. But it seems likely that our genetic potential is also being warped towards dominance by evolutionary selection pressures in modern civilization that reward the most competitive and aggressive, if not the most physically violent.

The statistics reveal that violence and mental illness are prevalent in every aspect of life and every area of society. And, like a rising tide, they threaten to overwhelm our civilization. But we tend to turn a blind eye to what is happening, claiming our violence and aggression are normal, and blaming human nature for it. Our genes undoubtedly play a part, but our experiences play at least as big a part, and probably a bigger one. We are not helpless victims of our genetic inheritance, but creators of our own destiny. Trauma is a powerful root cause that we ignore at our peril.

22. The Collective

Collective Trauma and the Pain Body

Collective trauma drives many of the atrocities and tragedies of the world, and is transmitted from generation to generation. World War II grew out of the pain inflicted on Germany after the First World War, and the nation is still coming to terms with its history.[1] Part of that history is the Holocaust, the trauma of which underlies Israeli intransigence and brutality in its dealings with the Palestinians. Past events were used to fan the flames of ethnic cleansing in Bosnia, genocide in Rwanda, and atrocities elsewhere. Around the world, ethnic, racial, sectarian, caste and class conflicts arise from past domination, exploitation and violence. At a smaller scale, strife between families and gangs often have their roots in past events, and perceived wrongs.

Before The Fall, we believe there would have been much less collective trauma because hunter-gatherer societies often released the energy of potentially traumatic events through ceremonies and ritual. In post-Fall civilizations, however, it has been more normal to repress emotional pain, and exploit it in the service of nations and empires. Unless it is healed, this trauma builds up during the individual's lifetime, and is passed on through learning, collective consciousness and epigenetics to following generations. Each generation, therefore, starts with a legacy of pain, to which is added whatever trauma occurs in its lifetime. Some traumas naturally fade with the passing of time, but others linger on, and can accumulate through the generations. While it remains suppressed and unconscious, trauma saps the inner vitality of the culture, and creates a powder keg that may explode in external violence.

A similar view is expressed by spiritual teacher Eckhart Tolle in his description of the 'pain-body':[2]

The remnants of pain left behind by every strong negative emotion that is not fully faced, accepted, and then let go of join together to form an energy field that lives in the very cells of your body. It consists not just of childhood pain, but also painful emotions that were added to it later in adolescence and during your adult life ...

This energy field of old but still very-much-alive emotion that lives in almost every human being is the pain-body.

The pain-body, however, is not just individual in nature. It also partakes of the pain suffered by countless humans throughout the history of humanity ... This pain still lives in the collective psyche of humanity and is being added to on a daily basis ... The collective pain-body is probably encoded within every human's DNA, although we haven't discovered it there yet.

Every newborn who comes into this world already carries an emotional pain-body.

This shared trauma, whether it be a grievance, grief, loss, or a desire for revenge, often forms the nucleus around which a group coalesces. Driven by their common pain, the gang, military unit, crowd, or nation may act in ways that would be unthinkable for most individuals, including arson, looting, raping, torturing, lynching and massacring. Alternatively, the pain and despair may cause collective depression leading to poverty, ill health and cultural breakdown. As Tolle notes, by far the greater part of the violence that humans have inflicted on each other is not the work of criminals or the mentally sick, but of respectable citizens in the service of the collective. Indeed, the collective ego often has a touch of paranoia as reflected in modern American visions of the wars against the evil empire of communism and the Islamic 'axis of evil'.

Indigenous Peoples and Generational Trauma

Perhaps the clearest examples of collective, intergenerational trauma are provided by numerous indigenous peoples around the world. Following European contact, they were decimated by epidemics of new diseases, hunted down by genocidal settlers, expelled from their lands and spiritual homes, taken from their families as children to be put into missions and residential schools, and pressured to assimilate into western culture. These traumas were accentuated by their loss of ceremonial freedom, language, dance, song and other customs that would have helped them to express and heal their pain. The burden was made all the heavier by being stripped of their dignity, leaving them ashamed to be Natives. As a result, indigenous peoples carry a heavy load of pain accumulated over the centuries of European exploration and colonization; pain that is only now beginning to be healed as they reclaim their heritage.

Across North America, 90-95% of the indigenous population died of disease soon after the white man came. On the Island of the Haidas, off the coast of Alaska, a society of 80,000 was reduced to just 500.[3] Yet despite this devastation, and the genocide and oppression that followed, Native American peoples preserved their traditional teachings and ceremonies in the homes, minds and hearts of the survivors. Spirituality is the key to this resilience. Their spirituality is based upon the connections between all things that ripple outwards from the family until they encompass the whole universe; upon circles of relationship that extend through time as well as space, linking past, present and future. The traumatic grief and loss of epidemics and genocide flowed outwards through this network until they affected everything, and the trauma became part of the very land itself.

Many individuals rose above the trauma, and held the spiritual web for posterity. They honored the Creator's sacred instructions to protect their languages, beliefs and ceremonies. Now they are able to revive their fragmented traditions, learning once again how to access the realms of spirit through dreams and visions. This guardianship required great humility and faith, generation after generation. When Europeans came to Australia, they began to kill male Aborigines. In order to save the male lore for future generations, the men humbled themselves, and took the momentous decision to transfer responsibility for its keeping to the women. It was only a few years ago that this responsibility was returned to the men.[4]

In their study of historic Aboriginal trauma in North America, Cynthia Wesley-Esquimaux and Magdalena Smolenski argue that deep rivers of unresolved grief continue to flow beneath the remembering of ceremonies, traditions and beliefs.[5] It is, they claim, as if a dark curtain has fallen over part of their collective memory which prevents the trauma being seen in their dreams and visions. It is a collective amnesia; a collective dissociation. But the trauma is real, and can be felt. They suggest that the peoples may be unable to flourish as whole and healthy societies because of the effects of this hidden trauma which may be embedded in their genes through epigenetic mechanisms. The future of indigenous peoples may depend on accessing this stream of the collective unconscious, and healing it mentally, emotionally, physically and spiritually. Until then, their children will continue to build defense mechanisms to help them survive; defenses that also create unbalanced people who may blame themselves, and act out their legacy of abuse in dysfunctional ways.

A Case Study of Sri Lanka

The erstwhile island paradise of Sri Lanka provides a more recent illustration of the effects of collective trauma. The country was torn by sporadic civil war for over a quarter of a century, with some of the fiercest fighting taking place shortly before the war ended in 2009. Some areas suffered additional trauma when the 2004 tsunami wiped out coastal settlements. Psychiatrist Daya Somasundaram described the severe and deep impacts on society while the war was still raging.[6]

The trouble began as an ethnic conflict between the Tamil minority and the majority Sinhalese. It led to the destruction of the village culture that was the foundation of Tamil life. Many villages ceased to exist—due both to the war and the tsunami. Villagers were dispersed, thus fracturing the sustaining network of relationships, structures and institutions. Even where people returned, the villages were not the same. There were many newcomers, and the social fabric had disintegrated. Within each village, the family home had always been a place of security and peace, like a womb; a place where the ancestors' spirits still dwelt and were honored. But when displaced people returned, they found their relationship with their homes had been broken. Many did not repair them, living in makeshift arrangements, and with an emergency bag packed ready to move.

Traditional relationships were also irrevocably changed. The authority of parents, elders and community leaders was undermined by their submissive response to the military. Elders came to be seen as powerless and incompetent in the face of the war and its consequences. Parents had to watch what they said in front of their children in case they inadvertently made some dangerous remark. Huge gaps were left in the family structure by members missing due to death, injury or displacement, particularly when they had been the breadwinner. Often the fate of the 'disappeared' was unknown, adding grief and uncertainty to dysfunctional family dynamics. The loss of leaders, entrepreneurs, professionals, engineers and skills of all kinds had devastating consequences. Many left to escape the trauma, joining the 'brain drain'. Others stayed, only to be targeted by would-be rulers, often from factions within militant Tamil organizations. Those with leadership qualities were killed, intimidated into leaving, or forced into silence.

Young people were particularly affected. They had spent their whole lives immersed in violence and terror. They had watched the horrifying deaths of loved ones, seen countless mutilated bodies and decaying remains. They had seen their homes and villages destroyed. They had been bombed, shelled and shot at. They had learned to survive, but had lost hope for the future. At first, youths were active in rescues and organizing camps, but later grief and guilt at the loss of family members overwhelmed them. There was nothing for them to do in the camps. Deprived of mature leaders and traditional authorities, adolescents formed their own rival gangs, resorting to violence and crime—the only models of social life they had learned. And many younger children, less able to see through the propaganda and manipulation of recruiters, were induced to become soldiers.

Not surprisingly, Somasundaram found psychological disturbances, particularly depression, were much more common in displaced families than in those still living in their own homes. Separation anxiety, cognitive impairment, conduct disorders and sleep disturbances were frequent in displaced children. Economic stress and lack of privacy in overcrowded camps increased quarrels between parents. War traumas directly affected family relationships. The loss of a limb often brought feelings of inferiority and shame that made family life difficult, and sometimes led to the husband leaving. Survivors of torture were often withdrawn, had difficulty with intimate relationships, were irritable, and not motivated to work or be active. In one area, Somasundaram found 92% of children had been exposed to potentially terrorizing experiences including combat, shelling and witnessing the death of loved ones. The lives of 57% were significantly disrupted by these experiences, and 25% were suffering from PTSD. A larger survey of school children found 47% of those exposed directly to the tsunami as well as war had PTSD, compared to only 15% of those exposed to war alone.

Somasundaram observed more general psychological effects as well. Many reactions to trauma came to be accepted as normal, including tension, extreme vigilance, irritability, being easily startled, poor sleep and nightmares. People suffered from ennui, impairment of mental functions, a preoccupation with death, and a narrowing of outlook and worldview. Their thinking became petty, mundane, rigid, focused on daily survival and self-interest, with a lack of concern or planning for the future. They lost trust in relationships, fearing that they would be betrayed, and that others would not fulfill their responsibilities and undertakings. And they lost trust in social structures and institutions, justice, law, values, cultural beliefs—even in themselves and their families. Many became so resigned and lacking in motivation that they refused resettlement, preferring the security of the camps.

Violence, terror and counter-terror became structural, institutionalized elements of the system, entrenched in law and pervading all relationships and activities. Initial resistance to discrimination and inequity led to emergency and anti-terror legislation, militarization of society, and the targeting of Tamils, especially youth. There were mass arrests, detention, disappearances and killings, with counter-violence by Tamil militants. Those responsible for atrocities have never been punished. Torture became a routine tool to break individuals and coerce communities into submission. Those who survived were broken before release; and the maimed bodies of those who died were put on display as a warning to others. A "fluid and shifting terror was there just below the surface, subtle and covert" and a major cause of collective trauma. By contrast, the tsunami was a one-off natural disaster that left a trail of destruction and loss but was relatively short-lived, and did not cause such severe trauma.

Some catastrophic events transformed the lives of individuals, families, communities and societies in fundamental ways. Immortalized in stories, folklore, songs, poems and drama, they will continue to impact on future generations. One such incident in 1996 was a mass exodus in which more than 400,000 people abandoned their beloved homes and villages to trek through a night of rain and shells. In terror, with few possessions, they moved slowly along the crowded roads, the elderly and less able falling by the wayside. They arrived at their destination only to find makeshift accommodation with poor facilities or none. They not only lost their homes and communities, but also their identities, pride, dignity and hope.

The war ended as we were writing in May 2009. The last remnants of the Tamil Tigers were ruthlessly crushed by government forces. Thousands of civilians were killed and hundreds of thousands displaced amid international condemnation. It remains to be seen if Sri Lanka can move forward to peace and reconciliation in the aftermath of such trauma, but the prospects are not good. In early January 2009, shortly before he was assassinated, Lasantha Wikramatunga wrote the following words in an editorial in The Sunday Leader:[7]

> ... a military occupation of the country's north and east will require the Tamil people of those regions to live eternally as second-class citizens, deprived of all self respect. Do not imagine that you can placate them by showering "development" and "reconstruction" on them in the post-war era. The wounds of war will scar them forever, and you will also have an even more bitter and hateful Diaspora to contend with. A problem amenable to a political solution will thus become a festering wound that will yield strife for all eternity.

Collective Trauma as a Weapon and a Tool

Today, there is a tendency to use collective trauma as a deliberate weapon to subdue a society by breaking their social bonds, values and norms. The mass public raping of Bosnian women and girls, for example, has been described as a "psychological grenade" intended to destroy a culture in which virginity and fidelity were central. At the same time, the traditional role of parents as protectors was shattered when they were forced to witness brutal sexual assaults on their daughters.[8] Part of this process was exploitation of the ancient trauma of the battle of

Kosovo as propaganda to unite the people against a modern 'enemy', and to justify atrocities against Muslims today. The charity Save the Children Fund graphically described how modern warfare targets civilians in this way:[9]

> *Civilians are no longer 'incidental' casualties but the direct targets of violence. Mass terror becomes a deliberate strategy. Destruction of schools, houses, religious buildings, fields and crops as well as torture, rape and internment, become commonplace. Modern warfare is concerned not only to destroy life, but also ways of life. It targets social and cultural institutions and deliberately aims to undermine the means whereby people endure and recover from the suffering of war. ... A key element of modern political violence is the creation of states of terror to penetrate the entire fabric of economic, sociocultural and political relations as a means of social control.*

Arlene Audergon argues that the nightmares of history do not erupt spontaneously.[10] The flames of revenge are fanned for political ends. The appeal of revenge lies in the vain hope of a collective purging of trauma that will bring an end to pain by hurting others, by making them pay, by letting them know how it feels. Sadly, revenge does little but store up more injustice and trauma to inflame future conflicts. In order to heal, we need to break through the emotional repression and numbness, and reconnect with our traumatic history. But we need to do it not out of revenge, but as an act of love towards the dead, and of reconciliation with the innocent descendants of our enemies.

More positively, Mary de Young notes that collective trauma can bring people together in a way that regenerates culture. Traditional western death rituals lose their value and meaning in the face of overwhelming events such as the 9/11 attack on the World Trade Center, the death of Princess Diana, and similar public tragedies. In response, people have spontaneously created memorials with symbolic mementos left at the site—flowers, toys, signs, letters, poems. These represent "efforts to create a new, meaningful and public ritual that acknowledges the grief and fear of the larger community, lifts constraints on the duration of mourning and the expression of emotion, and offers the role of mourner to anyone who participates."[11]

The importance of rituals is highlighted by the experience of African- and Asian-American veterans of the Vietnam war who suffered more from PTSD than white Americans. A major reason for this may have been racial prejudice that denied them full participation in public ceremonies.[12] Similarly damaging can be the impatient desire of the majority to move on before the minority has healed its trauma, and without integrating their story into the larger cultural narrative. In extreme cases, the dominant group may even cut the events from its version of history, or at least sanitize them, as has happened to indigenous peoples in the USA, Australia and elsewhere.[13] Often, the survivors feel a duty to bear witness so that the trauma will never happen again. But society seldom wants to hear the truth, and they end up telling socially acceptable myths that turn the horror of mud and blood into a heroic tale of courage and nobility.[14]

Reflection

Our focus has been on the victims of collective trauma, but we should not forget that the perpetrators are also affected, and need healing too. They are often left with a collective sense of guilt and shame that echoes down the generations. This is apparent in Australia and other countries with a colonial past as they apologize for their treatment of indigenous peoples, and seek reconciliation. It is also evident in Germany, where many are still coming to terms with their history.

Both perpetrators and victims are often left with a sense of betrayal. Betrayal by governments, the military, police, and other authorities. And betrayal by friends and neighbors, family and community who failed to support them, or turned against them.

But in today's global society we are all guilty of betrayal. Too often, we turn away when victims call to the world for help. Too often, we watch the TV news and go on with our lives, banishing events from our personal and collective awareness and concern. Too often, we seek safety and freedom from emotional pain by allowing ourselves to be silenced by authority, and the demonizing of others by the media. But by our silence we contribute to the trauma.[15]

In the affluent, western world, we are fortunate to have suffered no major collective trauma in the last half-century. But many of the world's peoples are not so lucky. Their cultures, societies, communities and families have been, or are being, shattered, and will have to be rebuilt from the ground up in the decades and centuries to come. It is impossible to foresee all the consequences of these traumas in the years ahead, but we can be sure they will be massive. It is vital that we reduce and heal the incidence of collective as well as individual trauma in the interests of creating a peaceful, sustainable future.

Closure to Part V

This Part of the book has been heavy going for us as researchers and writers, and no doubt for you, our readers. It contains a mass of complex information which is hard to absorb and integrate. And it dives deep into dark corners of the human psyche and culture. It reveals how trauma is a major fact of human existence in all cultures, and at all ages from before conception until death. It demonstrates the huge impact which this trauma has on the lives of individuals, families, communities and nations. So great is its effect that we believe trauma is the root cause of the multiple crises facing our civilization. Even if this turns out to be an exaggeration, it is clear that humanity and Earth would benefit greatly from a reduction in human trauma.

We deliberately presented this overview of current knowledge in a factual way, with few dramatic personal stories or case studies. One reason for this was brevity. Another was that we felt a cool appraisal was more appropriate to our aims than an emotional outpouring. But in our research, we have been exposed to many harrowing stories in the media and books—both fiction and non-fiction. At times, we have become traumatized ourselves, suffering sickness, exhaustion, and despair. At times we have been tempted to give up. We have had to acknowledge and discharge our rage at the stupidity, insensitivity, greed and cruelty of our species, our civilization, our society, and individuals, including ourselves. We have had to process and release our grief at what we collectively have done, and are doing, to each other, all life, and our living planet. We have had to face our fears for the future, and the future of our children and grandchildren. But running like a healing stream through the horrors is another strand. A strand of courage, creativity, imagination, compassion, love, selflessness and beauty. A strand of vision and hope.

The children whose lives contain a thread of hope are the ones who survive whatever life throws at them. This also applies to us as mature individuals, and as a culture. In the last Part of this book we explore what each of us can do, individually and collectively, to minimize the creation of fresh trauma, and to heal old wounds. In that way we can create hope for humanity.

Part VI. Healing into Partnership

There is nothing more personal than traumatic experience that shakes you to the bone, tears apart your identity, our community, spirit and meaning of life. Traumatic experience frays and fragments the psyche of an individual, the spirit of whole communities, nations and the meaning of history. The ghosts of history want not only accountability and to be included into history, but also to be relieved, to take their place beyond space and time. Time and again, those among us who have seen the very worst of humankind, seem to touch some place in their own hearts, beyond all polarization, beyond even life and death, and from here inspire us to keep believing in humanity.
Psychologist Arlene Audergon[1]

Lasting peace among warring peoples cannot be accomplished without first healing the traumas of previous terrorism, violence and horror on a mass scale.
Trauma Therapist Peter Levine[2]

In order to create a partnership future for humanity, we must break out of the self-perpetuating dominator culture which began at The Fall. This does not mean turning the clock back to a mythical Golden Age, but moving forward into a new era of sustainability, peace and justice. Earlier parts of the book have revealed a clear message from prehistory, biology, indigenous peoples and spiritual teachers: such a future is possible. We are not doomed by evolution or our genes to perpetuate the tragedy of the last six millennia. What is not so clear is how to redirect the tide of history towards partnership.

At its simplest, the human predicament can be represented as a self-reinforcing cycle of trauma and domination. Trauma produces both fearful, submissive people who are readily

269

dominated, and dominators who are aggressive and hungry for power, wealth and status. The power hierarchy closes the loop by traumatizing those who are subject to it. The first and second waves of reaction to The Fall, which we described in Chapter 15, were unplanned and unconscious. They tried to weaken domination by countering the ego and pressing for humane social reforms. But the fundamental structure of power remains intact. It defends itself by:

- Adapting to changes that do not threaten its core values;
- Crushing opposition by legal and financial means if not by physical violence;
- Subverting, manipulating, distracting and co-opting reform movements; and
- Using trauma to feed the system with both dominators and subservient individuals.

The result is entrenched patterns of beliefs, values, ideologies, emotions and behaviors that obstruct the paths to a partnership society, and block access to the wisdom and inner harmony of higher states of consciousness. We will remain trapped in this dominator way of being until we find a way to start a self-sustaining positive spiral of lessening trauma and increasingly egalitarian, peaceful social systems. In order to survive, these systems must be resilient, and difficult to crush, control, manipulate or subvert. This is a tall order, to which we do not have complete answers. However, some elements of a strategy are presented in the following chapters. In summary, these are to:

- Reduce the number and intensity of potentially traumatic events;
- Increase the resilience of individuals and communities;
- Heal traumatized individuals, families, communities and societies;

- Develop non-hierarchical, decentralized, self-sustaining communities; and
- Limit or resolve the arms races due to mutual fear of other nations, races, and ethnic groups.

This strategy may appear to divert attention away from the urgent needs of peace-making, peace-keeping, curbing climate change, reducing poverty and injustice, conserving natural resources, cutting our addiction to oil, healing mental illness, and more. Humanity and the Earth call out to each one of us to play our part in tackling these issues with all our gifts, knowledge, energy and experience. But trauma will continue to undermine and taint our efforts unless we combine our work for peace, justice and sustainability with personal and collective healing. This inner work will bring us the courage, strength, confidence, humility, wisdom, empathy and compassion needed to transform ourselves and our families, communities, nations, civilization, and the human species.

Can we change our world to create fewer traumatic memories to carry into the next generations—fewer traumatic events to shape our children who will create our future social structures?

How can we heal the scars of individual and group trauma that haunt us today? Can we ever make racism, misogyny, maltreatment of children—distant memories? There are solutions. These conditions are not the inevitable legacy of our past. When an individual becomes self-aware, there is the potential for insight. With insight comes the potential for altered behavior. With altered behavior comes the potential to diminish the transgenerational passage of dysfunctional or destructive ideas and practices.

And so it must be for groups. As a society, we cannot develop true insight without self-awareness. ... The challenge for our generation is to understand the dynamics and realities of our human living groups in a way that can result in group insight—which, inevitably, will lead to the understanding that we must change our institutionalized ignorance and maltreatment of children.

Bruce Perry, The ChildTrauma Academy[3]

23. Reducing Potentially Traumatic Events

The Importance of Second Wave Reforms

Potentially traumatic events are a part of life and cannot be eliminated. There will always be natural disasters, accidents, sickness, bereavement, and the break-up of relationships. But we can do a lot to reduce their number and severity, and to increase the resilience of individuals and communities so that fewer people become traumatized. This is vitally important as there are far too many people in need of help to be able to provide therapy for them all. However, it is also important not to go too far, and remove the challenges of life that enable us to grow and mature. Our psyches and nervous systems need to succeed in meeting challenges in order to stay healthy. Today, those of us in rich nations seldom face physical threats, but danger still exhilarates and energizes us. Without it, we lose vitality, and fail to engage fully with life.[1]

Efforts to reduce potentially traumatic events are typical second wave activities arising from compassionate concern for human rights and well-being. Over the last two centuries, they have made major inroads on many sources of trauma, and continue to do so today as shown in Table 18. (A more specific agenda for political reform at the national level is outlined in Chapter 29, and Table 23.) A mass of information on these issues is available in books, films and the internet, and there is a huge number of organizations worldwide dedicated to such tasks. These reforms are vitally important, and it is essential that as many people as possible become engaged in such campaigns. It is also vital that the campaigners work simultaneously on healing their own traumas, thus increasing their effectiveness by weakening inappropriate emotional and behavioral patterns, and enhancing their positive qualities.

Table 18: Some Areas of Action that Reduce Potentially Traumatic Events

Early warning and rescue systems for natural disasters	Grassroots economic development
	Shelter and housing
Safer transport technologies	Education
Increased food production	Democracy and suffrage
Famine relief	Campaigns against racial, ethnic,
Anti-slavery campaigns	religious and sexual discrimination
Campaigns to end child labor	Peace-making
Regulation of working hours and conditions	Revision of the rules of warfare
	Campaigns against torture
Social security provisions	Elimination of political detention
Improved human rights	Prison reform
Women's rights	Abolishment of capital punishment
Birth control information and methods	Environmental protection
	Action on climate change

Trauma and the Rights of the Child

It is clear from Chapters 17-20 that we cannot reduce trauma in the population at large unless we protect our young from traumatic experiences. Trauma, particularly during early development, can result in lifelong emotional, intellectual and physical impairment. Compensating adjustments are sometimes possible later in childhood, but established patterns become progressively more difficult to change, and may become fixed in adulthood. At best, adult therapy is a slow process.[2] Together with the high incidence of childhood trauma, this means, as Bruce Perry put it, that "Our society is creating violent children and youth at a rate far faster than we could ever treat, rehabilitate, or even lock them away."[3] It is also clear that not enough is being done to prevent child trauma, and that it must be given high priority in any strategy to reduce trauma in general.[4]

Not surprisingly, there is widespread agreement that

prevention is better than cure. Besides reducing the number and severity of potentially traumatic events, prevention may include healing incipient trauma before it becomes trapped, and increasing the child's resilience (the subject of the next chapter). Preventing early trauma has long-term cumulative effects, since children with sensitive, nurturing caregivers learn how to be good parents, and are less likely to maltreat their own offspring. They also are more likely to have successful intimate relationships, thus reducing the risk of exposing their children to scenes of domestic violence, and coincidentally reducing adult trauma.

Most policies aim to prevent maltreatment by adults close to the child. However, as Richard Reading and his co-authors point out, this omits collective harm caused by communities, social institutions, laws, policies, traditional practices, social disruption and war.[5] They argue for a more inclusive goal based on the UN Convention on the Rights of the Child (UNCRC). This provides not only for protection from harm, but also for provision of basic needs, and participation by the child in actions and decisions that affect it, as summarized in Table 19. Reading et al interpret these principles as including emotional harm, even though it is not specifically listed.

The broad scope of these principles is necessary given the diversity and prevalence of child trauma today, but it presents a number of practical difficulties. It is almost impossible to monitor infringements of such a wide range of rights in order to identify victims or children at risk. Similarly, it is hard to imagine how any child-welfare service could intervene and enforce standards across such a spectrum, particularly in relation to issues such as war. Not surprisingly, therefore, there is resistance to further widening of the definition of maltreatment.[6]

Another difficulty is posed by cultural differences. The African charter on the rights and welfare of the child, for example, states that "children have a responsibility to work for the cohesion of the family, to respect parents and elders at all

Table 19: Key Principles of the UN Convention on the Rights of the Child

(Source: Reading et al 2009)

The Right to Protection from:

Physical, sexual or mental abuse, neglect or exploitation

Discrimination for any reason, including disability

Exposure to drugs

Abduction and transfer abroad

Economic exploitation, or harmful work

Torture or inhuman punishment

Armed conflict, including recruitment to armed forces before 15 years of age

Traditional practices prejudicial to the health of children

The Right of Participation:

In decisions and actions that affect them

To express their views freely

To have their views heard and given due weight

To have access to information and ideas of all kinds

To freedom of association

To the freedom to practice a minority culture

The Right to Provision of:

Education

Health care

Social security

Leisure and cultural activities, including play

Family care, with the child's parents or an alternative if deprived of parents

A standard of living adequate for the child's physical, mental, spiritual, moral, and social development

General Rights:

To life, survival and development

To preserve his or her identity

To freedom of thought, conscience and religion

To privacy

The right to help to recover from any neglect, exploitation, abuse, or violence

times, and to assist them in case of need."[7] The last clause allows the child of a subsistence farming family to mind the chickens, or an urban slum child to help her family scavenge from rubbish dumps. But both these activities might be regarded as exploitation in an affluent western society. Corporal punishment is similarly controversial. In many cultures it is still the norm, and it is hard to draw a clear line between what is legitimate discipline, and what is physical abuse. Even more difficult is the question of female genital mutilation. There is no doubt in western minds that it represents severe abuse, but it is still a cultural tradition in many countries. By acknowledging the right of these peoples to retain their cultures, we run the risk of failing to protect children from serious harm. Conversely, ignoring the social context of child-rearing may lead to inappropriate actions which could worsen the child's relationship with its family and community.

Closely linked to cultural differences is the issue of poverty. This is often associated with maltreatment, and relatively high rates of mortality, teenage pregnancy, criminal activity, drug and alcohol abuse, and sexually transmitted diseases. The UNCRC places a responsibility on states to provide an adequate standard of living for children, but some countries are more economically able to do this than others. Clearly, a poor African nation cannot be expected to provide child welfare support at a level appropriate in a rich country. And even rich countries such as the UK are often criticized by the UNCRC for unequal provision. The other side of this coin is that maltreatment causes huge costs for society which effective intervention can reduce substantially in the long term.

Yet another challenge faced by democratic countries is to balance protection of the child against the invasion of family privacy. The provision of family support services and financial benefits to low-income families can go a long way to ensuring that parents have adequate resources. But further intervention is sometimes needed to prevent maltreatment, including moving the child to a foster home. What rights should parents have in this situation? And how can the child's right to have a say in its own future best be recognized?

Family Support Services in Theory

A serious weakness of the UNCRC as a tool for preventing child trauma is that it defines life as starting at birth. But trauma can occur during gestation, and even before conception. There is also a tendency to transform the broad UNCRC principles into standards, accompanied by monitoring and intervention programs. In general, social science research shows that positive support for good behaviors is more effective than punishment for poor performance. This means that effective prevention of child trauma requires an integrated program of education, training and support for both parents and children that starts before conception and continues until the child is through adolescence. Intervention by medical or government authorities should be a last resort. Unfortunately, there is little reliable information on how to design such a system, and the large number of social, economic and cultural variables makes it difficult to know whether or not an effective program can be transferred successfully to another context.[8]

A first step in trauma prevention is to reduce the number of unwanted babies, and the number of immature girls who have them. It is also important to help adolescents and young adults form stable, loving relationships so that children are welcomed into a nurturing environment. These goals can be pursued through school education, training and support services provided in the family home or community, and personal counseling. Ideally, such programs should include:

- Opportunities for personal development, counseling and trauma therapy;
- Education and training in:
  - Healthy intimate relationships;

- Contraception;
- The needs of the fetus and infant;
- The responsibilities of parenthood;
- Good parenting practices; and
- Ready availability of contraceptives.

Once a woman becomes pregnant, income support, social services and training classes should be available to help ensure that the needs of the fetus are met as far as possible, and that the mother is well prepared for the birth. Birth is often one of the most traumatic experiences of the baby's lifetime, and the newborn is very vulnerable. Birthing practices vary widely, and it is important that they be chosen to minimize infant trauma. This can be difficult to do as many well-established practices are now widely regarded as harmful, as described in Chapter 17.

After the birth, continued support is needed until at least the end of infancy at around 2-3 years. Often, such services are made available only to families that are assessed as being at-risk due to poverty, low socio-economic status and other factors. However, universal availability would help to protect all children from emotional neglect and sub-clinical effects as well as active abuse. Income support is also highly desirable as necessary to enable one parent to become a full-time caregiver, or single parents to pay for high-quality day-care.

Various types of program have been tried, but the most successful are regular home visits. Experience suggests that, during infancy, visits should last 1-1.5 hours and be made at least monthly by a university-trained professional nurse or social worker. Paraprofessionals have not proved as effective in this role.[9] Support should cover a broad range of issues including the health of the mother and child, the needs of the fetus or infant, the mother's emotional well-being, her relationship with her partner (if she has one), her support network of family and friends, how she would like to parent her child, the family's economic situation, future plans, or any other problems. The visitor also might facilitate the formation of community mutual-support groups, and refer the family to financial, housing and other services as necessary.

It is imperative that the support-person not be seen as an authority figure who issues orders and can punish failure by taking the child away as this creates hostility and resistance to suggestions. Rather, the aim should be for the visitor to develop a long-term relationship with the mother and other family members as a trusted mentor who helps them become good parents. However, forming such a relationship can be difficult, particularly in cases of substance abuse. After infancy, the intensity of support required declines, but regular follow-up visits are highly desirable until the child reaches maturity at 18. These can be used to reassess the family's needs, and refer them for further support as necessary.

Family Support Services in Practice

Richard Rhodes noted that children who survived severe abuse without becoming 'violentized' often were not rescued and removed from their families, but were supported, valued, and shown alternatives to violence. Teachers were often their lifelines.[10] Similarly, Bruce Perry argued that we need to transform our culture to make childrearing the responsibility of the whole community rather than just the overburdened nuclear family. As he put it: "Children belong to the community; they are entrusted to parents."[11]

Unfortunately, however, many home-visiting programs have failed to show significant benefits in practice. Some may have succeeded because they were research projects rather than service programs, used tertiary-trained staff, and invested heavily in ensuring the program was delivered faithfully. One of these success stories was for poor and single mothers in New York State. This dramatically reduced the number of verified cases of maltreatment, and visits to hospital emergency departments. A similar program in New Zealand was also effective.[12] A follow-up study in New York when the children were 15 years old found that those who had been in the program were doing far better than those of unassisted mothers. They had half the number of arrests and one-fifth the number of convictions for criminal offences. They smoked and drank less, and had fewer sexual partners.[13]

Many other approaches have been tried for preventing maltreatment, and minimizing the impairment caused. According to Prof. Harriet MacMillan and her colleagues, very few of them have been properly evaluated, and even fewer have been shown to be effective.[14] One of these is the Positive Parenting Program, or Triple P as it is known.[15] This aims to create stable, supportive families that have positive relationships between parents and children, and are able to resolve conflicts and deal with problem behaviors. It does this by improving parental understanding of how the family works using simple routines and small changes in thoughts, feelings and behaviors. Parent Child Interaction Therapy (PCIT) has been found to reduce repetition of physical abuse. It aims to improve the attachment relationship, and train parents how to use commands and behavioral discipline rather than violence. Similarly, Cognitive Behavioral Therapy (CBT) is effective both for preventing repeated abuse and healing the child. However, few other psychotherapeutic approaches were considered in the studies reviewed by MacMillan and her colleagues.

The overall impression from the literature is that prevention of maltreatment is not working well because those on the front line often become social police rather than friends and mentors, and because the approach is fragmented, focusing on parts of the whole problem. It seems likely that programs would be more cost-effective if services were integrated, and networked with volunteers, churches and charitable organizations in the local community. Increased investment in community development and local networks of mutual support might pay big dividends. It could improve the relationships between service providers and families, and make it easier to ensure that they receive assistance tailored to their needs.

Partnership Parenting

The long-term aim is to ensure that all children experience good parenting. Research indicates clearly that certain childrearing methods consistently tend to produce partnership characteristics such as non-violence, peacefulness, tolerance, caring, sharing, cooperation, gender equality and independence of mind.[16] Unfortunately, growing up in most parts of the modern world is largely a matter of learning dominator roles. Despite the efforts of the feminist movement, there is still strong gender differentiation from an early age. Many boys are taught to be little men: strong, tough, dominant, action-oriented, insensitive, aggressive and violent. They get to play with guns, machines and war games. Many girls, on the other hand, are dressed like mini fashion models, and are expected to play at traditional female roles. They rapidly learn that women are submissive, passive, weak, soft, nurturing, and empathic. Comparisons between cultures and research on childrearing show that these are learned behaviors, not innate gender differences. This is also apparent from the fact that gender roles are changing. More men today are taking on nurturing, childrearing and home-making roles, and choosing 'women's' careers such as nursing. Meanwhile, women are more often becoming truck drivers, construction workers, engineers, corporate managers and politicians.

The key to successful partnership parenting is loving and informed care that is attuned to the child's needs from conception, through gestation, and infancy. Beyond infancy, love remains the key, but how it is expressed must change as the child develops. Important needs are:

- Freedom to choose her own interests rather than those of her parents;
- Freedom to achieve her goals within emotionally and physically safe boundaries;
- Discipline based on reason, explanation and distraction rather than punishment;
- Early assignment of responsibility;
- Toys, games and entertainments that encourage peaceful cooperation; and
- Modeling of partnership behaviors by adults, particularly parents.

Aggression is linked to frustration. Hence, it is important that children are given the autonomy and resources to achieve their legitimate, acceptable personal goals. However, they also must learn to inhibit aggressive feelings, consider the needs of others, and avoid danger. Partnership parents provide freedom within clear boundaries by being firm and directive as well as warm and responsive. They treat their children as individuals whose feelings, preferences and questions matter. They explain the reasons for limits, encourage empathy, and divert attention away from inappropriate desires rather than simply imposing rules. Partnership parents try to balance their needs and rights with those of their children by providing firm control when necessary without hemming the child in. Paradoxically, a failure to set limits may appear to the child as indifference or lack of love, leading to insecure attachment.

Limits to freedom must be enforced when the child's desires are dangerous or inappropriate. But the belief that children must be punished to drive out innate badness, or original sin, is counter-productive. Harsh discipline may get conformity in the short term, but it demonstrates that might is right, and teaches the roles of domination and submission. Children learn that being good means obedience rather than following their inner beliefs and values. By contrast, peaceful societies and partnership parents believe in the inherent goodness of children, and aim to draw the best out of them. They rarely use physical punishment, preferring to tolerate, laugh at, or divert unwanted behavior. They praise and encourage good behavior, and allow a certain amount of verbal give and take. They reason with the child, and help him to develop empathy by explaining the effects of hurtful actions. However, success depends on living the values espoused. Parents who embody the dictum 'do as I say, not as I do' are a source of confusion and stress.

In order to become integral parts of their family and community, children need to be given real responsibilities from an early age. This happens naturally in traditional societies where they are part of the family economy, looking after the hens, or cleaning the floor. When coupled with praise and encouragement, these tasks increase self-confidence and independence, as well as fostering cooperation and sharing. Such roles have disappeared from western society, but many people have argued the need for reintegration of children into family and community life, including the workplace. Children's contributions should not be pretend work, but include tasks that are genuinely important, and that require judgment, decision and risk. Adults must trust the child, refraining from following up, and being willing to accept occasional failures without punishment.

Toy weapons and war games encourage violent play. They teach children that these are normal parts of life, and that violence is an acceptable way to resolve conflicts. Less well-known is the fact that competitive sports also have negative effects. Contrary to popular beliefs, participating in, or watching, competitive sports does not discharge aggressive energy. Research shows, for example, that people care and share less after watching a football match than after watching gymnastics. If we want children to grow up peaceful, cooperative and caring, we need to encourage activities that pit the child against herself or her environment rather than others, and that require cooperation rather than individualism or competition. However, the media and peer pressure often make it difficult for parents and schools to encourage appropriate toys and equipment. In order to be attractive, toys and games must be exciting and challenging, require physical action, involve some risk, and facilitate imitation of adult activities.

Classroom studies have shown that cooperation rather than competition amongst students improves learning and achievement, particularly where student teams have responsibility for working out how best to carry out the assigned task. The social skills learned through interaction also enhance self-esteem, and encourage trust, sensitivity, communication, caring and sharing. Similarly, course materials such as reading practice can be chosen to reinforce partnership values and behaviors.

Adopting a partnership mode of parenting is more challenging than these brief guidelines imply. We all have conditioned patterns, and consciously or unconsciously we tend to repeat our childhood experiences in our relationships with our children. We also do not want to be seen as different or strange by family, friends and neighbors. But it is important that we do our best. As Buddhist psychology puts it, the mental seeds we water are the ones that grow. If we water aggression and violence, greed and competition, these are the characteristics our children will develop. Conversely, if we water the seeds of love, peace and cooperation, they will flourish.

Reflection

It is a truism that our children are our future. If we are to overcome the multiple challenges facing humanity, we must give top priority to loving the children of the world, reducing their load of trauma, and raising them in a partnership way of being. Responsibility for change rests primarily upon parents, extended families and communities. But government involvement is needed as well. This can take the traditional form of monitoring and enforcement of minimum standards of care. Or it can focus on encouraging good parenting through education, training, income support and professional services that are integrated with community organizations. The first approach is authoritarian, and hierarchical. It grows out of, and models, the dominator system we are seeking to replace. By contrast, the second is a model of the partnership society we wish to build, based on the principles of cooperation and sharing.

24. Developing Resilience

Efforts to reduce potentially traumatic events need to be complemented by action to increase resilience, or the ability to bounce back rather than succumb to trauma. There are some people who emerge without obvious emotional or psychological impairment from the most extreme traumatic events. This was true of some survivors of the Holocaust. Today, it is true of some of the refugees who resettle in western countries, and become good community members with stable family relationships. And it is true of a significant fraction of the children who suffer maltreatment. An outstanding example of resilience was Sri Lankan journalist Lasantha Wikramatunga who was undaunted by violence and death threats before he was murdered. The following quotation is from his last editorial for *The Sunday Leader* newspaper in January 2009.[1]

> *It is well known that I was on two occasions brutally assaulted, while on another my house was sprayed with machine-gun fire. Despite the government's sanctimonious assurances, there was never a serious police inquiry into the perpetrators of these attacks, and the attackers were never apprehended. In all these cases, I have reason to believe the attacks were inspired by the government. When finally I am killed, it will be the government that kills me. ...*
>
> *I have done nothing to prevent this outcome: no security, no precautions. I want my murderer to know that I am not a coward like he is, hiding behind human shields while condemning thousands of innocents to death. What am I among so many? It has long been written that my life would be taken, and by whom. All that remains to be written is when.*

In this chapter, we explore what makes people resilient and how to develop this quality.

Factors that Increase Resilience

Trauma Therapist Babette Rothschild observes that "Well-cared-for babies become adults with resilience who are able to swing with the punches dished out by life. … On the other hand, babies raised by caregivers unable to meet significant portions of their needs are at risk of growing into adults who lack resilience and have trouble adapting to life's ebbs and flows."[2] More specific factors associated with resilience have been identified in a number of studies. One project in Hawaii has followed 698 children since their birth in 1955. Emmy Werner analyzed the results for the first 32 years, together with data from other long-term projects.[3]

Almost a third of the Hawaiian children were assessed as being at risk due to chronic poverty, birth difficulties, low parental education, family discord, desertion, divorce, alcoholism and/or mental illness. Some of these children experienced four or more risk factors before they were two years old. Of this sub-group, two-thirds either developed serious learning or behavioral problems by the time they were 10, or were delinquent, had mental health problems or were pregnant by 18. However, the remaining one-third proved to be resilient, and became competent, confident and caring adults. Werner set out to discover why they were different.

A key factor turned out to be the child's personality. Infants who become resilient are active, affectionate, cuddly, good-natured, and easy to manage. As a result, adults find them attractive, and respond with nurture. By the time they go to preschool, these children combine autonomy with the ability to ask for help when they need it. They typically have a special interest or hobby which they share with a friend, and which is a source of pride. By adolescence, they are outgoing, independent, caring and sensitive. Family religious beliefs also may provide stability and meaning during hardship and adversity. Louise Harms identified a more extensive list of personal characteristics that protect against trauma, particularly in adulthood, as shown in Table 20.[4]

Table 20: Personal Characteristics that Protect against Trauma
(Adapted from Harms 2005)

Easy temperament	Low tolerance for outrageous
High IQ	behavior
Interpersonal awareness and	Open-mindedness
empathy	Courage
Superior coping style	Personal discipline
Strong sense of autonomy and self-	Creativity
esteem	Integrity
A willingness to plan	A constructive philosophy of life
A sense of humor	that gives meaning
Insight into oneself and others	A willingness to dream dreams
Ability to learn from experience	that inspire hope
High tolerance for distress	

Despite their troubled family situation, the personalities of resilient children means that they usually form a close bond with at least one person who is caring, competent, emotionally-stable, and attuned to their needs. This relationship gives them a good role model, and a sense of trust in the world. Often these surrogate parents are family members of the same gender such as a grandfather or grandmother, or an older brother or sister. Later, these children may be called on to provide the same care for a younger sibling, or a sick or disabled family member. Resilient children also rely on people outside their families for emotional support, advice and comfort in times of crisis. These may include neighbors, older mentors, youth workers and peers. Particularly important in many cases are teachers who listen, challenge and champion them.

Resilient children are not necessarily gifted, but those with higher IQ are better at assessing stressful situations and working out coping strategies, either through their own efforts or by asking for help. Also important is self-confidence, and a belief in their own competence. After a troubled adolescence, many resilient children get a second chance in their 20's and 30's. They may enroll in adult education, volunteer for military service, participate in church activities, or find a supportive friend or spouse. Broadly similar, but more detailed, conclusions were drawn by Bruce Perry. He divided factors which influence the development of PTSD in children into three categories: the characteristics of the child, the nature of the event, and the family and social context, as shown in Table 21.[5]

The Importance of Hope and Meaning

Many of the factors that increase resilience can be subsumed under the headings of meaning and hope. From his own and others' sufferings in a Nazi death camp, Viktor Frankl concluded that life has meaning even in the most absurd, painful and dehumanized situations. He discovered this meaning in every moment of living, even in suffering and death, and he believed the key to survival of the inner self, or soul, is faith in the future. Once that was lost, prisoners were doomed.[6]

Bruce Perry similarly emphasized the importance of hope for maltreated children:[7]

We are trying to understand how it is that one child can be beaten and humiliated and end up being a caring and productive (but depressed) person and how another with apparently similar childhood trauma can end up being a remorseless predator. ...

While we don't understand completely, it is becoming increasingly clear that the children who can carry the abuse without becoming violent and predatory have had some element of "hope" in their lives. Hope is the internal representation of a better world — "hope" that somewhere, sometime, things will be better.

Table 21: Factors that Increase or Decrease the Risk of Developing PTSD

(Adapted from Perry 2000)

The Child	The Event	The Context
Increased risk		
Being female	Multiple or repeated	Distant caregiving
Low IQ	Long duration	Absent caregivers
Perception of physical harm	Physical injury to child	Trauma directly affects caregivers
History of previous trauma	Physical injury or death to loved one, particularly mother	Continuing threat and disruption to family
No cultural or religious anchors	Seeing disfigured or dismembered bodies	Primary caregivers anxious
Isolation; no shared experience with peers	Destroys home, school or community	Physical isolation
Age (Young children are more vulnerable)	Disrupts community infrastructure, e.g. earthquake	Chaotic, overwhelmed family
Pre-existing mental illness	Perpetrator is family member	
Decreased risk		
Able to understand abstract concepts	Single event	Intact, nurturing family support
Good coping skills	Short duration	Non-traumatized caregivers
Knows about post-traumatic responses	No disruption of family or community structure	Caregivers know about post-traumatic responses
Immediate post-traumatic intervention	Perpetrator is stranger	Mature, attuned parenting
Strong cultural or religious beliefs		Strong family beliefs

Likewise, Daniel Goleman identified hope and optimism as key attributes of emotional intelligence:[8]

> *Hope ... does more than offer a bit of solace amid affliction; it plays a surprisingly potent role in life ... Hope ... is more than the sunny view that everything will turn out all right. ... (It is) believing you have both the will and the way to accomplish your goals, whatever they may be. ...*
>
> *Optimism, like hope, means having a strong expectation that, in general, things will turn out all right in life, despite setbacks and frustrations. ... optimism is an attitude that buffers people against falling into apathy, hopelessness, or depression in the face of tough going.*

Hope entails the possibility of an alternative path, and a better future beyond the traumatic situation. It brings the possibility of choice and change. Hope implies that we have some power over the situation; that we can change our attitude to it, even if we cannot improve our circumstances. Viktor Frankl chose the higher path of service to his fellow prisoners. Lasantha Wikramatunga, quoted earlier in this chapter, chose to stand up for his beliefs despite the certainty of death. Abused adolescents, according to Bruce Perry, face the option of living with their pain rather than inflicting it on others through violence. Critical to this choice is a sense of support, and the rightness of the chosen path, whether that support comes from family, friends, peers, the community, God or some other being.

Strategies to Increase Resilience

From her study of resilient children in the Hawaii project, Emmy Werner argued that interventions should aim both to decrease exposure to risk and to increase resilience. Consistent with the conclusions of the last chapter, she found that:[9]

(Effective programs) typically offer a broad spectrum of health, education, and family support services, cross professional boundaries, and view the child in the context of the family, and the family in the context of the community. They provide children with sustained access to competent and caring adults, both professionals and volunteers, who teach them problem-solving skills, enhance their communication skills and self-esteem, and provide positive role models for them. ... There is an urgent need for more systematic evaluations of such programs to illuminate the process by which we can forge a chain of protective factors that enables vulnerable children to become competent, confident, and caring individuals, despite the odds of chronic poverty or a medical or social disability.

Bruce Perry also strongly urged community involvement in order to provide the wounded child with a safe haven, nurturing by a caring adult, stability, encouragement and hope.[10]

We are all in this together. If we cannot structure our schools, our communities, and our social agencies in a manner that will identify, protect, and, at a minimum, provide hope to our children, we will be swept away by the inevitable decay of (society and culture). ...

So many children from abusive settings have lost hope. Even brief interactions with respectful, honest, and nurturing adults can be helpful to the abused child, allowing them to know that some adults can be kind and honest and predictable. There are many ways to find children who need your time: Volunteer to be a foster parent; to rock the crack-addicted infant in the hospital; to teach a child to read; to be an aide in the local public school; to answer phones at a battered women's shelter. In all of these settings, you can enrich the life of a child. You can give a child hope.

Good schools are an essential part of this framework. As Lonnie Athens put it: "Although the community cannot guarantee a good family to every child, it can guarantee them a good school," and "a good school can go a long way in making up for a bad family."[11] From this perspective, education about maltreatment, and training in social and emotional skills are important elements of good schooling. Daniel Goleman describes how, in the 1980's, early school programs on sexual abuse focused on basic information, such as the difference between 'good' and 'bad' touching. However, this did little to help children avoid being victimized, whether by a school bully or a potential child molester. Children who were also trained in emotional and social competencies were better able to protect themselves, and were more willing to report abuse. The most effective programs repeated the courses at different levels of the curriculum, and enlisted the assistance of parents. They aimed to:

- Develop self-awareness and a positive attitude to life;
- Teach children how to identify, express and manage feelings, control impulses, delay gratification, and handle stress and anxiety;
- Develop interpersonal skills such as reading body language, listening, taking others' points of view, non-violent verbal communication, and understanding what behaviors are acceptable in different situations.[12]

Babette Rothschild identified several types of resource that trauma victims can use to reduce risk and stress, and increase resilience:[13]

- Functional resources are practical ways for victims to reduce the risk of repeated traumatic experiences, for example by making sure their home is secure, their car is reliable, or they are cautious when out at night.
- Physical resources: many people find that increasing their strength and agility by weight training or self-defense classes gives them more confidence.

- Psychological resources include intelligence, humor, creativity, and most defense mechanisms (see Chapter 3).
- Interpersonal resources include partners, family members, friends and wider social networks. Pets, and significant figures from the past such as grandparents or teachers can also be powerful supports.
- Spiritual resources may include a belief in God, following a spiritual teacher, performing religious practices, or simply communing with nature.
- An oasis is an absorbing activity such as a hobby, complex knitting or a computer game that distracts attention from a stressful problem.
- Pleasant memories of a person, place, pet, object or activity can bring relief from stress and a surge of pleasurable endorphins in the brain. Rothschild calls them 'anchors', while William Bloom labeled them 'strawberries'.[14]
- A safe place is a particularly powerful anchor that is associated with protection and security. Conjuring up the sights, smells, sounds and feelings it evokes can bring temporary relief from traumatic memories.

One of the best ways to increase resilience is to release the traumatic experience and wind down the stress response before it becomes trapped as trauma. This is the aim of post-trauma counseling and psychological debriefing methods such as Critical-Incident Stress Debriefing. These encourage victims to express their thoughts and feelings soon after the event. However, there is little evidence that such approaches reduce the incidence of PTSD.[15] More effective for children, according to Bruce Perry, is education of the family and child about symptoms that are expected after a traumatic event. This can reduce anxiety, increase the sense of competence, and help them identify abnormal responses that require therapeutic help.[16]

Adapting the approaches of indigenous peoples and

shamanic cultures may lead to more effective ways of defusing potentially traumatic events. Because these cultures accepted the reality of trauma, there was less need for the victims to pretend to be unaffected by their ordeal. They could cry, shake and talk endlessly about what had happened within a supportive community. They could re-enact events in dramatic narratives, and release pent-up tensions and emotions through drumming, dancing, chanting, trance, sweat-lodges, and other rituals. We need to move back towards social systems that can provide such support.

Reflection

Emma Werner found a link between infant personality and resilience, implying that there is a strong genetic factor involved. However, next to nothing is known about the effects of pre-birth and birth trauma on personality. It is possible that infants who are less outgoing, affectionate and easy to manage become that way as a result of trauma before or at birth, and that this makes them more vulnerable to future trauma. Even if genetic predisposition is significant, much can be done to ameliorate its influence. The individual can develop skills and resources for defusing potentially traumatic events. And their family and community can provide an understanding and supportive context in which to face life's challenges. Particularly important community contributions are appropriate rituals and ceremonies for releasing trauma, and an atmosphere of meaning and hope in the future—something that is hard for parents to provide if they are suffering from depression themselves.

25. Healing is a Universal Need

We All Need Healing

If asked, few people readily acknowledge that they are trauma-tized and require healing. But very few people could say they are free of all the symptoms and effects associated with trauma that are listed in Table 3. This does not mean that every case of every symptom is directly caused by trauma, but it is a significant factor in many of them. Hence, it seems likely that all, or almost all, of us are affected. Therapist Peter Levine maintains that trauma affects everyone, and can remain hidden for years.[1] In support of this claim he cites studies showing that:

- 40% of Americans had experienced a traumatic event in the previous 3 years;
- 75-100 million Americans have been sexually or physically abused in childhood;
- 30% of married American women and 30% of pregnant women have been beaten by their partners, coincidentally traumatizing their fetuses as well;
- War and violence affect nearly everyone on Earth;
- Many communities are devastated by natural disasters; and
- Trauma is the underlying cause of much mental illness, including widespread depression and anxiety.

There is another reason for believing we all need healing. In Chapter 14, we argued that The Fall was triggered by the traumas of climate change and violent conflict over dwindling resources. The response led to the dominator civilizations of Saharasia, whose traumatized way of being spread throughout the world in the millennia that followed. We still inherit the legacy of these times from our ancestors. We share the psychic disharmony that gave rise to hierarchy, war, competition, gender discrimination and sexual repression. We continue to compensate for alienation from our inner selves, each other, and nature by seeking status, power, wealth, prestige and distractions from the suffering of existence.[2] So embedded are these characteristics in our culture that we regard them as normal, and do not recognize them as distortions of our true nature brought about by trauma.

Peter Levine brings a slightly different perspective, arguing that our culture's emphasis on the cognitive mind is the result of separation from our more primitive instinctive and emotional selves. Lacking this connection, we lose our sense of belonging— to the earth, our families, or anything else. This, he believes, is the root of trauma, the source of our existential loneliness, and the cause of our distrust, competition and war. In order to be fully human, to be our naturally loving, cooperative selves, we need to reintegrate these three parts of our triune brains. As Levine put it, "The transformation that occurs when we do this fulfils our evolutionary destiny. We become completely human animals, capable of the totality of our natural abilities. We are fierce warriors, gentle nurturers, and everything in between."[3] This reintegration of the parts of our brains may also unblock access to higher states of consciousness.[4]

One of the main reasons we are so reluctant to recognize our own trauma is that our culture tends to reject its reality—a symptom of collective denial. As a result, we may fear that we are going crazy; our doctors may think we are hypochondriacs because they cannot find a physical cause for our problems; and our families and friends may urge us to move on before we are emotionally ready. Hence, we recoil from the healing process, and attempt to repress and deny our symptoms with the power of our rational minds. But, argues Peter Levine, this effort does us a disservice.[5]

If we attempt to move ahead with our lives, without first yielding to the gentler urges that will guide us back through these harrowing experiences, then our show of strength becomes little more than illusion. In the meantime, the traumatic effects will grow steadily more severe, firmly entrenched, and chronic. The incomplete responses now frozen in our nervous systems are like indestructible time bombs, primed to go off when aroused by force. ... Real heroism comes from having the courage to openly acknowledge one's experiences, not from suppressing or denying them.

The Challenge and Benefits of Healing

Most of us find that our physical, mental and emotional selves resist opening what we fear may be a can of worms. We prefer to leave whatever lies beneath the surface safely locked away rather than confront our traumas. It takes conscious intention and determined will to enter the healing path. It takes courage to delve into the dark places in our souls, and face the possibility of emotional pain. It often takes persistence and perseverance to achieve healing because our subconscious systems lock the trauma memories away so securely, and invent so many distractions to divert us from that goal. But the potential benefits of healing make the effort worthwhile. Not only may we rid ourselves of emotional, physical and mental dysfunctions, but also we may open up undreamt of possibilities. We may gain confidence and self-esteem, courage and personal power. As we become more sure of who we are, our egos may drive us less strongly towards power, status and wealth. The compulsion to acquire material goods and to be constantly distracted may fall away, along with substance addictions. We may lose our emotional buttons, and become less volatile. We may become less aggressive, angry and violent, and more at peace with ourselves, our lives and our circumstances. We may become more spontaneous and creative; more open to change.

Peter Levine claims that releasing the contained energy of trauma can "propel us into new heights of healing, mastery and even wisdom. Trauma resolved is a great gift, returning us to the natural world of ebb and flow, harmony, love, and compassion." He offers the image of an injured young tree that grows around its wound, forming gnarly burls and misshapen limbs. "The way a tree grows around its past contributes to its exquisite individuality, character and beauty."[6] Similarly, according to shamanic healer Sandra Ingerman: "To be in universal flow, one must understand the concept of power *with* the forces of nature, not power *over* them. True power is transformative; it can transform any energy. With true power we can transform the energy of any illness. ... Ultimately with true power we can learn to transform suffering into joy."[7]

When we dissociate during trauma, a part of our core self, or soul, becomes separated and lost. Sandra Ingerman retrieves these parts for clients. After a period of adjustment, most people find this reintegration brings feelings of being more present in their bodies, seeing colors more vividly, having more energy, power and strength. Frequently, they are able to stop abusing themselves, others and the planet. They become less critical and judgmental, and accept others more easily. They become more realistic about relationships, and their marriages may improve as they become more independent. They may attract new people into their lives who reflect their new wholeness. Through such personal transformation, individuals are prepared for effective non-violent action for social and planetary change. They gain inner strength, courage, confidence, commitment, empathy, compassion, and the ability to work humbly with others. They lose the need to dominate without becoming submissive. In the words of Peter Levine: "I believe that we humans have the innate capacity to heal not only ourselves, but our world, from the debilitating effects of trauma."[8]

Choosing a Healing Path
In our view, the aim of therapy is to transform the past, not to

wallow in it. It is to heal dysfunctions caused by trauma as quickly, permanently and painlessly as possible, and to move on in life. In other words, it should be focused in the present, rather than the past, with an eye to the future. We need to reach the point of saying: "It is over, that was a long time ago, I survived."[9] In similar vein, psychiatrist Judith Herman aims to enable clients to revisit the memories of trauma and to put them aside at will like other memories. This frees us to build a new life based on beliefs that meaningfully integrate the suffering.[10]

There are hundreds of different healing modalities, based on a number of theoretical perspectives. They range from simple self-help methods, through a smorgasbord of alternative therapies, to long-established psychotherapies and psychiatry. Choosing a therapy is made even more confusing by the fact that many therapists combine two or more methods. According to trauma psychotherapist Babette Rothschild: "Each available therapy helps some clients, and each of them also fails at times. Every modality has strengths as well as weaknesses. ... there is no one-size-fits-all trauma therapy. In fact, sometimes it is the therapeutic relationship, not any technique or model, that is the primary force for healing trauma."[11]

It is a good idea to look for a healing path that suits your personality and philosophy of life. Equally important, possibly more important, is to find a therapist that you trust, with whom you feel a rapport, and who gets results rather than encouraging dependence on a paid listener.[12] Many of the therapies available today are relatively fast, and do not require expensive years of talking. There is not space here, nor are we qualified to provide a detailed comparison of modalities. Rather, we have sought to give some general guidance based on our own limited training, experience (as both healer and client), and reading.

Research-based evidence for the effectiveness of most trauma therapies is scarce. An exception is Cognitive Behavioral Therapy. CBT is the most widely respected therapy amongst mainstream psychotherapists because it has a solid theoretical base, and has been well tested.[13] It aims to change patterns of feeling, thinking and behaving through systematic procedures that question established beliefs and thoughts, gradually confront avoided situations, and introduce new ways of behaving. Also well-researched is Eye Movement Desensitization and Reprocessing (EMDR) whose distinctive feature is the use of eye movements to simulate the natural dream state. This stimulates recall of painful memories and helps process them.[14] Most other methods are harder to evaluate scientifically because they are more subjective, and depend significantly on the intuition of the therapist. Mainstream scientists also tend to reject out-of-hand the validity of any methods that are spiritual or mystical, such as shamanic soul retrieval, or prayer. Nevertheless, client feedback indicates that many such approaches are highly effective.

Some therapies focus primarily on helping clients function better in everyday life by suppressing, stabilizing or reducing their symptoms. Psychoactive therapeutic drugs are often used for this purpose. They create a cork that prevents the genii of terror and uncontrollable rage from escaping the bottle. But this same cork may prevent the release required for healing.[15] Another way of tackling the symptoms is to change the client's thought and behavior patterns, as in CBT. This undoubtedly helps many people to lead more or less normal lives, but may leave the original trauma unresolved. Clients' lives may continue to be limited by the trauma, even if less severely than before.

Many therapies rely on evoking memories of the traumatic event, and re-experiencing them in some way. Regression therapies and hypnotherapy seek to recover lost memories, and shamanic soul-retrieval often has a similar effect. But these practices are controversial, and sometimes lead to false 'memories' of events that did not happen in reality. Once a memory has been evoked, the associated trauma must then be released in some way. Psychoanalysis and some other modalities believe that this requires an intense catharsis.[16] However, Peter Levine's experience has taught him that catharsis may actually evoke false memories and renew the trauma rather than heal it.[17] The roles of false memories and re-experiencing the trauma are discussed in more detail in the next chapter.

These and other controversies surrounding trauma healing can be very confusing. Bruce Perry describes how conflicting advice is often given on the treatment of children with PTSD. Some recommend talking about the event, for example, while others focus on dealing with practical social or educational problems arising from it.[18] In choosing a healing path and therapist for yourself, it is a good idea to seek out independent information and client testimonials on the modalities and therapists available in your area. Ultimately, however, you have to trust your intuition and experience. Do not be afraid to try a few therapies and therapists until you find one that works for you. This may not mean choosing the one you find most comfortable, as comfort may actually indicate that it is not challenging your inner resistance.

Babette Rothschild claims that when a therapist simply follows the client's process without intervention, it usually results either in avoidance of traumatic memories, or in overwhelm by them. What is needed, she argues, is a therapist who directs the client quite strongly, but whom the client trusts completely to regulate the process and keep him or her safe.[19] After trying a therapy, check in with yourself: "Has this helped? Am I calmer and better able to handle daily life? Did I feel safe to go into memories of terror?" The bottom line is: if it helps you, it's OK.

There is widespread agreement that the support of family, friends and community is vital to successful healing. It is highly desirable to have at least one close relative or friend who understands the process, and is ready and willing to provide support between therapeutic sessions, and to ensure that you are given proper care if you need it. Studies of Vietnam veterans have also shown the importance of wider community acceptance and support. The returned soldiers desperately needed to have their stories of horror and shame heard over and over again, and to have their experience validated by being told that others would have reacted the same way in their shoes.[20] Instead, many veterans struggling with PTSD were rejected as crazy. Sandra Ingerman found that soul retrieval could be a great help to them, but only if their communities were ready to help them integrate their lost parts. Today, many of us have no community support to draw upon, and this isolation is itself a major cause of trauma and soul loss.[21]

A Word about Safety

Babette Rothschild states that the prime duty of the therapist is to avoid doing harm, and to create a sense of security for the client. But no therapy can be guaranteed 100% safe. She likens unresolved trauma to a pressure cooker. If it is opened up too fast, the internal pressure may cause an explosion. When powerful emotions are released or re-lived, much depends on the experience and intuition of the therapist. A vital skill is to be constantly aware of the client's state of arousal, and to know how to slow the process down when necessary before it gets out of control. Failure can lead to a panic attack, flashback, breakdown, serious illness, or even suicide. It is impossible to confine such processes to the duration of a therapy session, and they may emerge or continue in between times. That is why a personal support system is so important.

It is the responsibility of the therapist to ensure, as far as possible, that the client is safe to leave and re-enter normal life at the end of the session. Risks include self-harm or suicidal thoughts; accidents due to emotional and mental turmoil; or hospitalization if they become severely dysfunctional. If they are diagnosed as psychotic, drugs may be used to reduce the symptoms, potentially blocking completion of the healing process at least temporarily. If problems do arise, it may indicate that the healing modality is unsuitable for the client. For example, some trauma sufferers cannot handle therapies that evoke memories, and do better with ones that aim simply to relieve symptoms and increase coping skills.[22]

Reflection

The therapies discussed in this chapter have been developed for adults who can evaluate alternatives, choose an approach that suits them, and talk about their experiences or symptoms. But many of the most significant traumas happen before or at birth and in infancy, before language and cognitive memory develop. Often, these early traumas remain trapped until adulthood. Healing at this stage is possible, but by this time traumas may be so deeply embedded that healing is very slow and difficult.

An alternative is to heal traumas as they happen in infancy. A vital aspect of healing a distressed infant is simply to provide the nurturing he or she needs: gentle touch, rocking, loving eye contact, and a prompt response to distress, as described in Chapter 18. There are also many alternative therapies that do not rely on language that can be used on young babies as well as adults. These include massage and manipulation to release muscular tensions, and stimulation of acupressure points by gentle tapping or rubbing. There are also spiritual or energy healing methods in which the therapist uses his or her own bio-energy and consciousness fields to calm the infant and release the distress of trapped arousal.

26. The Healing Process

The aim of trauma healing varies widely between therapies. As a minimum, all therapies aim to cure dysfunctional thoughts, emotions or behaviors that affect daily activities so that the victim can lead a normal life in the community. Many also include existential healing that helps victims to find meaning in their suffering, and to integrate it into their belief systems and sense of personal identity. A smaller number of therapies seek to facilitate transformation, thus enabling their clients to achieve self-actualization, or to realize their full potential as human beings, unlimited by trauma. Ideally, we believe, healing also should open transpersonal pathways to higher consciousness and to what many spiritual traditions call enlightenment. As we argued in Chapter 6, this is the level of healing necessary to empower humanity to overcome the crisis of civilization, develop a new partnership culture, and evolve the possible human. However, this is more commonly the domain of spirituality than psychotherapy.

This chapter outlines a healing process for pursuing this ambitious goal. It is a process that feels intuitively right to us from the perspective of our beliefs and values, and our limited knowledge and experience of both trauma and healing. It is based primarily on the well-established approaches of *Focusing* developed by Eugene Gendlin, and *Somatic Experiencing* developed by Peter Levine, together with the ideas of Babette Rothschild.[1] The approach is holistic, aiming to get mind, body, emotions and spirit working in harmony so that we may achieve our highest potential. It avoids intense catharsis and the use of drugs, and seeks to release the trauma gently. Some components are suitable for self-help, but inner resistance is often so strong that healing requires the assistance of a therapist. At the very least, a good therapist undoubtedly speeds the process and makes it safer.

Remembering and Re-experiencing Trauma

When we are aroused by a potentially traumatic threat to our survival, explicit memory is suppressed, and no factual recording is made of what happened, where and when. Hence, we may be left with nothing but powerful and confusing implicit memories of emotions and sensations. This is particularly true of trauma in the womb and during infancy when the capacity for explicit memory has not yet developed. Despite this limitation, many therapies rely on evoking memories of the traumatic event by various means including talking about the past, or regression to past events using guided imagery, controlled breathing, or hypnotherapy. Sandra Ingerman has found that lost memories also may return following shamanic soul retrieval.[2] Sometimes clients appear to regress to times before birth or to other lives, and it has been possible to verify some such accounts against medical, family or historical records.[3] Given the importance of pre-birth, birth and early-infancy trauma, the possibility of connecting with such events and healing them is highly significant. However, experiences before about age three are usually remembered as a holistic 'felt sense' without factual details.

In many cases, people have 'remembered' things that turned out not to be true. There seems to be little doubt that suggestions about what happened can distort memories, and even create 'memories' of things that never occurred.[4] Trauma therapist Peter Levine states that "the dynamics of trauma are such that they can produce frightening and bizarre "memories" of past events that seem extremely real, but never happened."[5] He goes on to argue that some of the memories stimulated by regression or hypnotherapy are genuine, and others are misinterpretations of metaphoric body messages or images. For example, a memory of rape may not be literally true, but mean that the experience felt like rape. The actual event might have been a car accident, a medical procedure, or child neglect. Indeed, Babette Rothschild points out that medical examinations, rectal thermometers, suppositories, surgery and other procedures in early infancy are often mistaken for abuse. She warns both clients and therapists against leaping too easily to conclusions, and recommends regarding all recovered memories as suspect unless they can be verified.[6]

Such distortions of memory arise from the way information is stored and recalled. Levine stresses that memory is not like a recording. It is comprised of sets of different, but associated stimuli. Thus, when the mind recalls an event, it selects a combination of colors, images, sounds, sensations, smells, interpretations and other data, that reflect its present state. Each bit of information may well be accurate, but the overall memory is a compilation of real experiences together with information from newspaper stories, books, films, conversations and dreams. In the case of trauma, the mind may use anything that has the same emotional tone and level of arousal as the original event.[7] Boris Cyrulnik paints a similar picture when he says our memories are not lies but reconstructions of the past, shaped by the impression we want to make. Every element is true, but the whole is an "autobiographical chimera" by which we give meaning to the past.[8]

Given this situation, Peter Levine warns that persistent searching for the truth of what really happened can actually impede healing. The trick is to accept that memories are not literal, and that they can give us only a hazy sense of what may have happened. Even if a memory is true, he argues that explanations and interpretations are not as important as the sensations and feelings associated with them. Accuracy is not as important as whether the memory enables completion of the arousal cycle, bringing a sense of resolution, empowerment, and healing.

The unreliability of memory casts doubt on the value of re-experiencing traumatic experiences as advocated by many therapies. In Peter Levine's view, it is not necessary to dredge up old memories and relive their emotional pain. In his experience, cathartic methods may actually re-traumatize rather than heal, encouraging dependence on repeated catharsis and the emergence of false memories.[9] He believes the key to healing is not cognitive memory, but awareness of emotions and associated body sensations and thoughts. He argues that it is not the intense, dramatic emotional outpouring that heals, but the discharge of the trapped energy of arousal. If we confront trauma directly, it may seize us again. Instead, we should slide gently into the trauma, and then draw ourselves gradually out.[10]

A slightly different perspective comes from Sandra Ingerman's experience with soul retrieval. The soul's return is often gentle, but can be very painful because the lost part still carries the pain that made it leave. In order to avoid overwhelming her client, she limits the number of parts she retrieves in one session, and allows a few months before attempting to recover further parts. During that time, memories may return, emotions may intensify, dreams may become more vivid, and the returned parts may need active care to ensure they do not leave again.[11] In other words, care must be taken that the client does not dissociate again.

Renegotiation and the Felt Sense

Part of the natural healing process is what Peter Levine calls renegotiation. He describes how three cheetah cubs escaped a lion by climbing a tree. Afterwards, they repeatedly re-played the experience with one cub taking the role of the lion while the others practiced various escape maneuvers. In this way, they built their confidence and developed better survival strategies for the future. Daniel Goleman relates how young children similarly make games out of traumatic experiences, such as a playground shooting.[12] He suggests that this repetition in a non-threatening context gradually desensitizes their memories. It also provides an opportunity to magically change the outcome, for example by killing the perpetrator. Levine argues that the energy of arousal must be discharged before such playful renego-tiation is possible. Unfortunately, in modern civilization we often have no opportunity to release the experience before we tell our story. Thus, we review the event while still aroused, leading to painful re-enactment rather than lighthearted learning. Once the energy has been trapped in this way, we experience repeated re-enactments and develop trauma symptoms.

The way out of this cycle is to develop what Eugene Gendlin called the 'felt sense'.[13] Peter Levine defines this as "a medium through which we experience the fullness of sensation and knowledge about ourselves" or "the totality of sensation."[14] The felt sense is a body awareness or physical sensation, not a mental construct. It may be influenced by thoughts, but is a feeling, not thought. It includes the five senses of sight, sound, taste, smell and touch, and also encompasses the inner senses of body posture and movement, muscle tensions, temperature and so on. Emotions are part of it, but are not an important component.

The felt sense integrates and gives meaning to a mass of infor-mation from our whole organism: body, mind, instincts, emotions, intellect and spirit. It relays "the overall experience of the organism, rather than interpreting what is happening from the standpoint of the individual parts."[15] In other words, it is like seeing the image on a TV screen rather than the individual pixels, or hearing the music instead of the individual notes. It is the essence of being alive. Often vague, it varies in intensity and clarity, constantly shifting and transforming. It serves "as a portal through which we find the symptoms, or reflections of trauma," and when we experience an event as a whole it "can bring revela-tions about how to undo the trauma."[16] It also can be a doorway to spiritual states. As Peter Levine notes, we use this sense every day, but few of us are aware of it or cultivate it. It has no place in western culture, and is not generally taught. The best way to learn how to develop it is through the books and other resources by Eugene Gendlin and Peter Levine.[17]

Using the felt sense, we can learn to know ourselves, letting our instincts clarify the pattern of trauma and the blockages to healing. We can initiate renegotiation and keep the pace of healing to a tolerable, gentle discharge of energy. Peter Levine likens his *Somatic Experiencing* process to peeling an onion to reveal the traumatized core. "For each of us, the mastery of trauma is a heroic journey that will have moments of creative brilliance, profound learning, and periods of hard tedious work. It is the process of finding ourselves a safe and gentle way of coming out of the immobility of the freeze reaction without being overwhelmed."[18]

There are several key steps in this process, according to Levine. First is development of the felt sense. After this skill has been mastered comes surrender to the flow of feelings, including trembling and other spontaneous discharges of energy. No attempt is made to dredge up memories, emotions or insights. If they come, they are simply observed and let go without worrying about their source, or whether or not they are true. Out of this emerges, in its own time, a single image or word that symbolizes the meaning of the traumatic event, and which arouses strong emotions such as hurt or rejection. As we allow these feelings to be there, without trying to understand or control them, they gradually shift towards more positive emotions. Entering the felt sense of these new emotions again produces change. As this cycle continues, excitement gradually separates from anxiety. We start to distinguish the joyful challenge of living from the fear arising from trauma. We gain a new felt sense of strength and resilience as we ground this energy in our bodies and social world. Step by step, the helplessness of trauma is renegotiated for empowerment, and mastery of the skills to handle future threats. Finally, comes re-orientation to our circumstances and environment arising from this new perspective.

Some other approaches concentrate on directly strengthening

our positive emotions, particularly joy, as a way to reduce unhappiness and the re-enactment of trauma. These include ancient Buddhist practices for overcoming the suffering of life, the field of positive psychology (e.g. Martin Seligman's book *Authentic Happiness)*, William Bloom's *Endorphin Effect*, and Jacquelyn Aldana's *15-Minute Miracle* practice of gratitude.[19] The authors are currently associated with a group that is developing an approach which combines an emphasis on joy with the felt sense and other techniques in order to heal trauma with less discomfort and resistance. It is based on the idea that, beneath the limitations caused by our traumas, we each have core strengths that are underlain by pure joy. We can heal more gently, rapidly and with less pain if we can connect with this joy, and learn to expand it.[20]

Boris Cyrulnik's approach to healing centers on expressing the traumatic experience in some way.[21] At first sight, this appears to be quite different to Levine's *Somatic Experiencing*, but there are similarities between the two processes. Before the trauma can be expressed in words, pictures, drama or children's play it is necessary to allow the feelings to surface, and to rework the experience as an 'image' that may be visual, verbal or an action. This corresponds to the first stages of *Somatic Experiencing* that culminate in an image or word. Whereas Levine recommends simply allowing this image and associated feelings to be there, Cyrulnik encourages its expression. This arouses emotions which shift as the process unfolds. In Cyrulnik's experience, if children are left alone to do this, their memories will keep returning to haunt them. But if they can share their drawings, stories, thoughts and plays with someone who responds with tears, laughter and comments, their emotions will calm and their images will be reshaped. Representing our tragedy may facilitate the renegotiation process, helping us to rework our feelings and reconnect the parts of our divided self.

Meditation and Healing

There are many similarities between *Somatic Experiencing* and the healing effect of Buddhist meditation. Like *Somatic Experiencing*, meditation focuses inwards on awareness of the spontaneous flow of thoughts, feelings and bodily processes, which are simply observed and let go. Meditation teacher and psychotherapist Jack Kornfield describes in *A Path with Heart* how we must develop a feeling awareness of what is actually going on in all parts of the body, and particularly note areas of constriction that prevent the free flow of energy. As we observe them with kindness, the tensions and muscular armoring gradually release, and energy begins to move. Sometimes, he notes, this may be accompanied by vibration and shaking as Levine describes, or by heat, labored breathing or other physical symptoms.

If we stay with this process, gradually the painful emotions and memories fade, and more positive states arise as the practitioner becomes less trapped in the past, and more present to the here and now. "What we find as we listen to the songs of our rage or fear, loneliness or longing, is that they do not stay forever. Rage turns into sorrow; sorrow turns into tears; tears may fall for a long time, but then the sun comes out. A memory of old loss sings to us; our body shakes and relives the moment of loss; then the armoring around that loss gradually softens; and in the midst of the song of tremendous grieving, the pain of that loss finally finds release."[22]

This process is illustrated by the experience of a Vietnam veteran who went on a meditation retreat after suffering eight years of frequent nightmares and flashbacks. At first, vivid, horrific memories filled his days as he fully lived the emotional impact of his experiences for the first time. He began to face memories of which he was not consciously aware, and simultaneously to deal with his fear that he would be unable to control the demons he was letting lose. But the visions of horror gradually gave way to other memories: "the entrancing, intense beauty of a jungle forest, a thousand different shades of green, a fragrant breeze blowing over beaches so white and dazzling they seemed carpeted by diamonds." There also arose deep, enduring compassion for himself which grew to encompass those around him over the months that followed. "While the memories have also stayed with me, the nightmares have not."[23] This may sound simple, but it takes great courage and strength, a warrior spirit, to face our traumas in this way.

Research has shown that meditation reduces arousal and metabolic level, changes patterns of brain activity, reduces sensitivity to stressful stimuli, and helps break old habits. Not surprisingly, therefore, it can improve many conditions associated with trauma, including anxiety, aggression, stress, insomnia, phobias, addictions, mild depression, psychosomatic illnesses, asthma, heart problems and chronic pain. It also increases awareness of our present reality, enhances self-esteem, self-confidence, self-control, empathy, creativity, academic achievement and intimate relationships.

There may be as many as 100 million practitioners of meditation in the East, and there are now several million in the West. However, it is not without its difficulties as a healing modality. One is the simple fact that it can be slow, and may require a lifetime of practice to achieve significant results. Jack Kornfield notes that there are many areas of personal development and healing where good Western therapy is faster and more successful than meditation.[24] This is generally the case for healing dysfunctional thoughts, feelings and behaviors, and for some aspects of existential healing. However, meditation is likely to be more effective at facilitating self-actualization and transpersonal or spiritual healing, which are not addressed by many Western therapies.

Another difficulty is that meditation can cause emotional volatility, with episodes of anxiety, agitation, depression and euphoria.[25] Occasionally, meditators experience extreme terror which, unlike the veteran quoted above, they cannot handle. They may have no knowledge of what happened because the trauma occurred early in life before the formation of conscious memories, and yet be unable to sleep or continue meditating. Without skilful management, such experiences can spark severe depression or suicidal feelings. Few eastern meditation teachers know what to do in such situations. Strong physical sensations can also occur. Jack Kornfield describes how some people feel they are having a heart attack as they make contact with locked-up energy, and their hearts open. When this happens, it is a challenging judgment for the teacher to decide whether or not to send them to hospital.[26]

Another type of experience is spiritual emergence — sometimes referred to as a spiritual emergency. In this case, the person enters an altered state of consciousness in which they experience vivid images, and deep insights into the nature of reality, possibly due to an extreme form of dissociation from terror. The process is best allowed to run its course provided a safe space and supervision are available. In this case, it can produce powerful healing and reintegration of the fragmented soul. Unfortunately, psychiatrists often misdiagnose the condition as psychosis and suppress the symptoms with drugs before the process can complete itself. John Weir Perry observed that people treated in this way frequently relapse and often became chronically ill.[27] There is a need for more meditation teachers to be trained in managing trauma, and for psychiatrists and therapists to be trained in meditation.

The opposite situation may also arise when a practitioner is consistently unable to go deeper into the meditative space. For example, Jack Kornfield comments that "we frequently find meditators who are deeply aware of breath or body but are almost totally unaware of feelings, and others who understand the mind but have no wise relation to the body."[28] Similarly, when the relaxation induced by meditation brings trauma close to the surface, the reptilian brain is extremely clever at finding ways to protect us from what it sees as a threat to our survival. The felt sense process and meditation practices both encourage practitioners to allow painful thoughts and emotions to remain present until they dissipate naturally. However, Kornfield himself found that even after many years of intense meditation training and practice he would still use his mind to suppress anger, sadness, grief or frustration without even being aware he was feeling them. As he put it: "Meditation and spiritual practice can easily be used to suppress and avoid feeling or to escape from difficult areas of our lives. Our sorrows are hard to touch. ... there is much pain in truly experiencing our bodies, our personal histories, our limitations."[29] Thus, as noted earlier, trauma can block access to higher states of consciousness.

A final difficulty with meditation as a healing technique is that people suffering from PTSD, anxiety, depression or other more severe trauma symptoms may be quite unable to calm their minds enough to meditate. When Jack Kornfield tried to teach meditation to inmates of a mental hospital, he quickly found it was not what they needed. "These people had little ability to bring a balanced attention to their lives, and most of them were already lost in their minds."[30] In such cases, it may be necessary to undertake progressive healing, working first to reduce pathology and improve daily functioning, then to tackle issues of meaning and identity, before moving on to the transformational and transpersonal levels.

Trauma, Transformation and Higher Consciousness

The renegotiation and expression of trauma transforms us. It requires fundamental changes in the nervous system, emotions and perceptions to move from trauma to peace; from immobility, fear and constriction to fluidity, courage and receptivity. As we transform, we find that rage and the desire for justice and revenge fade away. We no longer need to forgive because there is no more blame or judgment, just acceptance of what is. As our fears dissipate, we learn to trust more, and face challenges with confidence. We gain a surer sense of self, greater resilience and spontaneity. We relax and live life more fully, joyfully and passionately.[31]

A beautiful illustration of this process is Aba Gayle's story that she told at a Conference on Forgiveness at the Findhorn Foundation some years ago.[32] Her story began on the day her daughter Catherine was brutally murdered. With little support from her family, friends and colleagues, she entered a 'journey of darkness.' Believing that finding and executing Catherine's killer would make everything OK, she entered eight years of rage, hatred and lust for revenge. The turning point came when she learned to meditate, and began a spiritual quest. Guided to forgive her daughter's killer, she wrote him a letter on death row. "I was surprised to find that I could forgive you. This does not mean that I think you are innocent or that you are blameless for what happened. What I learned is this: You are a divine child of God." Finding true forgiveness in her heart finally gave her the healing she needed. "All the anger, all the rage, all the lust for revenge—simply vanished in that instant. In its place I was filled with this incredible feeling of Joy and Love and Peace." Aba Gayle went on to meet Douglas on death row in San Quentin, and became an active campaigner for the abolition of the death penalty. She traveled around the world sharing her story in the hope that it would inspire others to heal themselves. As she said at the conference, "Remember ... forgiveness is a gift you give to yourself." And also remember that forgiveness can happen only when the heart is ready. It cannot be forced.

Trauma resolved is a blessing. As Boris Cyrulnik expressed this idea: "I am no longer the man who was tortured ... I am becoming a man who can transform the memory of his sufferings into an acceptable work of art." And, for those who survive the ordeal, "misfortune becomes the evening star that shows the way to the miracle."[33] Trauma has the power to destroy our lives, or to renew them. Depending on our response, we may be turned to stone, or set upon a higher path. The felt sense is like the cast that supports a broken bone, enabling us to bridge the gulf between destruction and renewal. But we must be willing to challenge our core beliefs, and trust instinctive responses and novel sensations that we do not understand. We must be willing to let go of preconceptions and fixed ideas, and allow ourselves to flow in harmony with the spirit of life.

Another level of healing is possible beyond this existential transformation. This happens when we open to the transpersonal realms of existence and higher states of consciousness through spiritual practices such as eastern meditation or yoga, or the similar Christian practice of contemplative prayer. Meditation develops the ability to control our minds, and true yoga adds ethics, intellectual study, lifestyle, body postures and breath control. When practiced consistently, these can lead to deep insights into the nature of mind, consciousness and identity, and help develop optimal well-being and consciousness. Greed, anger and aggression fade, to be replaced progressively by love, compassion, peace, joy, generosity and service to others. The way is opened to achieving our true potential.[34]

Reflection

The healing journey is often long, and the going is rough at times. We embarked on our own slow voyage many years ago, and are still far from being fully healed. Along the way, we have explored several types of therapy, and trained in a few. Even now, there are dark places that our bodies and psyches resist entering for fear that they will not survive. But we have no doubt that the on-going journey has been, and will continue to be, worthwhile. We have benefited greatly from both self-help and professional therapies, and our inconsistent practice of meditation. Our fears and anxieties are much weaker than they were. Our self-confidence and self-esteem are stronger, if not yet strong. Tensions and some physical ailments are gone or reduced. Our self-awareness and understanding of our inner selves are deeper, and our relationship with each other is deeper and more secure. And our level of consciousness is increasing, particularly in our relationship with the natural world.

27. Healing Generational and Collective Trauma

Collective traumas vary widely in scale and impact. Some, such as a fatal car accident, may affect a single family and a few close friends. A major fire or shooting incident may expand involvement to the local community. An earthquake or storm may spread across a city or region, as when hurricane Katrina hit New Orleans. The bombing of the World Trade Center mainly affected New Yorkers, but had a smaller and less direct traumatic impact on the whole of the USA and beyond. At still larger scales, war and genocide can devastate the lives of whole nations for decades, and some native peoples have suffered collective and generational trauma for centuries since colonization.

Most of those involved in a collective trauma suffer personal pain and loss. Many may experience individual trauma symptoms, such as rage and a desire for revenge. Collective healing is not possible unless the personal traumas of most of those involved are also healed. As individuals heal and become more willing to share their experiences, so collective healing becomes easier. And as the collective heals, awareness of their common suffering provides a supportive context for individual healing. Thus, the two levels of healing intertwine and are complementary. But there are also differences that demand different approaches. It is impossible to heal collective traumas one by one when thousands or millions are affected. Often in such cases, a whole way of life has been destroyed, and it is necessary to establish new beliefs, values, myths, rituals and patterns of behavior. Similarly, peaceful coexistence of different religious, racial and ethnic groups may not be possible until deep fears and distrust have been resolved, and centuries of generational trauma in the form of conflict, exploitation and prejudice have been overcome.

Healing Generational Trauma

Generational trauma is a factor in both personal and collective trauma. Some traumas are passed down through a single family as a result of an accident, abuse or other tragedy to an earlier generation. If other families were not involved, these may be treated as normal individual cases, or perhaps by group therapy with affected family members. When the original event impacted a whole community, city or nation, however, collective trauma is inherited through cultural beliefs, attitudes, customs, rituals and so on. Boris Cyrulnik refers to the "classic three-generation pattern" in which the first generation survives the trauma and makes an effort to adapt, the second profits from their efforts, and the third looks for its roots.[1]

Once again, there are both personal and collective aspects to this process. At the individual level, many children in the generation after World War II were traumatized by fathers who had been in combat or prison camps, and who suffered uncontrollable rage, violence, withdrawal or other symptoms. Their grandchildren are often affected by anxiety and other trauma symptoms as well—a fact recognized by the Australian Government which provides some free therapy for both the children and grandchildren of war veterans.

The collective level of this three-generation pattern is reflected in the experience of Germany. At the end of the Second World War, the German people suppressed their traumatic experiences and got on with rebuilding the country. They created a culture of silence about what had happened that penetrated the souls of the post-war generation.[2] It was not until the third generation that it became possible to start expressing and healing the wounds.[3] As Joanna Macy wrote: "the German people determined that they would do anything to spare their children the suffering they had known. They worked hard to provide them a safe, rich life ... They gave their children everything—everything but one thing. They did not give them their

321

broken heart. And their children have never forgiven them."[4] But now, as the children age and the grandchildren mature, healing is happening.

A step towards this was taken in September 2007. Six hundred people gathered one evening for a meditation on the collective consciousness of Berlin guided by Thomas Hübl. The participants clearly sensed the shadow of the Second World War, and an atmosphere of unity emerged that they felt had the potential to bring reconciliation, healing and transformation.[5] Then, in May 2008, a second, day-long event was held. It began with invited speakers sharing their life stories, most of whom were directly affected by World War II. The aim was to deepen participants' knowledge and understanding of the past, and particularly to evoke their feelings about the collective shadow so that they could engage with the process with open hearts, not just with their minds.

After lunch, the 500 participants divided into groups of five to discuss questions set by the organizers. After each question, they changed groups to maximize interaction. The questions focused mainly on feelings and included issues such as: What touches you most about Germany's Nazi past? How much does it still influence Germany today? What can we personally do to make sure nothing similar happens again? Many people found it hard to stay with the stark reality of the past, and wanted to bring in positive aspects. The event culminated with a guided meditation on the German and Jewish souls during the Second World War, which were then meditatively united. This proved to be a very powerful experience, with many tears. The day closed with the group singing tones and chants together, rapidly achieving harmonic effects. Importantly, advisors were available throughout the event and afterwards to help participants who experienced difficult emotions.

Collective Trauma and the Cultural Fabric

One of the most important factors in collective trauma is the depth of its impact on the culture. When the World Trade Center was destroyed on 11 September 2001, hundreds of thousands of New Yorkers were directly affected. Many millions more across the nation and around the world were traumatized by the replays on television, their emotional identification with the dead and injured, and their fears for the future of themselves and their loved ones. This sparked a national search for meaning and answers to questions such as: Why did this happen? How does it make sense within my philosophy or religion? Did it have any positive outcomes?

Two months after the event, two-thirds of Americans were still trying to make sense of it. Many persisted for the following year. Those who succeeded in finding meaning suffered significantly fewer trauma symptoms than those who failed. However, despite this soul-searching, the fabric of American culture was not fundamentally torn, and most people dealt with their trauma as individuals with the support of their social networks. After a couple of weeks, they tended to stop talking about it for fear that others were no longer interested. This may have been because everyone was affected by 9/11, so that talking became a sharing between victims rather than recounting a personal experience to someone who was not involved. This also may explain why those who chose not to express their feelings coped better than those who did.[6]

Terrible as they were, the events of 9/11 and the response to them was relatively mild compared to the cases of Sri Lanka and indigenous peoples, described in Chapter 22. The traditional family- and village-based Tamil society has been shattered, and now must be rebuilt from scratch. Similarly, as the indigenous peoples of North America, Australia and elsewhere emerge from centuries of epidemics, genocide, displacement, and cultural assimilation, they are beginning to re-member and re-create their ceremonies, traditions and ancient beliefs. Healing requires reintegration of the fragments of past traditions with present conditions and future hopes; and reestablishment of the links between family members, ancestors, community, and culture. Of particular importance to many peoples is the connection to their land, which is still the home of their ancestors, and which also needs healing from the pain in which it is soaked.

As described in Chapter 22, Cynthia Wesley-Esquimaux and Magdalena Smolewski claim that indigenous peoples continue to suffer unconsciously from deep, unresolved grief. They suggest that the peoples may be able to connect with, and heal, this grief once the Elders have resurrected their collective memories, and these have been reclaimed by the young people. But until that happens, the unacknowledged trauma will continue generation after generation to blight their ability to flourish as a whole and healthy people. When asked how best to promote community well-being, most Native American women answered 'by returning to traditional ways'.[7] A similar deep grief and cultural blight may haunt the Tamils for decades or centuries to come.

The Importance of Ritual and Expression

Familiar cultural rituals are an important part of both individual and collective healing. They facilitate expression of emotions, guide behavior, and strengthen community bonds while offering a sense of meaning and completion. For example, veterans of the Vietnam War from the Native American Navajo tribe found the traditional 'Enemy Way' ritual of their tribe restored harmony, balance and connection to the community. This lasted 7 days and involved their family, clan and community. By contrast, Mary de Young suggested that one reason why African-American and Asian-American veterans suffered more from PTSD than those of European extraction was that racism and prejudice effectively barred them from the restorative rituals of the white culture.[8]

Today, the meaning of most traditional rituals and ceremonies in the western world has been lost, and we often engage in collective denial. As a result, trauma victims are silenced. As Boris Cyrulnik put it, "We can only say what our culture wants to hear. But the wounded soul's compulsion to bear witness is so great that it becomes a form of torture. If he does not bear witness, he will become a traitor. But he can speak only if he conforms to the expressive criteria that are laid down by his culture."[9] This need drives the spontaneous emergence of new forms of collective expression, such as the laying of flowers, poems and gifts after the tragic death of Princess Diana, and the horror of 9/11.

Reconstruction of Tamil society in Sri Lanka will succeed only as social structures and practices are restored and collective trauma is healed. Daya Somasundaram described how, even before the end of the war, large groups were being taught culturally-familiar relaxation exercises. These not only released tension, but also connected them with their childhood, community and religious roots. At the same time, children were being encouraged to build friendships and express their emotions through play, art, dance, stories, and yoga; and schools were holding regular ceremonies for the dead with pictures, flowers and candles. Refugees were similarly being urged to use traditional funeral, anniversary, and other rituals and ceremonies as reminders of their loss, and to celebrate their heroes. Communities were also being encouraged to erect memorials at mass graves so that they would become sacred places, imbued with meaning, where public ceremonies could facilitate collective expression of their grief.[10]

Small Group Processes

Many approaches to large-scale collective healing make use of work with small groups to elicit deep sharing and the release of trapped emotional energy. Such groups are normally facilitated by a therapist, or someone skilled in group dynamics. We described above how a small-group process helped several hundred Germans come to terms with their collective generational trauma. A rather different process was used by Joanna Macy to facilitate the psychological healing of victims of the Chernobyl disaster of 1986.

The town of Novozybkov was heavily contaminated by radioactivity from the Chernobyl nuclear reactor when the government seeded clouds to produce heavy rain in order to protect the people of Moscow. Joanna Macy, known world-wide for her work on despair and empowerment, went there to help the inhabitants understand and respond creatively to their massive collective trauma.[11] On arrival, the Mayor told her that intense anger was simmering below the surface, ready to explode. They had always been people of the forest, but now they dared not venture into it. They had always lived close to the Earth in timber buildings, but now they were being re-housed above it in concrete apartments. They had always been healthy, but now their children were sick.

The workshop was limited to 50 participants so that they could sit in a circle, able to see and speak to each other. For a day and a half, structured processes built trust and openness in communicating personal experiences. These included interactive exercises in pairs and small groups that encouraged participants to risk telling the truth about their thoughts and feelings, and to listen to others without interruption or judgment. During this time, nothing was said about the contamination, radiation sickness, or birth defects. Joanna Macy then led the group on a guided journey to connect with their ancestors, and imbibe their strengths. Once immersed in this wonderful past, they did not want to return to the disaster, and the present. As they drew pictures of the journey and shared them with each other, memories were unlocked of the searing wind, their children playing in the white ash falling from a clear sky, and the drenching rain that followed. With the memories came anger at what had been done to them, and confusion about the point of letting out this pain when they could do nothing to prevent their children dying of cancer. The next day, a mother spoke of her breaking heart, and how she felt this breaking connected her to everything, to everyone, as if they were all branches on the same tree. And a father, whose little daughter was in the hospital, told how hard it had been to feel the pain and speak it out. Now he felt clean for the first time in a long time.

Community-Building

From his experience of working with people in Sri Lanka affected by civil war and the 2004 tsunami, Daya Somasundaram concluded that collective trauma and social breakdown are best dealt with at the community level.[12] Relief, reconstruction and development work all need to include the psychological dimension rather than it being another separate program. The main aim of this integrated approach is to strengthen and rebuild families and village social structures, and to help the survivors find a shared meaning for their suffering. To this end, it is important to empower the community to look after itself. Rather than providing outside aid, the community should be encouraged and supported to re-establish community processes, organizations, traditions, rituals and relationships.

One way to do this is through leadership development—a challenging process in Sri Lanka when potential leaders were being intimidated or killed. Nevertheless, Somasundaram describes a program in which a trainer carefully selected a core group of 15-20 men and women from amongst teachers, university students, farmers and other villagers. He or she then worked with them to develop skills in identifying and solving problems, raising community awareness and mobilization, running children's activities, forming support groups, and so on. The trainer then withdrew, apart from follow-up monitoring and evaluation, and providing back-up if difficulties arose.

In addition, grassroots community workers were trained in basic mental health knowledge and skills, and given a manual on the mental health of refugees that had been adapted for the local culture. Amongst the trainees were primary health care workers, teachers, village leaders, traditional healers, priests, monks and nuns as well as staff from government bodies, and non-government organizations. These workers raised awareness of trauma, carried out preventive and promotional work, and referred more severe cases for specialist treatment. Self-help groups were also formed within communities for specific categories of victim, such as widows, survivors of torture, and landmine casualties.[13] Each group was encouraged to share their stories and provide mutual support leading to practical action. Similarly, extended families were supported to reunite and stay together, to re-establish traditional roles, and seek ways to generate an income.

Forgiveness, Reconciliation and Justice

In the last chapter, we illustrated the importance of forgiveness to individual healing with Aba Gayle's story. Forgiveness, reconciliation and justice are equally important in collective healing. Communities and nations that have been in conflict will be unable to live in lasting harmony as long as feelings of distrust, hatred and the desire for revenge continue to exist. It is a common experience that these feelings fade when trauma is healed, and it is then possible to move naturally towards forgiveness and reconciliation. This does not mean that the actions of the perpetrators are condoned or their accountability is lessened in any way. Rather, the power of the past to blight the future is diminished. Amongst other things, healing must deal with issues of responsibility and accountability for what happened, and bridge the gulf of distrust that conflict and trauma open up. Some reconciliation processes work with small groups at the community level, and others at the national or international level.

During the war in the former Yugoslavia, both Serbs and Croats committed atrocities. This left a deep legacy of distrust, discrimination and suspicion between ethnic groups that impeded reconstruction. Arlene Audergon and her colleagues used Process Work in small multi-ethnic groups to break through these barriers, and "to repair the fabric of society, thread by thread."[14] Process Work is based on the assumption that the group itself contains all the resources it needs to transform its past. The facilitators contribute a sense of hope and confidence that it is possible to go into the heat of the fire with awareness, and come out the other side transformed. They help the group to open up, expose their fears, and reveal their polarized positions. They help them to stay with the hot issues rather than avoiding or falling into them; to assemble the story of what happened; and to find a creative way forward, rather than replaying the conflict and trauma.

Audergon recalls how extraordinary transformations took place when people spoke of their personal and group roles in the horrific events. Resolution occurred when people shared their inner conflicts; their questions and doubts; their ethical dilemmas and struggles; their guilt about not doing enough to stop the atrocities; and the terrible choices they were forced to make that affected their families and friends as well as themselves. Audergon expresses amazement that such intimate sharing was possible amongst a mixed group of Serbs, Croats, and Muslims. "The highly tense and explosive atmosphere of suspicion and judgment, and fear of re-triggering old wounds, and tripping on volatile issues transformed into a sense of deep concern and respect for one another and all they had gone through ..."

Peter Levine and Eldbjorg Wedaa have developed a beautiful approach to breaking through distrust that makes use of the natural bonding between healthy babies.[15] They bring a group of mothers and infants together from opposing sides who start by teaching each other folk songs from their cultures while the facilitators enhance the rhythm with simple instruments. Holding and rocking their babies, the mothers sing and dance. The movements, rhythms and singing produce peaceful alertness, and soothe the mothers' hostilities. Meanwhile, the babies become entranced, and, when given a rattle, will often join in generating the rhythm with squeals of glee. Seeing their babies' delight, the mothers start to feel more secure and happy. Putting them on the floor, they allow their infants to explore. The barriers of shyness melt away as the babies contact each other, and the mothers form a supportive circle around them. Later, the group divides into fours, each group having a mother from each side with their babies. As they gently swing the infants between them in a blanket, the babies become 'blissed out', filling the room with a love that infects the mothers. At last they begin to smile at each other and enjoy bonding with the people they had feared earlier. Levine and Wedaa then teach some of the most sensitive mothers to become facilitators.

At the national level, the drive for reconciliation has taken two forms. One is exemplified by the South African Truth and Reconciliation Commission which sought to uncover the truth and encourage reconciliation rather than to punish perpetrators. It offered an amnesty for politically-motivated crimes if there was full disclosure, thus encouraging people to come forward and fill the gaps in knowledge. By bringing the whole story into the public arena, they hoped to impart a sense of justice, thus facilitating reconciliation and enabling the community to move forward. So successful was this model that it has now been used in at least 16 other countries. It demonstrates that punishment is not an essential prerequisite for reconciliation and collective healing to occur.[16]

The second approach is through international tribunals such as those set up by the UN for Yugoslavia and Rwanda. While they see their work as helping communities come to terms with their recent history, their aim is judicial. By holding individuals accountable and bringing war criminals to justice, they hope to deter future leaders from committing similar actions, to prevent whole groups being stigmatized by the actions of a few, and to aid the process of reconciliation.[17]

Worldview

Every culture is based on a set of fundamental beliefs and assumptions about the nature of reality. These constitute its worldview, and determine how that culture perceives and experiences the world and life. In a very real sense, our worldview actually creates our reality by determining how we interpret and understand the world we sense around us. It also legitimates and justifies cultural institutions, social structures and norms of behavior. Today, the emerging global civilization rests on worldviews that evolved out of, and are rooted in, our dominator history. As such, they perpetuate trauma and block the path to a partnership culture. We must let go of these outdated and outworn beliefs before we will be able to resolve the crisis of civilization. We must embrace the new worldview that is struggling to be born, and that facilitates healing and the evolution of a partnership society.

Today, the world is divided between two major categories of worldview. On the one hand, is the scientific, rational perspective. It is secular and materialist, and rejects the reality of non-material phenomena. For instance, consciousness is seen as a mere by-product of the workings of the brain, and most scientists vehemently reject the possibility of paranormal phenomena. On the other hand, western cultures are steeped in religious traditions dating back to Old Testament beliefs in a male creator God who is angry, judgmental and punitive. Both science and the Judaic religions (Judaism, Christianity and Islam) tend towards dogmatic belief in their version of the Truth, thus bringing them into conflict. Even democratic countries still view hierarchies of status, wealth and power as the natural order of things. Our culture also views evolution and social progress through the lenses of individualism and brutal competition. As a result of these unacknowledged biases, the world is riven by conflict and exploitation. To facilitate healing of the collective trauma of modern civilization, and to move towards partnership, we need a worldview that integrates consciousness and the spiritual realm with the material realm into a coherent whole. We need a worldview based on the principles of love, compassion, justice, equity, freedom, cooperation, peace, harmony and similar qualities. And we need a more open attitude to truth that accepts the limitations of what we can know.

This is not the place for a detailed discussion of what is wrong with our worldview, or what might replace it. If you would like to explore the issue further, you might like to read Malcolm Hollick's earlier book, *The Science of Oneness: A worldview for the twenty-first century.*[18]

Reflection

Genocide, wars, terrorism, revolutions and riots reveal the price we will continue to pay if we do not break out of the trauma cycle. In the words of Peter Levine: "Untraumatized humans prefer to live in harmony if they can. Yet traumatic residue creates a belief that we are unable to surmount our hostility, and that misunderstandings will always keep us apart. ... We must be passionate in our search for effective avenues of resolution. The survival of our species may depend on it."[19] It is vital that we, as families, communities and societies, create safe times, places and processes in which individual, collective and generational traumatic experiences can be expressed and heard. Only in this way can the victims fulfill their duty to society to bear witness to events from which we must learn, and that must never be allowed to happen again. All too often we keep silent, and deny what happened in our desire to forget and rebuild their lives. This is a mistake.[20]

28. Meeting the Overwhelming Need

If our argument in this book is correct, then the world must take urgent, effective action towards healing billions of people. But the current capacity to provide therapy for those in need is already overwhelmed, even in rich nations. Only one-fifth of the tens of millions suffering depression and anxiety each year in the USA receive professional help today. Keith Oatley and his co-authors concluded that, even using group therapies, there are simply not enough resources to go around.[1] When undiagnosed, sub-clinical needs, and the plight of heavily traumatized people in poor countries are included, it is clear that far more needs to be done. Governments should take the lead by massively expanding financial support for therapy students and training organizations for a wide range of effective mainstream and alternative therapies. Similarly, health insurance funds and government health systems should include trauma therapy amongst approved treatments as part of a strategy to improve well-being.

However, simply expanding existing services will not solve the global problem. They require too many human resources, and take too long to work. Attempting to meet the challenge in this way would bankrupt the economy without resolving the problem within the foreseeable future. A radically different but complementary approach is also called for which can heal large numbers of people with limited input of human resources, and low per capita costs. A few possibilities are described in this chapter.

The Pros and Cons of Drugs

In this age of genetics, molecular biology and neuroscience, it is natural to look to drugs for the answer to the epidemic of trauma. If only the pharmaceutical industry could come up with a pill that gives us resilience to face life's challenges, commits the traumas of the past to oblivion, and brings us happiness no matter what our circumstances—and all without side-effects!

The current and potential role of drug therapy is highly controversial. At one extreme are psychiatrists who still rely heavily on treating specific symptoms with cocktails of drugs. Together with the pharmaceutical industry, they are optimistic about the potential. At the other extreme are experienced psychotherapists who are scathing about the value of drug therapy. In between are many practitioners who see a valuable, but limited, role for drugs.

Unfortunately, despite progress, it is not clear that drugs will be able to play a major role in either prevention or healing of trauma in the foreseeable future. Nevertheless, there is little doubt that drugs can help many trauma victims in the short term. They can calm hyper-arousal, reduce anxiety, and help them sleep. Children with PTSD, for example, have difficulties with relationships and school performance as a result of hyper-arousal. This leads to low self-esteem and inappropriate behaviors which are hard to treat as long as the child is anxious, impulsive, and unable to concentrate. In these circumstances, Bruce Perry argues, medication to 'contain' the symptoms can enable other therapies to tackle the problems of self-esteem, competence, social skills and mastery of fears.[2] Similarly, Peter Levine advocates judicious short-term use of drugs to buy time by stabilizing severely traumatized individuals.[3]

Problems arise when drugs are used as a long-term solution rather than as a short-term complement to other healing modalities. Used in this way, many drugs permanently suppress the symptoms of fear, anxiety and anger which remain trapped in the body. Further, according to Levine, both legal and illegal drugs can prevent the shaking and trembling that is an essential part of the healing process. Drugs are also a blunt instrument that may dampen positive emotions such as joy and pleasure as well the negative ones. As Candace Pert makes clear, the way neurochemicals work in the body means that all drugs will have unwanted side effects.[4] Thus, drugs may enable the sufferer to function in a minimal way, but do not facilitate achievement of their potential.

Knowledge of neurochemistry is advancing rapidly, and there remains the hope that drugs will have genuinely healing effects in future. In 2006, the Royal Society of Chemistry reported that the body's own stress hormone, corticosterone, had potential as a treatment for PTSD if administered soon after the traumatic experience.[5] Based on studies of mice, they argued that high levels of corticosterone stimulated the brain to make a new memory that lacked the traumatic experience. If similar results occurred in humans, it might be possible to develop a therapy in which a flashback to the trauma was stimulated, followed by extinction of the memory. A few years later, New Scientist reported that the common blood pressure drug, propanolol, could increase resilience to a traumatic event.[6] Other recent studies of soldiers under extreme stress have shown that those who perform best actually have the highest levels of stress hormones. Their edge comes from also having unusually high levels of the stress-lowering chemicals DHEA and NPY which reduce the mental confusion caused by stress. NPY also reduces dissociation under extreme stress, and hence may provide some protection against PTSD.[7]

These and many other research findings point towards more subtle and effective drugs in future that may help heal trauma rather than simply control its symptoms. What is needed is a drug that facilitates release of the trapped energy and associated emotions, thus enabling the traumatic events to be relived, renegotiated and healed at a manageable pace. However, all drugs have side-effects, and long-term treatment regimes should be avoided.

Self-Help Therapy

Does self-help therapy work? Can we learn to heal ourselves, either individually or in groups, or do we need the help of a trained therapist? There is no definitive answer to these questions. A good therapist is always beneficial, but this does not necessarily mean that we cannot make progress without one. Psychotherapist Babette Rothschild does not address this question directly, but she argues that trauma therapy must be highly directive. As noted earlier, she believes that following the client's lead without intervention results either in avoidance of the trauma or overwhelm by it. This strongly implies that self-help therapy is a waste of time.[8] Shamanic healer Sandra Ingerman says that self-healing sometimes works, but that the shaman is often needed to do things that the client cannot. She does not recommend doing your own soul retrieval without careful training as it can be dangerous, but she does provide exercises to prepare for the soul's return.[9] Peter Levine has greater faith in our ability to retrieve our own soul parts and reintegrate them into our core selves. He believes we can succeed if we have a strong desire to be whole, and supportive friends and family.[10]

In contrast to these cautious views is a growing number of therapists who believe in self-healing. While they continue to argue the benefits of having a good therapist, they are willing to train people in DIY methods, and often distribute basic techniques free of charge on the web or in other media. Examples include Eugene Gendlin's *Focusing* technique, Peter Levine's *Healing Trauma Program*, Gary Craig's *Emotional Freedom Technique* (EFT), William Bloom's *Endorphin Effect*, and Byron Katie's *The Work*, to name just a few.[11] All these can be done individually, and some of them can be used in mutual support groups. Similarly, in many countries there is a wide range of mutual support groups for specific problems, such as alcoholics and incest survivors.

Apart from these and other established self-healing techniques, there are many other things that we can do to help ourselves. They are sufficient to fill a book on their own and a few examples will have to suffice here.

- Physical exercise can relieve anxiety and depression, and induce a flow of 'feel-good' hormones.[12] Non-competitive activities are best, such as mountaineering, rock climbing, sailing, running, cycling, swimming, yoga, tai chi, and gardening. Competitive sports are not so good because they encourage the stress of aiming for the top.
- Loving relationships help to build self-esteem and support us through potentially traumatic experiences. They have a powerful effect on our emotions and health. The quality of our relationships can be improved in many ways, including by learning non-violent communication.[13]
- Biofeedback, or even simple focused breathing exercises, can improve cardiac coherence, and the balance between the flight or fight and relaxation responses of the nervous system.[14]
- Appropriate hobbies and computer games can bring relief from the stress of life, reducing arousal and interminable mental discussions.
- Both creative and expressive arts can induce healing through the expression of buried emotions and memories. They have given birth to a variety of therapies, but can also be practiced in private.
  - Words have power as we know from songs, poems, prayers, charms and spells. Expressive writing about traumatic experiences and life stress has been shown to boost the immune system, reduce sickness, and improve mood, memory, asthma and arthritis.[15]
  - Painting, pottery, sculpture, textiles and other visual arts have long been recognized as therapeutic, and Art Therapy is a well-established approach. The emotional brain is highly tuned to symbolism, and potent

memories surface in the art.

- Music and dance are similarly powerful, often evoking emotional release through the physical vibrations of music, and/or rhythmic movement of the body. Examples of their use for healing include Toning, Gabrielle Roth's 5 Rhythms, and Biodanza.[16]
- Drama is also a recognized therapeutic approach that enables people to explore difficult and painful issues indirectly.[17]
- One of the most powerful healing activities is to spend time connecting with nature. This can take many forms. Walking in the countryside, or, even better, in wild areas. Scuba-diving in the ocean. Gardening and growing food. Watching wild birds and animals. Eco-tourism vacations. Interacting with pets, or working with animals in a caring environment. Even a bonsai tree and a goldfish in your apartment.

E-Therapy

'E-therapy' is developing rapidly as a means of mass healing with the potential to reach millions for a few cents per head. In this approach, clients interact with computer programs online, with varying amounts of human support. Most such programs are based on Cognitive Behavior Therapy (CBT) which encourages people to change their emotions and behavior by changing the way they think. The software can deal not only with physical health issues such as managing diabetes or quitting smoking, but also with a widening range of mental health problems.

Typically, new users are asked to complete a questionnaire. On the basis of the responses, the software may accept the person, decide they are unlikely to benefit, or refer them to a doctor for face-to-face emergency care. Those accepted as clients work through a series of tailored educational modules and exercises. These are spaced out over weeks or months so that they have time to digest the material and act on what they learn. Along the way, they complete evaluation forms and receive personalized feedback and instructions. Sometimes, online support groups, and email or phone contact with a live therapist are available.

A wide range of problems related to trauma are already being tackled. In late 2008, MoodGym was being used by over 250,000 depressed people from more than 200 countries. At the time of writing, the UK had formally approved FearFighter for treating panic and phobia, and Beating the Blues for mild to moderate depression. Still under development was a diagnostic program for mental disorders called E-couch which, for example, can identify depression and offer a choice of five different therapies.

Until recently it was assumed that clients with more complicated disorders such as PTSD, or panic with agoraphobia would need extensive contact with a human therapist. However, research suggests that this may not be the case. One study compared clients with panic disorder, with or without agoraphobia. They were treated using CBT either by a therapist or a program called Panic Online which includes regular email contact with a therapist. The results showed Panic Online to be just as effective as a human therapist, and one email a week was as good as many. Research is also investigating the use of a program to treat bipolar disorder. This is more challenging as clients are not always in touch with reality.[18] Clearly, there is great potential for software to handle at least the pathological level of trauma symptoms.

Another approach makes use of computer games. Research has shown that playing Tetris soon after a traumatic experience can reduce the incidence of flashbacks, even though narrative memory of the event is unimpaired. It seems that occupying the brain's capacity to process images may temporarily prevent it from laying down permanent visual memories. Following the report in New Scientist magazine, a reader with PTS wrote to say that she played Tetris night and day for many months, and found that "it requires such extensive spatial and visual brainpower that it disengages my capacity for verbal thought and brings relief from anxiety and flashbacks—until such time as exhaustion overtakes me. Upon waking from my restless sleep, disturbed by nightmares born of terrible memories, I turn immediately to the Tetris I keep on my bedside table, which provides further relief until I pass out once again." This constitutes a distraction rather than healing, but might be useful as an alternative to drugs for damping trauma symptoms.[19]

Meditation and Religious Practice

Meditation already helps tens of millions of people around the world, and could help many more if its benefits were advertised, and training was made available through national health systems. Its appeal could be widened further if Christian and Islamic contemplative and spiritual practices were promoted more strongly alongside those from Buddhist and Hindu traditions. Meditation also can be used as a mass or collective healing technique. Many studies have shown that a group trained in Transcendental Meditation (TM) can significantly decrease crime, traffic accidents, violent deaths, terrorism and even warfare. It seems that just 1% of the population of a city or region practicing regularly may be effective. It is also claimed that far fewer are needed if the practitioners are highly trained and experienced.[20] However, most of this research has been done by members of the TM organization, and independent validation is needed.[21] Several other organizations also hold mass meditations for peace. For example, the World Peace Prayer Society uses teleconferencing to synchronize prayers in over 70 countries.[22] Many studies also show the benefits of healing prayer for the sick.[23]

Despite being published in reputable scientific journals, such studies often attract controversy. However, criticism frequently seems to arise from a belief that the results are impossible rather than because of methodological flaws in the research. This is a common problem with all investigations into the paranormal. Such criticism has raised the quality of the research, and resulted in standards of proof that are often higher than those for the effectiveness and safety of pharmaceutical drugs.[24] The potential of such methods is so great that they should not be dismissed lightly.

Other religious practices also have the potential to contribute strongly to healing. Faith healing is an obvious example. Even if its effectiveness is due to the placebo effect, it has a valuable contribution to make.[25] Another example is confession—a kind of story-telling in which bizarre, embarrassing, and shameful symptoms can be shared anonymously and confidentially. Like shamanic soul retrieval, exorcism of evil spirits may also help some people. Large numbers probably could benefit from rejuvenation of moribund religious and cultural rituals, or the conscious creation of meaningful new ones. As well as being designed to heal traumatic life events such as bereavement, sickness, and family breakdown, these could be used to strengthen resilience by celebrating life and joyful events, and giving thanks for what we have.

Reflection

Recent research is revealing another mechanism which may help to meet the need for healing. According to Nicholas Christakis and his team at Harvard Medical School, emotions and behavior patterns, including empathy, altruism, happiness and depression, are infectious, spreading through social networks like a disease.[26] The key to effective diffusion is to have a critical mass of interconnected people who influence one another. The effect extends not only to friends, but also to friends of friends. So anyone who is popular and well-connected has a disproportionate influence on those around them. If they enter therapy, or otherwise start a healing journey, many other people may benefit, or at least be encouraged to engage in healing themselves as well. And as others in their network heal, the originators will benefit too. Perhaps it will be possible to develop strategies that consciously exploit and enhance this effect through the burgeoning online social networks? This idea potentially opens up new areas of social responsibility, and new possibilities for social action.

29. Evolving a Partnership Civilization

Until we prevent and heal trauma, the dominator civilization will simply go on reproducing itself, albeit in different forms. But dealing with trauma is not enough. In order to create a sustainable future for humanity we must build a new culture based on partnership values and ways of life. However, as the history of reactions to The Fall demonstrates, there is a danger that even a concerted reform campaign will be suppressed by the power hierarchy. Rich and powerful individuals, institutions and corporations will not stand idly by while the structures of power and status from which they benefit are dismantled. They will use their power to control information, subvert democratic processes, restrict civil liberties, and obstruct economic equality. Table 22 gives a few examples of the defensive actions the powerful are already taking on a daily basis.

We cannot confront the dominator culture directly. This would invite defeat or co-option, and be playing by the rules of power, rather than replacing them—as so many revolutions throughout history have done. Instead, attacks by the power hierarchy must be avoided and resisted like a martial artist who does not seek a fight, but, if it comes, yields and uses the strength of her opponent against him. We must challenge the power hierarchy indirectly, aiming to undermine it by evolving and growing radically different social systems which are as inconspicuous as possible, and difficult to control or subvert.

One possible strategy is to develop cooperative networks of small, independent, egalitarian groups that communicate, share information, and cooperate with each other. Flexible and adaptable, with no structure to be destroyed or key leaders to be eliminated, such systems are resilient to external attack. They need no master plan or strategy that can be disrupted, but work through fluid processes driven by shared core values and goals.

Table 22: Actions in Defense of the Power Structure

Control of Information	Political Influence	Restriction of Civil Liberties and Economic Equality
Give limited, biased coverage and analysis of current events in the media, and use them to spread propaganda.	Make campaign donations to political parties and candidates.	Indulge in covert surveillance of private citizens.
Distract the people with sport, entertainment and consumerism (The ancient Roman strategy of bread and circuses.)	Heavily lobby government to support 'dominator' policies, and oppose 'partnership' ones.	Police suppression of legitimate citizen protests.
Promote popular culture (TV, film, video games, etc) that glorifies physical and emotional violence, and supports inequalities of gender, race and wealth.	Give gifts to key people.	Discredit leading opponents.
	Covertly rig elections at home and abroad.	Incite fear of terrorism to gain acceptance of 'security' systems.
	Promote arms races with competing hierarchies of power.	Support religious fundamentalism and intolerance.
Fund front organizations and 'scientific' journals that give false legitimacy to opponents of reforms, e.g. on climate change, or smoking.	Support violent, repressive regimes.	In many countries, promote police violence, disappearances, torture, detention without trial, and murder (or the threat of them.)
	Use military power to protect threatened interests, such as energy resources.	Support the growing gap between rich and poor within and between nations.

However, such systems are vulnerable to self-destruction due to internal conflicts and development of a new power hierarchy. This is the fate of most popular revolutions, which end by replacing one oppressive regime with another. To avoid this, the new system must be based on a worldview, values, norms, and social processes that encourage personal and collective healing, constrain ego, and prevent the re-emergence of hierarchical leadership. Members should also be committed to a path of healing.

Creating a Partnership Community

Most children growing up in our dominator society are traumatized to a greater or lesser degree by aggressive, controlling adults, and become either submissive or aggressive themselves. Thus, a self-perpetuating cycle of domination is established. The best hope of breaking this cycle is to create a sub-culture of assertive, self-confident, empowered individuals within non-hierarchical, cooperative, egalitarian social structures. Initially tiny, this sub-culture must be robust enough to resist domination by mainstream society, and to constrain the inevitable pressure from individuals within it for power, wealth and status. These internal constraints must be based on democratic processes, and not rely on a hierarchy of power. No individual, group or institution within the system should have *power over* others. Instead, all members should share *power with* others.

This may seem unrealistically utopian, but many hunter-gatherer and agricultural societies evolved social controls that worked through shared beliefs, values and norms of behavior supported by peer pressure. For example, some societies regarded anyone who sought power as unsuitable for leadership, and did not empower their leaders to make unilateral decisions for the whole group. Re-creating similar social structures is not easy, but it can be done as demonstrated by hundreds of intentional communities and ecovillages around the world. Most of these are small, like hunter-gatherer bands. Some, particularly religious ones, are ruled by the authority of their leaders, but most use consensus decision-making methods that encourage open disagreement and a search for creative alternatives.[1]

In its simplest form, consensus requires that every member of the group agree on every decision. Even in small groups, this can be frustratingly slow, and some actions may be blocked when an individual holds out against the majority. Overall, the outcome may reflect the least common denominator rather then the group's highest potential. As a result, many communities use modified consensus processes. One simple change is to require 'consensus minus 1', '90% majority', or a similar criterion. This prevents one person or a small minority from holding the community to ransom. A more sophisticated approach is to bar any individual or minority group from blocking action for personal reasons. In this system, anyone who votes against a proposal must do so in the interests of the whole community. They may be overruled if the group believes the reasons are personal, not collective. A similar approach is to ask opponents to form a 'loyal minority' which supports implementation of the majority decision unless they feel so strongly about the issue that they feel compelled to oppose it. In this way, discussion and the search for creative solutions becomes focused on the most controversial issues.[2]

A little closer to modern democratic governance is delegation of certain powers and responsibilities to individuals or committees, on condition that any decision can be overturned by a vote of, say, 10% of community members. Delegating overall community management in this way minimizes the time and energy taken by decision-making, and gives the management team a strong incentive to ensure that their decisions are in line with community wishes. Another approach used by some hunter-gatherer societies is known as heterarchy. In this case, members of the group share responsibility for decisions, and leadership changes fluidly so that the person best able to deal with the needs of the moment assumes the lead. This ad hoc, short-term delegation makes best use of available knowledge, skills and experience, and is an effective means of handling complex situations. Consensus and heterarchy work well if there is unity of purpose, backed by the commitment of all members to the stability of the group. There also must be shared values of non-violence and cooperation, combined with an atmosphere of trust, mutual respect, patience and individual empowerment. These are all solid partnership virtues.

In reality, such groups are not without leaders, who ideally practice what John Heider called Taoist leadership.[3] Compared to leaders of hierarchical systems, Taoist leaders seem passive and inactive. They do not push to have their ideas implemented, nor use coercion. Instead, they lead by example, and facilitate and guide what is emerging from the group. They have influence, but allow the group to manage itself, and the process to unfold as it will. The Taoist leader is humble but confident, with a strength that comes from inner silence and reflection. She has no need to impress others, nor to appear to know everything, nor to control what happens. Her power comes from willing cooperation by her 'followers'. She is happy to stay in the background, allowing others to take the credit, and letting the group claim to have done it themselves. She offers opportunities rather than obligations. She seeks to serve rather than to control, and to facilitate the success of others rather than to succeed herself. Because her actions go unnoticed, they stir no conflict, and there is no resistance or resentment. Hence, energy can be used creatively instead of in fighting each other.

An example of a Taoist approach to leadership comes from the Findhorn Community in Scotland. This loosely-knit community of about 350 people is facilitated by two Listener-Conveners, one male and one female.[4] The function of these elected, paid positions is to listen, be attuned to what is happening in the community, and to bring together appropriate people to deal with issues that arise. They have no formal power—not even votes on the Community Council which they chair—but if they do their job well they unobtrusively enable the community to move forward.

Taoist leaders can be trained, and appropriate qualities tend to emerge naturally as individuals and groups heal. Patterns of dominance and submission weaken, and self-confidence, self-esteem, courage, resilience, empathy, compassion, service and other qualities come to the fore. People start to work together with less ego and less need for personal power. They gain strength to resist the structures of power non-violently, and their fear of being criticized, judged or imprisoned wanes. They also become less likely to cause trauma to others through their actions.

This brief discussion of leadership and decision-making gives a taste of what is involved in creating partnership communities. Many other skills and processes are also needed including conflict management and resolution processes; communication skills, both within and between groups; rituals, ceremonies, and celebrations for group bonding and discharging trauma; and skills in facilitating meetings such as active listening, non-violent communication, the use of silent reflection, and group attunement processes. There is a great need for more training opportunities in these fields. If you would like to delve deeper, some starting points are given in the Note.[5]

Building a Partnership Society

Strengthening and expanding the existing cooperative network of intentional communities and ecovillages is a vital step. It will provide diverse working models of partnership social structures, demonstrate cooperative ways of life, and increase resilience to pressure from the dominator system. But the ultimate aim is to facilitate the evolution of larger partnership societies that gradually replace the existing dominator ones. This will require reform of many existing laws and institutions so that mainstream society can converge with the growing grassroots initiatives. Hence, there is a continuing need for political action in the tradition of the Second Wave of reaction to The Fall.

This need is well illustrated by the practical difficulties of establishing alternative communities in developed nations within the existing framework of laws and regulations for urban and regional planning, building standards, health and safety and other matters. These are designed for mainstream, single-family residences and settlements, fully equipped with modern utilities and conveniences. As a result, they often make it difficult, if not impossible, to build dwellings designed to be shared coopera-tively by a group of individuals or families, and that are constructed from alternative but proven self-build materials such as cob or straw bales, and that incorporate green technologies such as composting toilets. This means that a significant task in creating grassroots partnership communities is to campaign for more flexible land use and building regulations.

Since she identified the patterns of partnership and domination in her classic book, *The Chalice and the Blade*, Riane Eisler has devoted her life to promoting a shift towards partnership. In *The Power of Partnership*, she defined "four corner-stones of the partnership political agenda" which provide a broad manifesto for reform. In her later book, *The Real Wealth of Nations*, she elaborated the requirements for a sustainable, caring economy. The Political Agenda outlined in Table 23 is based on Eisler's work, with the addition of community-building and some other items. This agenda is most applicable to the USA and other rich western nations, but also to the global community of nations to varying degrees.

Towards a Global Village
In order to create a viable future for humanity, we must go

Table 23: A Partnership Political Agenda
(Adapted from Riane Eisler (2002, 2007) and other sources)

CHILDREN FIRST

Today's children — tomorrow's citizens — must understand, experience, and value partnership.

Support campaigns to stop maltreatment of children, and promote partnership parenting. Teach children how to relate with empathy, compassion and love; without violence or domination. Work to end child poverty and to provide good nutrition and healthcare for all children.

Campaign for school curricula that are:

- Child-centered, multicultural, environmentally conscious, and gender-balanced;
- Help develop respect and care for self, others, and our natural environment; and
- Raise awareness of trauma, and develop self-help skills in dealing with potentially traumatic events.

Demand high quality childcare, with appropriate training, status, and remuneration for caregivers, whether women or men.

COMMUNITY BUILDING

Strengthen existing communities, and re-build community where it has been destroyed.

Encourage re-establishment of cooperative, mutually supportive communities, and community enterprises where they no longer exist.

Support the employment of community facilitators and organizers.

Campaign for local communities to be re-empowered to manage more aspects of their local environment, resources, social relationships and finances.

Encourage local businesses and employers to support the communities in which they are located.

Campaign for more flexible land use and building regulations to facilitate evolution of alternative communities.

EQUALITY

Develop family, social, economic, and political systems that are based on equal partnerships

Continued on next page

Table 23 continued

between male and female, and diverse racial, ethnic and religious groups.

Work to change cultural beliefs that males are entitled to control females in families and societies. Discourage the attitude that some activities are for men, and some for women; encourage equal status and value for all activities.

Work to disconnect the image of masculinity from domination and violence, and femininity from subordination and obedience.

Campaign locally, nationally, and internationally to stop violence against girls and women, and against minority racial, religious and ethnic groups.

Develop school curricula that value equally male and female, and diverse colors, cultures and systems of belief.

Campaign for balanced representation of men, women and diverse racial, ethnic and religious groups in policy-making positions, and introduction of more caring and empathic policies.

ECONOMICS

Develop economic systems that encourage empathy, creativity and sustainability, and value caring for self, others, and nature.

Campaign to reduce the influence of wealth on political processes, and encourage policy-makers to focus more on equity, sustainability and care.

Campaign for socially and environmentally responsible businesses.

Campaign for the use of economic indicators that focus less on productivity and more on quality of life, the needs of the poor, environmental quality, and the value of domestic and caregiving activities.

Support

Support development of an economic system that:

- Recognizes the vital contributions made by households, communities and nature;
- Is participatory and equitable;
- Invests in human capital;
- Promotes human development, equity, empathy, creativity and concern for the future and nature;

Continued on next page

Table 23 continued

- Values the work of caring for self, others, and nature, whether in the workplace, society, or at home.

BELIEFS, MYTHS AND STORIES

Create and strengthen beliefs, myths and stories that promote partnership and discard those that do not.

Support cultural traditions that encourage partnership, and work to reject those that promote domination.

Campaign to break up media monopolies and change media policies and management so that the diverse voices of partnership are heard.

Teach young people to understand the consequences of domination and the benefits of partnership, and to recognize beliefs, myths, and stories that promote one or the other.

Work to bring partnership values and perspectives into religious organizations, and to help them discard domination morality.

Nurture the spiritual courage that will sustain us on the journey to make partnership a reality for our children and generations to come.

beyond the community and nation state to consider relationships at the international and global levels as well. Dominator civilizations arose and flourished when the Earth seemed boundless, and there was no limit to imperial expansion. For most of history, war was an accepted way of boosting the Ruler's ego, distracting attention from domestic problems, and obtaining desired resources including land, slaves and soldiers. But today we are becoming acutely aware of the smallness of our planet, our interdependence, and our common humanity.

Natural resource extraction, manufacturing, knowledge and technology are now so global in scope that no nation could dominate the world through force of arms as the axis powers sought to do in World War II. Even the power of the US military is based on minerals from around the world, and electronic chips manufactured in Asia. Its actions are thus ultimately constrained by the tacit support of China and other nations. Similarly, even if China wished to conquer the world militarily, it could not wage war for long if imports of natural resources from far-flung countries were cut off. However, it has no need for conquest, having gained dominance through economic and financial power as the factory of the world.

We are learning that the security of rich nations no longer rests on territorial defense or armed conquest. It is more about limiting the spread of weapons of mass destruction, containing terrorist movements that have global reach, and ensuring supplies of key resources. We are beginning to realize that these objectives are best pursued through non-military means, including diplomacy, international law and institutions, trade ties, economic justice, and cooperation on common problems. Similarly, with the exception of hot spots like the Middle East, the massive purchases of arms by poorer nations are often more about image and internal affairs than realistic fears of invasion. Increasingly, armed conflicts stem from racial and ethnic hatreds, reactions to humiliation or deprivation, and efforts to suppress internal dissent by force. We are slowly moving towards a world in which national military defense is being replaced by conflict resolution, policing and law-enforcement by UN peacekeepers supported by an international legal system.

Meanwhile, it is becoming more difficult to unite national populations against foreign 'enemies' as travel, communications technologies, the internet, and shared concerns unite disparate peoples in their common humanity, and in campaigns to limit climate change, halt environmental destruction, curb the excesses of large corporations, end poverty and disease, and eliminate tyranny and torture. The realization is slowly dawning that true security will be gained only when equity, justice, dignity, human rights, and related issues are given high priority—in other words when we move towards a global partnership civilization.

Perhaps the greatest threats to peace and security in the long term are the perception of resource scarcity, and the ruthless exploitation of the weak, the poor, and the Earth. In an overcrowded world, we see ourselves as being in competition for depleting resources of land, fresh water, air, fisheries, fossil fuels, minerals and other resources. But as these get scarcer, our scientific knowledge and technological know-how are opening a cornucopia of new possibilities. Knowledge is a potentially infinite resource that is not depleted by use. Indeed, it grows all the faster when it is shared, and we are moving rapidly towards a world in which knowledge is free to those with an internet connection.[6] We are not so much in competition with each other as in a race between depleting physical resources, expanding knowledge, and the wisdom to use them both with justice, equity, and respect for all.

The goal of planetary partnership can be fostered by globalization. But it must be a globalization that brings unity and justice, not division, exploitation and domination as now. It must embrace the diversity of human culture, while being based on common core values, such as those enshrined in the UN Universal Declaration of Human Rights and the UN Convention on the Rights of the Child. It must be founded on the vision of a single global village rather than competing national interests, or corporate fiefdoms.[7] There can be no room in this village for winners and losers, in-groups and out-groups; for disrespect, disempowerment, exploitation or humiliation. We are all neighbors, members of the one human family, and must forge bonds of trust, equity, justice and dignity. This is far from reality today. Material and social inequalities breed frustration, resentment, humiliation and rage as Mustafa makes clear:[8]

We, the poor of the world hear that poverty is a humiliating violation of our human rights and dignity. We learn that we deserve enabling environments that empower us as human beings. We know how these enabling circumstances should look—access to clean water, health care, a flat, work, a refrigerator, a television set, and, one day, a car, vacation, and university studies for our children. All this is what our local elites and the people of the rich West have. Western tourists and soap operas are an ample source of information for us.

However, our reality, our poverty, gets worse. We are told that our humanity is debased, and then it is debased even more. This is perpetrated by the same people, those from the rich West, who say that they stand for human rights. In our eyes the West is worse than the worst hypocrite. This is the ultimate betrayal.

Each one of us can take action in our daily lives to promote the culture of a global village. In addition to the national political agenda of Table 23, we can:

- Cultivate a self-image as a citizen of Earth first and foremost.
- Cultivate international contacts and friendships through culturally sensitive tourism, social networking on the internet, and other avenues.
- Support justice and the reduction of poverty by buying fair trade products.
- Support a few of the hundreds of non-government organizations campaigning for change on a wide range of issues. Amongst the best-known are Save the Children, Amnesty International (human rights and justice), Friends of the Earth (environment), Oxfam (poverty and development), the World Peace Campaign, and Avaaz (key issues of the moment).

Reflection

The needs are so huge that it is easy to become discouraged. The actions of one person are but a drop in the ocean of need. But multiplied by millions, the effects can be dramatic in the long term, as Margaret Mead knew well when she wrote: "Don't think that a small group of awakened individuals cannot change the world. Indeed, it is the only thing that ever has."[9]

Our first responsibility to ourselves, our families and community, and to humanity, is to heal ourselves of whatever traumas we may be carrying. Every person who embarks on this journey represents a step forward for humanity. We can encourage our partners, families and friends to join us, and work to heal our relationships with them. Beyond that inner circle, we can treat every person with whom we come in contact, including dominators, with respect, warmth and dignity as a reflection of Cosmic Consciousness, or the Divine. And we can treat the Earth with the care our home deserves. If everyone did the same, humanity and the planet would be healed.

Closure to Part VI

Preventing potentially traumatic events and increasing resilience are almost certainly more cost-effective than individual or collective healing of trauma victims. And, despite the cost of therapy, healing is likely to be more cost-effective in the long term than dealing with the consequences of trauma. Investment in quality day-care for infants, family services, income support for poor families, parenting training, and better schools will pay many dividends. Reduced crime and delinquency will save policing and legal costs, to say nothing of the need for fewer jails. Improved physical and mental health and reduced domestic violence will save money on police, the war on drugs, medical doctors, therapists and hospitals, as well as improving workplace productivity and reducing the bill for social security payments. Fewer family breakdowns will save housing and infrastructure costs as well as cutting the bill for divorce. In the longer term, as trauma is reduced and partnership societies grow, the fear of 'enemies' and the threat of violent conflict will decline, producing huge savings in defense expenditure. Investment in trauma reduction is clearly justified on non-economic grounds, too. It will increase happiness, educational achievement, creativity, health, and longevity to name but a few benefits. And so the ripples will continue to spread outward as the world transforms.

Having said that, there are clear opportunities for improving the cost-effectiveness of actions to reduce trauma. Possibilities already exist for making more use of low-cost healing methods, ranging from self-help to e-therapy. And what little research has been done is pointing the way to more effective ways of minimizing child maltreatment. As the need is acknowledged and more attention is focused on it, there will undoubtedly be an upsurge in creative ways to reduce the incidence of traumatic events and boost resilience as well as to heal existing trauma.

If we want to see a more peaceful, harmonious, sustainable world, we cannot wait for 'them' to do something. Our responsibilities are clear. We must each commit to healing our own traumas—to ridding ourselves of our destructive anger, aggression and violent tendencies, and of our debilitating fears, anxieties, depression and withdrawal. We must each commit ourselves to improving our relationships with family, friends, and others, and to contributing in whatever ways we can to local, national and international reform. For 108 simple ways to contribute, from personal tools to global action, see Louise Diamond's *The Peace Book*.[1]

Part VII. Epilogue

Reprise

Our global civilization is in trouble. Our values, high ideals and achievements are being corroded from within by greed and corruption, addiction, mental illness, family breakdown, domestic violence, child abuse, crime, poverty, exploitation, fundamentalism, and more. Further, its sustainability is being challenged from without by terrorism, and the finiteness of the planet as reflected in resource depletion, the destruction of nature, and climate change. Normally, these are tackled as largely independent problems. But we have argued that they are underlain by a common cause.

There is a malaise of the human spirit that is undermining our intelligence, creativity and mental health. It prevents us from taking new directions, and blocks wise action to resolve humanity's multiple crises. We do not believe this is due to a fundamental flaw in human nature or our genes—a view that is supported by studies of apes and other mammals, of prehistoric societies, and of contemporary indigenous cultures. It is also supported by the growing understanding of our biochemical, genetic and neurological make-up. Some individuals and societies are violent, aggressive, and competitive; others are gentle, peaceful and cooperative. The human species embodies the potential to be saints or remorseless killers. Where each one of us ends up on this spectrum depends more on what we learn through our experiences, and on the experiences of our parents, grandparents and society, than it does on our genetic heritage. In particular, it depends on our exposure to traumatic events.

Trauma today is widespread in every segment of society. Few if any humans remain untraumatized. We are slowly becoming aware of the massive impact this has on our mental, emotional and physical development and health, on our relationships and patterns of behavior, and on the structure and operation of our society. By affecting our values, perceptions, emotions and thoughts, trauma hinders progress on major issues such as peace, environmental conservation, the elimination of poverty, and the achievement of justice. Preventing and healing trauma would not cure all our problems, but it would go a long way to resolving the crisis of civilization.

One of the strongest strands of evidence for our potential to be different comes from prehistory. In the mythical Golden Age of hunting and gathering, and even in the agricultural era, our forebears seem to have led largely peaceful, egalitarian, cooperative lives. But with the rise of so-called civilizations after The Fall, this partnership culture gave way to domination by the most aggressive, violent and competitive individuals and societies. Hierarchies of power, wealth and status emerged, and war became institutionalized. Many factors contributed to this transition, but the most significant trigger was probably the trauma of dramatic climate change, combined with the emergence of bitter conflict over dwindling resources. Once established, the dominator way of being became self-perpetuating, and the trauma was passed from generation to generation through cultural myths, upbringing, and the expression of our genes.

Trauma induces fear, anxiety, anger, depression and other negative emotional states. Our consciousness, whether as an individual or society, contracts around this terror or rage. We become stuck in old patterns of response to the world that may have been appropriate during a past traumatic event, but are inappropriate now. Unable to take a wide view or think creatively, we cannot change or move forward. Like a nervous dog, we become aggressive, snapping at strangers, fearful of anything new. We lock this terror and rage away behind layers of armor, together with painful memories and anything that might remind us of them. We distract ourselves from this hidden trauma with busyness, and preoccupation with consumerism, addictions, sex, entertainment, games, and so forth. The earlier in life we experience trauma, the more deeply these patterns become entrenched in our thoughts and emotions, as well as in the balance of our hormones, the expression of our genes, the structure of our brains and the form of our bodies. And the more entrenched they become, the harder it is to change. But healing is possible, as the success of many therapies demonstrates.

Growing awareness of the prevalence and impacts of trauma opens the way to effective action for change. Now that we understand its significance, it is possible to imagine whole nations implementing effective strategies to wind down trauma. There are at least four complementary strands to such a strategy. The primary aim must be to reduce the number and severity of potentially traumatic experiences, particularly in gestation, infancy, and childhood. There are many ways of doing this through better technologies and policies, education, parent training, and family support services. The second goal is to increase resilience to potentially traumatic events, again with a focus on the early years, through family support, good schools, training in emotional intelligence and self-help techniques, and so on. Third is to facilitate the discharge of the energy aroused by potentially traumatic events before it can harden into trauma. This can be done through aware relationships, counseling, and social rituals. Finally, many of those suffering from trauma can be healed, whether by a human therapist, self-help methods, e-therapy or some other means.

Reducing trauma would bring many benefits to both individuals and society as a whole. These include greater self-confidence, self-esteem, and vital energy; better intimate relationships; improved mental and physical health; and reduced crime, drug addiction, domestic violence and child abuse. In the longer term, these changes would lead to deeper social reform. Both submission to authority and the drive to dominate would weaken; the willingness and ability to cooperate would increase; aggression and violence would decline; gender and racial discrimination would fade; and the strength and courage to act non-violently against the structures of power and violence would grow. In other words, communities and civilization as a whole would move away from the dominator way of being towards partnership.

Those at the top of the pyramid of power, wealth and status will resist such reforms, and act to protect their privileged positions. There is thus a significant risk that the dominator culture will reassert itself, and the opportunity to create a new partnership civilization will be missed, as it was in the first and second waves of reaction to The Fall. That would be a tragedy for humanity and the Earth. Instead of moving forward to a culture based on interdependence, cooperation, non-violence, equality, democracy, compassion and love, we would remain stuck in individualism, competition, greed, addiction, aggression, violence, war, and centralized power. Instead of moving towards a cooperative relationship with our planetary home, we would continue to exploit and destroy it. Instead of cultivating higher spiritual values of empathy, love, compassion, service and wisdom, we would continue to worship cold rationality, economic exchange, and utility. What is needed is personal and collective awareness of the situation, and a commitment to healing and collective action for change.

One way to reduce the risk of the dominator culture reasserting itself is to subvert the power hierarchy by evolving alternative grassroots community structures that are based on partnership principles. But concentrating on such social reforms without working to heal trauma at the same time would be doomed to failure. Individuals and communities would continue to respond to unconscious emotional buttons triggered by past trauma. Hence, the world they created would still reflect their anger, frustration, aggression and desire for status. In order to create a partnership future, we must act from inner peace, love, and self-esteem.

Soul Healing

There are different levels of trauma healing. The most basic enables victims to function in daily life. This includes being able to hold a job, sustain an intimate relationship, and care for children without suffering violent rages, disabling flashbacks, anxiety or depression. Beyond this is existential healing in which the victim finds meaning in their suffering, and integrates it into their worldview and sense of personal identity. Success on these two levels represents a return to 'normal' human consciousness. But what we regard as normal consciousness is way below our potential. Indeed, Eckhart Tolle, amongst others, claims it is a form of insanity.[1]

We all have within us the seeds of higher forms of consciousness—ways of being that have been demonstrated by outstanding figures of history such as the Buddha, Jesus, Mahatma Gandhi, Martin Luther King Jr., Nelson Mandela, Mother Teresa and many more. As His Holiness the Dalai Lama has said: "the basic nature of human beings is gentle and compassionate. It is therefore in our own interest to encourage that nature, to make it live within us, to leave room for it to develop."[2] Louise Diamond points out that the words healing, holy and whole share the same linguistic root. Hence, "To heal is to remember who you really are—a child of the universe, divine, loving and inherently whole."[3] If we water these seeds, they will grow.

Another way of viewing the deeper levels of healing is as a process of integrating our fragmented being. The three parts of the triune brain operate quite differently to each other, 'thinking' with sensations, emotions and logic. Often these are in conflict, and need to be harmonized. For instance, we may crave alcohol despite the pain of a hangover, and be unable to resist the impulse. The brain also includes different kinds of memory—short and long term, implicit and explicit—that must be integrated into a coherent narrative of the past. Similarly, the subconscious and conscious minds must be coordinated, and parts of our consciousness that dissociate during traumatic events need to be reintegrated into the whole. Further, the many hormones, neurotransmitters and other biochemicals must be kept in balance, and the parallel chemical and neurological communication systems attuned to each other. And according to eastern philosophies, our energy centers, or chakras, must also be balanced. Ultimately, then, healing means integrating and balancing all our disparate systems, energies, and streams of consciousness into a coherent whole.

According to spiritual teacher and psychotherapist Jack Kornfield, our true nature is waiting to emerge whenever we let go of the contracted consciousness that results from trauma. "Gradually, we can cease to identify with these old patterns and allow for the creation of a healthier sense of self."[4] We can reclaim our abused or dissociated parts, our feelings, our unique perspective, the voice that says what is true for us. But this is not an easy task. On our spiritual journey, we often re-create the patterns that helped us survive the pain, trauma and dysfunction that we experienced in the past. We may claim to have renounced the world, while actually hiding from the challenges of life out of fear. We may get lost in spiritual visions just as we escaped from pain into fantasy as a child. Or we may seek spiritual purity as an extension of our pattern of being good to avoid blame. Our spiritual lives may mirror our childhood in many other ways, too, thus enabling us to avoid confronting the wounds that need healing.

Even after many years of deep work, many of us remain unaware of certain patterns, or are unable to heal particular wounds. Many of us are too damaged by early trauma to become completely whole, or to reach the highest levels of spiritual consciousness. We may remain blocked in some directions by our fears, anger, depression, or other negative responses to life. But we can all make progress. We can all relax certain contractions in our consciousness, and let go of some harmful patterns of emotion, thought and behavior. As we let go of our contracted identity, we can cultivate new qualities of kindness, patience, compassion, wisdom, integrity, and courage. That is all any of us can do. There is no ultimate level of healing, consciousness or enlightenment to attain, only a lifelong journey to take step by step towards the light.

To quote Jack Kornfield again:[5]

> Spiritual attainment is not the result of special esoteric knowledge, the study of great texts and sutras, and the systematic learning of great works of religion, nor is it found in the realm of control or power; it doesn't attach to things being a certain way; and it holds no blame. It involves neither the control over another person nor even control of ourselves. It stems rather from an abundant wisdom of heart. ... The wisdom of the heart ... arises not through knowledge or images of perfection or by comparison and judgment, but by seeing with the eyes of wisdom and the heart of loving attention, by touching with compassion all that exists in our world.
>
> The wisdom of the heart is here, just now, at any moment. It has always been here, and it is never too late to find it. The wholeness and freedom we seek is our own true nature, who we really are.

There are relatively few spiritual teachers who are equipped to facilitate the first two levels of healing. And there are relatively few therapists who are able to guide their clients on the spiritual journey beyond. Thus, as Jack Kornfield notes: "Many students come to meditation after a long course of therapy, seeking silence, depth of understanding, and freedom that they did not find there. Yet many meditation students discover the need for a healing in therapy and turn to it after years of meditation. It is our commitment to wholeness that matters, the willingness to unfold in every deep aspect of our being."[6]

Towards the Possible Human

Resolving the crisis of civilization requires nothing less than a transformation of the human spirit. We must transform ourselves or die as a civilization, perhaps as a species. We must become wise, responsible citizens of Gaia, or submit to her judgment. If we continue down the dominator path, the higher qualities and values that make us human will be whittled away, even if our biological descendants survive.

We have staved off the crisis for decades with cleverness, and technological and institutional fixes. We still urgently need creative new policies, laws, technologies, financial and political institutions, and economic structures. But these are no longer enough. No matter how clever we are, the future we create will inevitably mirror our beliefs, values, emotional patterns, and deep motivations. It will reflect the vision towards which we strive, and the intention with which we act. If we are motivated by dominator values and goals, our world will continue to be riven by violent conflict, competition, inequalities and environmental disasters.

Pragmatic reforms will not meet the needs of our time unless they are underpinned by new values and behaviors; by wisdom, love, compassion, forgiveness and other spiritual qualities. If we all lived and acted in accordance with these age-old values that are expressed in every great religious tradition, our problems would melt away. We would still experience challenging tensions between competing needs, desires and issues. And we would still experience climate change and other legacies of our past actions. But we would be able to handle them with greater wisdom, compassion and grace.

The vast majority of humanity wishes to live in both inner and outer peace and harmony. The potential to do so lies within each one of us, and yet most of us resist embarking on the journey of healing, spirituality and partnership. In our traumatized state, we prefer to keep our demons under lock and key, fearing the pain and repercussions of opening the prison doors. Whether consciously or unconsciously, we find ways to avoid the opportunities for healing. And yet the hope for humanity lies in each one of us grasping the nettle, and setting foot on the path.

In our own efforts to heal, we, the authors, are finding that the deep fears which lead us to resist healing work are often exaggerated and misplaced. When we persuade ourselves to engage, we often find that the emotional and physical pain are nowhere near as severe as we feared. And, as already mentioned, we are now working with healers who are learning to harness the power of the positive feelings that lie at the core of our being to heal trauma without the need to re-experience it.[7] In this way, healing can be joyful and peaceful, and, at worst, disturbing rather than terrifying. It is our hope that such approaches will blossom around the planet, helping us all to have the courage to heal.

Beyond the level of functional healing, the path branches into many ways ranging from mainstream religion to atheistic humanism, from New Age holism to ancient shamanism, from a life of devotional prayer and meditation to one of service. Whatever our path, if we set out with courage and determination, facing our fears and traumas, we will find ourselves transformed, sometimes suddenly but most often gradually. And as we transform, we will inevitably help to make the world a better place. It will never be perfect, but it will be better for the fact that we have lived. In *The Peace Book*, Louise Diamond put it this way:[8]

This is a choice each and every one of us must make in our own lives—in how we live our lives. Those of us choosing the path of unity and partnership are the pioneers of a new tomorrow. We are, literally, building a new world, even as the old one comes crumbling down around us.

Like any path, this peace road is carved by the actions of many hands; smoothed and widened by the passage of many feet. For humanity to move from a culture of violence to a culture of peace, those of us holding that intention must lead the way, with our thoughts, our words, and our actions ... now, more than ever.

As so many spiritual masters have proclaimed down the ages: Love is the answer. Love of ourselves. Love of our families. Love of our communities. Love of our society. Love of humanity. Love of the Earth and all living beings. Love made manifest in action, caring for each other physically, emotionally, mentally and spiritually. In the words of a beautiful friend, Celtic priestess and songwriter Phyllida Anam-Aire:

I am with you that I might heal
You are with me that you might heal
We are together that we might heal
We are healing that we might love

We are close to the edge of the cliff, but we are not doomed to fall. There is hope for humanity. That hope lies in each one of us, individually and collectively. Right now, that hope may appear to be no more than a tiny dried up seed. But it will swell and send out shoots and roots if we water it. In time it will blossom if we nourish it.

Hope is like the developing brain. If we do not use it and stimulate it, it will atrophy. We have suggested many ways in which hope can be put into action, and there are myriad more. Let's choose our paths and go with passion and creativity, with all our hearts and minds and souls. Then hope may blossom in us, our loved ones, our communities and around the Earth.

Appendix A: Post-Traumatic Stress Disorder

As the name implies, PTSD is classified as a psychiatric disorder by the American Psychiatric Association. The diagnostic criteria from the *Diagnostic and Statistical Manual of Mental Disorders* (commonly referred to as DSM-IV) are summarized below. Many people suffer post-traumatic stress (PTS) which is similar except that its symptoms may be less severe, and it heals itself within a month. Only about 20% of those suffering PTS develop full-blown PTSD.

The DSM-IV criteria have been criticized on several grounds. First, it has been argued that they turn the normal response to an intolerable experience into a psychiatric disorder. However, it seems reasonable to regard the natural healing of PTS within a month as the normal process, and on-going severe symptoms that disrupt the sufferer's life for years as abnormal. Nevertheless, the connotation of mental illness does cause some sufferers to feel stigmatized and avoid therapy.[1] Second, the criteria do not distinguish clearly between PTSD and other disorders. Research on severely depressed people, for example, showed that three-quarters of them had all the symptoms of PTSD whether or not they had actually suffered traumatic experiences.[2] Third, trauma may lead to a spectrum of effects ranging from anxiety, through depression, to full PTSD and psychosis with no clear division between normality and disorder.[3] Finally, the diagnosis focuses on cognitive symptoms, and neglects disruption to social and spiritual life, as well as common emotional reactions such as intense rage and a desire for revenge, a sense of injustice and violation, and guilt.[4]

Amazingly, the psychnet-uk summary of DSM-IV criteria for PTSD states that "The cause is not known, but psychological, genetic, physical, and social factors may contribute to it."[5]

Apparently experiencing extreme terror is not sufficient cause in itself!

Diagnostic Criteria for PTSD from DSM-IV

The person has experienced or witnessed an event that involved actual or threatened death or serious physical injury to the person or to others; and the person felt intense fear, horror or helplessness.[6]

The person repeatedly relives the event in at least one of these ways:

- Intrusive distressing thoughts and images
- Repeated distressing dreams
- Feeling that the event is recurring through flashbacks, hallucinations or illusions
- Marked mental distress in reaction to cues that symbolize or resemble the event
- Physical reactions to these cues, such as rapid heart beat, cold sweating, and elevated blood pressure

The person avoids at least three of these ways of stimulating memory:

- Thinking, feeling or talking about the event
- Activities, people and places that recall the event
- Cannot recall an important feature of the event
- Loss of interest in previously-important activities
- Feels detached or isolated from other people
- Restricted ability to love or feel other strong emotions
- Feels life will be brief and unfulfilled

The person suffers at least two of these symptoms of hyper-arousal:

- Insomnia
- Irritability
- Poor concentration
- Hyper-vigilance
- Increased startle response

These symptoms should have lasted longer than a month, be causing clinically important distress or impairing work, social or personal functioning.

Appendix B: Multiple Intelligences

Howard Gardner used two criteria for identifying independent modules of intelligence. First, for a mental attribute to qualify as a discrete, isolated intelligence, it must be possible to destroy it without impairing any other intelligence. Second, there must be a clear pathway by which it can be developed, and different degrees of development amongst different individuals. So far he has identified 9 such intelligences (see cells 1-9 in the Table). There may be others, particularly those described in cells 10-12 of the Table.[1]

It may be helpful to give a couple of examples of the way these modules facilitate learning. Linguist Noam Chomsky argues that infants have an in-built knowledge of the basic grammatical structures underlying all human languages. This is an aspect of Gardner's verbal/linguistic intelligence, and helps them learn to communicate quickly – a clear advantage for survival. In a similar way, young children learn very fast to understand how other people think and feel. This matches Gardner's interpersonal intelligence. It enables children to predict other people's behavior, thus helping them to integrate into their family and community – again a great survival benefit.

Table 24: Summary Definition of Multiple Intelligences
(Sources: 1-9 after Gardner 1993; 10 after Zohar and Marshall 2000; 11, 12 after Mithen 1996. Quotes in italics from Gardner)

1. Verbal/Linguistic
Thinks and learns with words and speech. Can memorize facts, do written tests, and enjoys reading. Core Operations: syntax, phonology, semantics, pragmatics. *The capacity to use language ... to express what's on your mind and to understand other people. Poets ... (and) any kind of writer, orator, speaker, lawyer, or a person for whom language is an important stock in trade.*

2. Logical/Mathematical
Thinks deductively applying rules and principles. Can deal with numbers and recognize abstract patterns. Core Operations: number, categorization, relations.
People with highly developed logical-mathematical intelligence understand the underlying principles of some kind of a causal system, the way a scientist or a logician does; or can manipulate numbers, quantities, and operations, the way a mathematician does.

3. Visual/Spatial
Thinks in images and pictures. Can visualize, create designs and communicate with diagrams. Core Operations: accurate mental visualization, mental transformation of images.
The ability to represent the spatial world internally in your mind .... can be used in the arts or in the sciences. If you are spatially intelligent and oriented toward the arts, you are more likely to become a painter or a sculptor or an architect ... Similarly, certain sciences like anatomy or topology emphasize spatial intelligence.

4. Musical/Rhythmic
Learns with rhyme and rhythm. Can recognize tonal patterns. Core Operations: pitch, rhythm, timbre.
The capacity to think in music, to be able to hear patterns, recognize them, remember them, and perhaps manipulate them. People who have a strong musical intelligence don't just remember music easily—they can't get it out of their minds.

Continued on next page

Table 24 continued

5. Interpersonal

Learns with others. Can facilitate groups, tell stories. Core Operations: awareness of others' feelings, emotions, goals, motivations

Understanding other people. It's an ability we all need, but is at a premium if you are a teacher, clinician, salesperson, or politician. Anybody who deals with other people has to be skilled in the interpersonal sphere.

6. Intrapersonal

Learns through self reflection. Can use meta-thinking, explore inner worlds. Core Operations: awareness of one's own feelings, emotions, goals, motivations.

Having an understanding of yourself, of knowing who you are, what you can do, what you want to do, how you react to things, which things to avoid, and which things to gravitate toward.

7. Body/Kinesthetic

Learns through movement. Can use body language, body memory. Core Operations: control of one's own body, control in handling

objects.

The capacity to use your whole body or parts of your body—your hand, your fingers, your arms—to solve a problem, make something, or put on some kind of a production. The most evident examples are people in athletics or the performing arts.

8. Naturalist

Learns through patterns in the natural environment. Can recognize and understand plants and animals in the natural world. Core Operations: recognition and classification of objects in the environment.

The human ability to discriminate among living things … as well as sensitivity to other features of the natural world … This ability was clearly of value … as hunters, gatherers, and farmers; it continues to be central in such roles as botanist or chef.

9. Existential

Learns through deep questioning. Can place self within time and space (cosmos). Sensitivity and

Continued on next page

Table 24 continued

capacity to tackle deep questions about human existence. The capacity to locate oneself with respect to the infinite no less than the infinitesimal, and with respect to the most existential features of the human condition: the meaning of life and death, the ultimate fate of the cosmos, such profound experiences as love of another human being or total immersion in a work of art.

10. Spiritual

This is about the meaning and purpose of life, creativity, discrimination, moral sense, good and evil, and envisioning a better future.

11. Physical

An intuitive understanding of the physical world. From an early age, children understand that physical objects are different to living things or mental concepts. They have an innate sense of solidity, gravity and inertia. They know that a dog is still a dog even if it has only three legs, but that a box can be a container, a seat or a table.

12. General

A general intelligence module that is flexible, and can be applied to acquiring any skill, or learning about any issue, and which includes general rules for making decisions. It is necessary for learning about things that do not fit within any of the other intelligences, particularly issues that cross the boundaries between intelligences.

Notes and Sources

Prologue

1   From *Waking the Tiger*, p.175

2   Levine and Frederick 1997, p.2

3   Ingerman 1991, p.18-9

4   From *Minding the Body, Mending the Mind*, quoted by Peter Levine in *Waking the Tiger* p.221

5   Medical doctors often refer to physical injuries as trauma, but we are concerned here with psychological trauma which may or may not be associated with physical injury. This definition from the MedicineNet website is for psychiatric trauma. URL

www.medterms.com/script/main/art.asp?articlekey=20130

6   Riane Eisler, in her classic book *The Chalice and the Blade*, first drew attention to the cultural gulf between prehistoric cultures and early civilizations. She called the former "partnership" cultures, and the latter "dominator" cultures (Eisler 1987). The characteristics of each of these are discussed at length in later chapters.

7   Steve Taylor, in his book of the same name, called this cultural discontinuity "The Fall" after the Biblical myth. But it was Riane Eisler, and later James DeMeo, who first documented the phenomenon (Taylor 2005; DeMeo 2006; Eisler 1987)

8   DeMeo 2006

9   Taylor 2005, Part 3

Introduction to Part I. Understanding Trauma

1   Levine and Frederick 1997, p.9

2   Perry 1997

1. What is Trauma?

1   Levine 2008, p.7

2   Adapted from MedicineNet, as quoted in the Prologue.

3   Post-Traumatic Stress Disorder (PTSD) is the best-known trauma diagnosis of this kind, due to its prevalence in returned servicemen from the Vietnam and Iraq wars. Diagnostic criteria for this are summarized in Appendix A.

4   We discuss the violentization process in more detail later in the book. It is described in detail in Rhodes (2000)

5   Levine and Frederick 1997

6   Rowe 2007a

7   Sarno 1998

8   Grant McFetridge of the Institute for the Study of Peak States (of consciousness) has identified many peak states, and associated trauma blocks (McFetridge 2004, 2008)

9   MacLean's claim that the triune structure reflects the evolutionary history the brain is controversial, but has been widely adopted as a useful metaphor (MacLean 1974).

10   This example is elaborated by Rothschild 2000, p.32

11   Levine and Frederick 1997

12   Brown 1978, p. 39ff

2. The Causes of Trauma

1   Levine and Frederick 1997, p.43

2   See Wikipedia for a brief biography. URL:
     http://en.wikipedia.org/wiki/Viktor_Frankl

3   Cyrulnik 2009, p.87

4   Levine and Frederick 1997, p.54

5   Becker et al 2003b

6   Lindner 2006, p.29

7   Lindner 2006

8   Cyrulnik 2009; Perry 2000; Levine and Frederick 1997

9   Evelin Lindner argues that humiliation is a major cause of war, as well as personal wounds (Lindner 2006)

10   Anon 2009

3. The Response to Potentially Traumatic Experiences

1   Levine and Frederick 1997, p.32

2   Lindner 2006

3   Cyrulnik 2009, p.25

4   See, for example, Sue Gerhardt (Gerhardt 2004)

5   Bishop 2007

6   Harms 2005

7   Cyrulnik 2009, p.286

8   Schlitz 2007, p.69; Harms 2005

9   Becker et al 2003b

10   Becker et al 2003b

11   Levine and Frederick 1997, p.6

12   See, for example, Shonkoff and Phillips (2000); Pariante (2003); Rothschild (2000); Siegel et al. (1999)

13   Landau 2009

14   Rothschild 2000

15   Rothschild 2000. The Committee on Adolescence of the Group for the Advancement of Psychiatry similarly comments that defense mechanisms such as repression, denial and dissociation may protect against development of full-blown PTSD.

16   This suggestion is made by Babette Rothschild. The discussion of dissociation is based mainly on Levine and Frederick (1997), Rothschild (2000) and Ingerman (1991)

17   Also known as Dissociative Identity Disorder.

18   Ingerman 1991, p.18-19

19   Cyrulnik 2009

20   This position is supported by trauma therapist Peter Levine (Levine and Frederick 1997), and shamanic healer Sandra Ingerman (Ingerman 1991)

21   Gerhardt 2004, p.143

22   Caplan 2007

4. The Symptoms and Effects of Trauma

1   These factors are drawn from many sources cited throughout the book, and too numerous to give here. There is some overlap with the causes of trauma listed in Table 1 because some factors can be both cause and effect.

2   Levine and Frederick 1997, p.155-69

3   Levine and Frederick 1997, p.47

4   Rowe 2007a

5   Szalavitz 2008

6   Rowe 2007b

7   Perry 1997

8   Perry 2002a, 1999, 2000, 1997

9   Perry 2002a

10   Sarno 1998

11   Rothschild 2000, p.71

12   The description of Reich's theories here is based largely on DeMeo (2006)

13   DeMeo 2006, p.28

14   Stephenson 2002, p.44

15   Perry 1996

5. Collective and Generational Trauma

1   Adapted from Ratnavale (2007)

2   Somasundaram 2007; de Young 1998

3   Turnbull 1972

4   Somasundaram 2007

5   de Young 1998

6   Somasundaram 2007

7   de Young 1998

8   Levine and Frederick 1997, p.225-6

9   Levine and Frederick 1997, p.226

10   Levine and Frederick 1997, p.169

11   This story, reported by Clancy Chassay, was published in The Guardian newspaper on 16 December 2008. It is

available at URL
http://www.guardian.co.uk/world/2008/dec/16/afghanistan-taliban-us-foreign-policy

6. Healing Trauma

1   Levine and Frederick 1997
2   Peter Levine recounts how three cheetah cubs narrowly escaped a lion by climbing a tree. Afterwards, they repeatedly replayed the event, taking it in turns to be the lion, and trying different escape strategies (Levine and Frederick 1997, p.174)
3   Trauma therapist Peter Levine describes the healing methods of indigenous peoples (Levine and Frederick 1997, p.57-8,183). Sandra Ingerman provides a good description of soul retrieval, and its relationship to trauma healing (Ingerman 1991)
4   Brown 1978, p.96-99

Introduction to Part II. The Human Brain and Mind

1   Bogucki 1999, p.xiv, 4

7. The Evolution of the Brain and Mind

1   This potted history has been gleaned from several sources, amongst them Mithen (1996), Bogucki (1999) and Wikipedia. The names of hominin species and the extent of their geographical range at different dates are still being debated by the experts.
2   Mithen 1996; Diamond 1998
3   Malcolm Hollick discusses the nature of the mind in depth in his earlier book, *The Science of Oneness* (Hollick 2006)
4   We have drawn on many sources for this section. Key references include Mithen (1996), Bogucki (1999), Diamond (1992), Lerro (2005)
5   Some people experience a phenomenon known as synes-

thesia in which, for example, sounds may be colored, and visual motion may be heard, indicating unusual communication between the parts of the brain that process sense data. The limited communication between conscious and subconscious mind is illustrated by the persistence of optical illusions even when we know they are illusions (Bateson 1979)

6 Gardner 1993

7 McFetridge 2004

8 Goleman 1995

9 McFetridge 2004

10 Mithen 1996

11 Mithen 1996

12 Taylor 2005

13 Gopnik 2009

14 Perry 1997

15 Diamond 1992, p.55

16 Diamond 1992

8. The Great Leap Forward

1 Diamond 1998

2 Levine and Frederick 1997

3 Oatley, Keltner, and Jenkins 2006; Goleman 1995

4 Goleman 1995

5 Goleman 1995

6 Pert 1997

7 Oatley, Keltner, and Jenkins 2006

8 (oleman 1995, p.43-4

Introduction to Part III. From the Golden Age to Agricultural Civilization

1 Quoted by Schmookler 1984, p.210

2 Roberts 1998, p.125

3 The Holy Bible, Revised Standard Version, Genesis Chapters

2 and 3. Quotation from 3:17-19.

4   This transition is documented particularly by DeMeo (2006), Eisler (1987), Taylor (2005)

9. Hunters and Gatherers

1   Key sources include Mithen (2003), Bogucki (1999), Lerro (2005), DeMeo (2006), Eisler (1987), Taylor (2005)

2   Robin Dunbar estimates that chimpanzees spend 20% of their time in social grooming. As group size increases, so does the need for grooming to maintain bonding. Dunbar argues that language is a more efficient means of communication, and essential for forming larger groups (Oatley, Keltner, and Jenkins 2006).

3   Mithen 2003, p.484

4   Oatley, Keltner, and Jenkins 2006

5   Gopnik 2009, p.211

6   A lot of this research is based on laboratory studies of structured games between students from rich nations, so its validity is a bit limited. Nevertheless it brings some very interesting insights. (Fehr 2003; Whitfield 2009a)

7   Lindner 2006, p.149

8   Rowlands 2008

9   Information on bonobos is drawn from several sources, including de Waal (2007, 2005, 1998, 1995), Kaplan (2006), Diamond (1992)

10   This account of early human sexuality draws heavily on studies of bonobos and some modern hunter-gatherer societies. (Fry 2006; de Waal 1998)

11   de Waal 2007

12   Bogucki 1999; Lerro 2005

13   For a study of herbal contraception and abortion see DeMeo (2006)

14   Yogis and Buddhist monks can control body temperature, heart rate, breathing and other functions. Faith healing is a

well-known phenomenon. So it seems quite possible that women's beliefs could control ovulation.

15 See URL http://en.wikipedia.org/wiki/Infanticide

16 For a description of child-rearing practices amongst modern hunter-gatherers, see Montagu (1978)

17 Lerro 2005

18 One case was in Northern Europe, which was a veritable paradise for two millennia after the retreat of the ice sheets. Human population expanded rapidly, particularly on rich estuaries and coastal lands. But by 9,000 years ago these areas were being drowned by rising sea levels in what are now the Baltic and North Seas. By 7,500 years ago the northward spread of farmers was adding to these pressures. The second case involved changes to the flow of the River Nile. Before 14,000 years ago, the Nile was a wide expanse of sluggish braided channels flowing through marshes. Bands of hunter-gatherers shared this bountiful environment, surrounded by inhospitable desert. Then, an increase in rainfall in the headwaters turned the river into a single, fast-flowing channel with a narrow floodplain. As a result, the previously peaceful inhabitants found themselves fighting for survival over greatly impoverished resources. The third case was the Murray River in Australia—a resource-rich strip surrounded by arid land. (Mithen 2003, p.175ff; Spinney 2008)

19 Fry 2006, Ch. 10

20 Diamond 1992

21 de Waal 1998, 2007

22 de Waal 1998, pp.1-2

23 Mithen 1996

24 Fry 2006

25 Horgan 2009. For a brief review of such studies see Taylor 2005, pp.31-5.

10. The First Farmers

1   Bogucki 1999; Mithen 2003

2   Mithen 2003

3   Mithen 2003, ch.34

4   Diamond 1998; Mithen 2003; Bogucki 1999

5   Steven Mithen envisages every traveler carrying precious pouch of seeds from place to place (Mithen 2003)

6   Mithen 2003, p.346

7   Much of the evidence for the health of early farmers comes from careful examination of their skeletons. The condition of bones and teeth can tell scientists a lot about diet, disease, longevity, physical stress and so on. (See works such as Mithen (1996), Bogucki (1999)). Some of the diseases they suffered were due to poor sanitation around permanent settlements. There is also evidence that many human diseases emerged when animals were domesticated and pathogens such as smallpox and tuberculosis jumped between species (Diamond 1998).

8   Bogucki 1999

9   Diamond 1992, p.184

10   Mithen 2003, p.179-80

11   Mithen 2003, ch.21

12   Bogucki 1999

13   Bogucki 1999

14   Bogucki 1999

15   Mithen 1996; Bogucki 1999

16   Mithen 2003, pp. 65-7

17   This account is based on Bogucki (1999) and Mithen (2003)

11. Agricultural Civilization

1   John Croft, pers. com.

2   This chapter is based on information from many sources, including Bogucki (1999), Mithen (2003), Lerro (2005), DeMeo (2006), Taylor (2005), Eisler (1987)

3   Eisler 1987

4   Mithen 2003, p.180

5   Bogucki 1999

6   Lerro 2005; Bogucki 1999

7   Lerro 2005; Bogucki 1999

8   This argument is made in detail by Bogucki (1999)

9   For brief reviews of differing interpretations see Taylor (2005), Mithen (2003), Lerro (2005), Eisler (1987), Bogucki (1999)

10 Mithen 2003, p.84

11 Mithen 2003, p.59; Fry 2006

12 The following description is based on several sources including Taylor (2005), Mithen (2003), Eisler (1987), Bogucki (1999), DeMeo (2006)

13 Mithen 2003, pp.92-6

Introduction to Part IV. The Fall

1   Eisler 1987

2   DeMeo 2006

3   Taylor 2005

12. The Great Drying

1   Brooks 2006; DeMeo 2006

2   Bogucki 1999; Brooks 2006

3   Bogucki 1999; Brooks 2006

4   Wade 1974

5   Lerro 2005

6   The Holy Bible, Book of Numbers, Ch. 31, New International Version

7   Archaeologist Maria Gimbutas claimed that the 'Kurgans' pioneered the use of horses and wheeled chariots about 6,500 BP. She identified three waves of 'Kurgan' invasions in about 6,300 BP, 5,400 BP and 4,800 BP (Eisler 1987). Many scholars derided these theories and counter-claimed that the

horse was not domesticated, the bit was not invented, and the spoked wheel did not exist until later than Gimbutas asserted (Lerro 2005). However, recent pioneering work by David Anthony and Dorcas Brown from the Institute of Ancient Equestrian Studies lend some support to Gimbutas' claims. They maintain that horses were ridden on the steppes with rope or leather bits before 6,000 BP, and that tribal raiding on horseback may have begun by then. 500 years later, relatively large horses from the steppes had spread over a wide area of southeast Europe and west Asia. And two-spoked chariot wheels have been found in the steppes dating back to around 4,000 BP.

Anthony and Dorcas believe that early bows were too big to be used on horseback, and smaller ones did not appear until 3,000 years ago. Similarly, horsemen cannot use swords and lances effectively without stirrups which were not invented until later. However, according to Maria Gimbutas, the Kurgans were making deadly daggers and battle-axes early in the Bronze Age, soon after they learned to ride (Eisler 1987). This suggests that at first they may have used their horses to launch swift, surprise attacks, but have done their fighting on foot. Once chariots were available, however, javelins appear that could have been hurled from a moving vehicle. The exact role of the horse in this period of history is still not clear, but it may have been highly significant. (Anthony 2007; Anthony 2008)

8   Deng et al. 2005

9   Eisler 1987

10   Bogucki 1999

11   The classic work on cranial deformation is Dingwall (1931). This account is based largely on DeMeo (2006, p.111-15). The practice seems to be extinct, but tight swaddling of babies to restrain their movements is still common in some parts of the world, causing them severe discomfort.

12 This is taken from DeMeo's summary of Colin Turnbull's book *The Mountain People*, Simon & Schuster, NY, 1972. (DeMeo 2006, p.77)

13 DeMeo (2006, p.78) quoting Carlson, D. (1982) *Famine in History: With a comparison of two modern Ethiopian disasters*, in Cahill, K. (Ed) (1982) *Famine*, Orbis books, NY.

14 DeMeo (2006, p.85) quoting S. Helms (1981) *Jawa: Lost City of he Black Desert* Cornell U. Press, Ithaca.

15 Vidal 2009

13. Agricultural versus State Civilizations
1   Lerro 2005
2   Lerro 2005; Fry 2006
3   Lerro 2005; Bogucki 1999
4   Abram 1996
5   Eisler 1987
6   Mithen 2003
7   DeMeo 2006
8   Lerro 2005

14. Causes of The Fall
1   DeMeo (2006, p.51) following a hint by psychoanalyst Wilhelm Reich.
2   Lindner 2006, p.139
3   Torrence 2002
4   Roberts 1998
5   Diamond 1998, 1992
6   Taylor 2005, p.22
7   Taylor 2005, p.115
8   Lerro 2005
9   See Chapter 8.

15. Reactions to The Fall
1   Taylor 2005

2   For a fuller discussion of this worldview, see *The Science of Oneness: A Worldview for the Twenty-First Century* (Hollick 2006). There are many modern teachers of these perennial truths. Amongst the most accessible and simple are the works of Thich Nhat Hanh and Eckhart Tolle.

3   McFetridge 2004

4   Taylor 2005

5   Lindner 2006

6   Rhodes 2000

7   http://www.wiserearth.org/

8   Eisler 2002

9   Eisler 2002, p.xxi

10   Lindner 2006, p.46

11   Schmookler 1984, p.21

12   Lindner 2006, p.xvi

13   Lindner 2006, p.8-9

14   Lindner 2006, p.169

15   Schmookler 1984, p.159, 163

Introduction to Part V. Trauma Today

1   Perry 1996

16. The Memory of Trauma

1   The disciplines of genetics, molecular and cellular biology, and neuroscience are mind-numbingly complex for the non-specialist. Consequently, this chapter leans heavily on sources written by experts for non-scientists. In particular, we have drawn on papers by Bruce Perry, and books by Candace Pert, Bruce Lipton, and Babette Rothschild. [Perry (1997, 1999, 2000, 2001, 2002), Pert (1997), Lipton (2005), Rothschild (2000)]

2   Nicholls 2009

3   Lipton 2005; Champagne 2008

4   Alberts et al. 2002

5   The term 'integral membrane protein' is used by Lipton (2005). This is a more inclusive term than 'receptor' as used by Pert (1997).

6   Pert 1997

7   Lipton 2005; Pert 1997

8   Lipton 2005

9   Lipton 2005

10 Media release by The University of Western Australia, and ABC News (McGilvray 2009)

11 Motluk 2009

12 Henderson 2008

13 Simon Baron-Cohen of the Autism Research Centre at Cambridge University suggests that increasing maternal testosterone 'masculinizes' the brain with consequent negative effects on the development of empathy, social skills and language, and positive effects on systematizing and mathematical abilities. Another study demonstrated that successful financial traders who have to make quick, confident decisions are likely to have been exposed to higher testosterone levels during gestation. Since autism is a predominantly male condition with similar traits, these findings suggest that one cause could be elevated fetal testosterone.(Chapman et al. 2006; Geddes 2009; Baron-Cohen 2009; Autism 2008)

14 Candace Pert illustrates this with the example of the anti-depressant Prozac and similar drugs. Depression is thought to be caused by a shortage of the brain messenger, serotonin. If a cell produces too much serotonin, it reabsorbs the excess. In order to boost the supply, Prozac inhibits this 'reuptake' mechanism, thus flooding the receptors with serotonin. But other areas of the body also use serotonin, including the intestines. Hence, Prozac can cause digestive problems.

15 Pert 1997, p.148

16 Gerhardt 2004; Sternberg 2009

17 Pert 1997

18 Robson 2009a

19 Pert 1997

20 Lipton 2005, p.131

21 Pert 1997

22 Rothschild 2000

23 Shonkoff and Phillips 2000

24 Shonkoff and Phillips 2000

25 Perry 1999

26 Gerhardt 2004

27 Schore 1994

28 Powell 2009

29 Perry 2002b

30 Thomson 2009

31 Perry 2002a; Gerhardt 2004

32 Levine and Frederick 1997

33 Cyrulnik 2009; Levine and Frederick 1997, p.211

34 Rothschild 2000

17. Before and at Birth

1 Most of the basic scientific information in this section comes from Alberts et al. (2002) and Gilbert (2000). More radical interpretations are from Lipton (2005)

2 Badcock and Crespi 2008

3 Lipton 2005, p.172-3

4 The main sources for this description are Alberts et al. (2002) and Gilbert (2000)

5 Anon 2008d

6 McFetridge (2008), Appendix F, provides a detailed list of developmental events at which he believes trauma may be experienced.

7 Grof 1990, p.34-5

8 Lipton 2005, p.176

9 Shonkoff and Phillips 2000, p.198

10 Quoted by Lipton (2005) p.173

11 Lipton 2005

12 Shonkoff and Phillips 2000; Gilbert 2000; Ellwood 2008

13 Grof 1990, p.37

14 Lipton 2005, p.173

15 Ellwood 2008

16 Gilbert 2000; Brown 2006

17 Anon 2008a

18 Brown 2006

19 Marchant 2004

20 BMA Board of Science 2007

21 Coghlan 2009

22 Gilbert 2000

23 Shonkoff and Phillips 2000; Brown 2006

24 Whitfield 2009b

25 Glover 2005

26 Champagne 2008

27 Anon 2007

28 Glover 2005

29 Anon 2007

30 Malaspina et al. 2008

31 Dutch Famine Study 2008) (Neugebauer 2005; Shonkoff and Phillips 2000; Roseboom et al. 1999; Lipton 2005)

32 Shonkoff and Phillips 2000

33 Neugebauer 2005

34 Scott, Duncan, and Duncan 1997

35 Grof 1990

36 Grof 1990, p.48-9

37 Grof 1990, p.51

38 Gaskin 2002

39 Grof 1990, p.67

40 Grof 1990, p.63

41 See Chapter 3. Also Rothschild 2000

42 Glover 2005

43 Weeks 2007; Anon 2009c

44 Brazier 2009

45 The use of painkilling drugs is controversial. Sandra Ingerman claims that infants whose mothers were drugged often come into the world disoriented—a state that may last throughout life (Ingerman 1991). In mid-2009, Denis Walsh, a prominent UK midwife, warned about the dangers of epidurals, and recommended alternative pain control methods. However, his position was strongly criticized by other midwives (Campbell 2009).

46 Wilhelm Reich cited by DeMeo (2006)

47 Tolle 2005, p.143

48 Kornfield 1993, p.334

18. Infancy

1 Oatley, Keltner, and Jenkins 2006

2 Perry 2001

3 Perry 2002b

4 Shonkoff and Phillips 2000

5 Perry 2001; Harms 2005

6 Schore 1994

7 Oatley, Keltner, and Jenkins 2006

8 Perry 2001; Harms 2005; Gerhardt 2004

9 Gerhardt 2004

10 Gerhardt 2004

11 Perry 2001

12 Champagne 2008

13 Perry 2001; Gerhardt 2004

14 Champagne 2008

15 Shonkoff and Phillips 2000; Gerhardt 2004

16 Champagne 2008

17 It is similar across English-speaking countries with 15-20% of toddlers showing avoidant insecure attachment, and another 10-15% forming resistant insecure attachments. However,

Israel has a high percentage of resistant insecurity, nearly half of Germany's toddlers are avoidant, but there is no avoidant insecurity in Japan.(Oatley, Keltner, and Jenkins 2006)

18   Gerhardt 2004; Harms 2005

19   Gerhardt 2004; Harms 2005; Perry 2001

20   Schore 1994; Champagne 2008

21   Schore 1994

22   Schore 1994

23   Rowe 2007a, p.76. Alison Gopnik also describes the newborn's ability to imitate poking out the tongue (Gopnik 2009, p.205)

24   Schore 1994; Gerhardt 2004

25   Perry 2002a

26   Highfield 2009

27   Harlow 1959

28   Suomi 1990

29   Champagne 2008

30   Gerhardt 2004

31   Gorski, Sweet, and Sehring 1990

32   Rausch 1990

33   Schore 1994; Wiess 1990; Lipton 2005

34   Gerhardt 2004

35   Shonkoff and Phillips 2000

36   Schore 1994

37   Schore 1994

38   Shonkoff and Phillips 2000; Gerhardt 2004

39   Gerhardt 2004

40   Shonkoff and Phillips 2000; Goleman 1995

41   Shonkoff and Phillips 2000; Gerhardt 2004

42   Gerhardt 2004

43   Goleman 1995

44   Gerhardt 2004

45   Schore 1994; Shonkoff and Phillips 2000

46   Schore 1994
47   Shonkoff and Phillips 2000

19. Childhood

1   Quoted by Rhodes (2000, p.236) from deMause, L. (ed) (1974) *The History of Childhood* Northvale, Jason Aronson.
2   Cyrulnik 2009
3   Cyrulnik 2009
4   deMause examined over 200 statements of advice on child-rearing written before the eighteenth century (Rhodes, 2000)
5   Rhodes 2000
6   Lindner 2006
7   Cyrulnik 2009
8   Goleman 1995
9   Gilbert et al. 2009
10   Zeanah and Scheeringa 1997
11   Perry 2000, 1996, 1997
12   Anon 2009a
13   Goleman 1995, p.233
14   Reading et al. 2009
15   Gilbert et al. 2009; Shonkoff and Phillips 2000; Zeanah and Scheeringa 1997; Gerhardt 2004; Perry 1997, 2000; Champagne 2008
16   Perry 1996
17   DeMeo 2006, p.6
18   Deng et al. 2005
19   Deng et al. 2005, p. 309-11
20   Goleman 1995, p.204
21   Perry 2000
22   Oatley, Keltner, and Jenkins 2006
23   Perry 2000. This confusion was also discussed by the Committee on Adolescence of the Group for the Advancement of Psychiatry (Becker et al 2003b)
24   Perry 2000

25 Perry 2002a, 2000, 1999; Goleman 1995; Rowe 2007a, 2007b
26 Perry 2000
27 Goleman 1995
28 Levine and Frederick 1997
29 Deng et al. 2005, p.301-2

20. Adolescence

1   Oatley, Keltner, and Jenkins 2006
2   Becker et al 2003a, 2003b
3   Perry 2000
4   Becker et al 2003a
5   Becker et al 2003a
6   Becker et al 2003c
7   Cyrulnik 2009, p.130
8   This section is largely based on Becker and al (2003b)
9   Gosline 2009
10 Ingerman 1991
11 Anon 2009b
12 Information on Wilhelm Reich's ideas is drawn mainly from DeMeo (2006)
13 McAnarney 1990
14 Prescott cited by DeMeo (2006)
15 DeMeo 2006, p.4
16 Quoted by DeMeo 2006, p.119
17 DeMeo 2006
18 Deng et al. 2005
19 DeMeo 2006
20 J. Lantier quoted by DeMeo (2006)
21 DeMeo 2006
22 Anon 2008c
23 Amnesty International 2009
24 Goleman 1995
25 Perry 1997; Gosline 2008
26 Gosline 2008

27   Perry 1997

28   Gosline 2008

21. Adulthood

1   Zimbardo 2007

2   Robson 2009b

3   Zimbardo 2007; Robson 2009b

4   Lindner 2006, p.61

5   Lindner 2006, p.61

6   Rhodes 2000

7   Perry 1997, p.141-2

8   Perry 1996

9   Landau 2009

10   Bond 2009

11   Bishop 2007

12   Bond 2009

13   Wyatt 2008

14   Travis 2009

15   Caplan 2007

16   Wyatt 2008

17   Personal communication regarding personnel at Fort George, Scotland.

18   Rhodes 2000

19   Caplan 2007

20   Quoted by Rhodes (2000, p.295)

21   The following description of military training is based mainly on Rhodes (2000)

22   Bishop 2007

23   Zimbardo 2007, p.417

24   Amnesty International 2009

25   Carvel 2008

26   Goleman 1995

27   Oatley, Keltner, and Jenkins 2006; Goleman 1995

28   Gerhardt 2004

29 Oatley, Keltner, and Jenkins 2006
30 National Institute of Mental Health 2008
31 Mental Health Foundation 2009
32 Oatley, Keltner, and Jenkins 2006, p.364
33 Gerhardt 2004
34 Anon 2008b
35 Eating Disorders Association 2009
36 Disordered Eating 2009; Anon 2009d; Eating Disorders Association 2009
37 Grieg 2009
38 Orbach 2009
39 Oatley, Keltner, and Jenkins 2006; Gerhardt 2004
40 Gerhardt 2004

22. The Collective

1 The efforts to heal collective trauma in Germany are discussed in more detail in the chapter on collective healing.
2 Tolle 2005, p.142
3 This section is based mainly on a report for the Canadian Aboriginal Healing Foundation on historic trauma and aboriginal healing (Wesley-Esquimaux and Smolewski 2004)
4 From a lecture by Aboriginal spokesperson, Noel Nannup, Perth, 2008.
5 Wesley-Esquimaux and Smolewski 2004
6 Somasundaram 2007
7 Wikramatunga 2009
8 Robben and Suarez-Orozco 2000
9 Quoted by Somasundaram (2007)
10 Audergon 2004
11 de Young 1998
12 de Young 1998
13 Audergon 2004
14 Cyrulnik 2009
15 Audergon 2004

Introduction to Part VI. Healing into Partnership

1   Audergon 2004
2   Levine and Frederick 1997, p.222
3   Perry 1999

23. Reducing Potentially Traumatic Events

1   Levine and Frederick 1997, p.43
2   Gerhardt 2004
3   Perry 1997, p.144
4   For a recent, in-depth review and analysis of the issue of child maltreatment, see the series of papers published in *The Lancet* in 2009 by Gilbert et al. 2009; MacMillan et al. 2009; Reading et al. 2009.
5   Reading et al. 2009
6   Reading et al. 2009
7   Reading et al. 2009
8   MacMillan et al. 2009
9   MacMillan et al. 2009
10   Rhodes 2000
11   Perry 1997, p.144
12   MacMillan et al. 2009
13   Gosline 2008
14   MacMillan et al. 2009
15   Triple P website http://www10.triplep.net/?pid=58
16   The main sources for this section are DeMeo 2006; Eisler 2002; Montagu 1978; Mussen 1977; Shaffer 1979; Bronfenbrenner 1972.

24. Developing Resilience

1   Wikramatunga 2009
2   Rothschild 2000, p.17
3   Werner 1995
4   Harms 2005
5   Perry 2000

6   Wikipedia
7   Perry 1996
8   Goleman 1995, p.87-8
9   Werner 1995
10 Perry 1996
11 Quoted by Rhodes 2000, p. 313
12 Goleman 1995, p.257ff
13 Rothschild 2000
14 Bloom 2001
15 Perry 2000; Seery et al. 2008; Harms 2005
16 Perry 2000

25. Healing is a Universal Need

1   Levine and Frederick 1997
2   Taylor 2005
3   Levine and Frederick 1997, p.267
4   McFetridge 2004
5   Levine and Frederick 1997, p.62
6   Levine and Frederick 1997, p.21, 33
7   Ingerman 1991, p.118
8   Levine and Frederick 1997, p.21
9   Rothschild 2000, p.150
10 Cited by Goleman 1995, p.210-3
11 Rothschild 2000, p.150
12 Oatley, Keltner, and Jenkins 2006; Rothschild 2000
13 Perry 2000; Oatley, Keltner, and Jenkins 2006
14 Servan-Schreiber 2004,
    http://en.wikipedia.org/wiki/Eye_movement_desensiti-
    zation_and_reprocessing
15 In 2009 it was reported that sedatives such as valium and
    diazepam are often prescribed to victims of traumatic events
    to reduce anxiety and help sleep. However, they seem to
    increase the incidence of PTSD. This may be due to inter-
    ference with the formation of memories (Geddes 2009a)

16 Harms 2005
17 Levine and Frederick 1997, p.10
18 Perry 2000
19 Rothschild 2000
20 Caplan 2007
21 Ingerman 1991
22 Rothschild 2000

26. The Healing Process

1 Gendlin 2003; Levine and Frederick 1997; Rothschild 2000
2 Ingerman 1991, p.158
3 For a scholarly discussion of past lives and their healing, see Roger Woolger's book "Other Lives, Other Selves". Stanislav Grof similarly verified some pre-birth experiences (Grof 1990). Sogyal Rinpoche retells the fascinating story of Arthur Flowerdew who had inexplicably detailed knowledge of the ancient city of Petra (Rinpoche 1992).
4 Loftus and Pickrell 1995; Rothschild 2000
5 Levine and Frederick 1997, p.47
6 Rothschild 2000
7 Levine and Frederick 1997
8 Cyrulnik 2009, p.33
9 Rothschild makes a similar point. She distinguishes between catharsis – a cleansing that happens when disturbing memories come to consciousness – and abreaction – an emotional discharge that often accompanies catharsis. Abreaction is of debatable value. It can cause disintegration and further trauma. She also advises against trying to resolve PTSD through flashbacks as this can reinforce terror and helplessness. (Rothschild 2000)
10 Levine and Frederick 1997
11 Ingerman 1991
12 Goleman 1995, p.208-9
13 Gendlin 2003

14 Levine and Frederick 1997, p.8, 68

15 Levine and Frederick 1997, p.69

16 Levine and Frederick 1997, p.66, 68

17 Gendlin 2003; Levine and Frederick 1997; Levine 2008. Further resources are available at http://www.focusing.org/ and http://www.traumahealing.com/

18 Levine and Frederick 1997, p.120

19 Seligman 2002; Bloom 2001; Aldana 2009. The basic idea of practicing gratitude as promoted by Jacquelyn Aldana is very beneficial. Unfortunately, in our view she puts too much emphasis on it as a means to financial success rather than on healing and spiritual values.

20 See http://alchemytechniques.com/

21 Cyrulnik 2009

22 Kornfield 1993, p.47

23 Kornfield 1993, p.28-9

24 Kornfield 1993a

25 Walsh 1993

26 Kornfield 1993

27 Grof and Grof 1989; Perry 1974

28 Kornfield 1993a, p.67

29 Kornfield 1993a, p.67

30 Kornfield 1993, p.9

31 Levine and Frederick 1997

32 The original conference record is no longer on the web, but Aba Gayle's story was still to be found at http://www.catherineblountfdn.org/abagayle.html – at least when I last accessed it on 13 July 2009.

33 Cyrulnik 2009, p.11, 25

34 Walsh 1995, 1993

27. Healing Generational and Collective Trauma

1   Cyrulnik 2009, p.242

2   Steininger 2008

3   Ilona Kaestner, personal communication

4   Macy 1995

5   www.globalawareness.info accessed 8 July 2009

6   Updegraff, Silver, and Holman 2008; Seery et al. 2008

7   Wesley-Esquimaux and Smolewski 2004

8   de Young 1998

9   Cyrulnik 2009, p. 201-2

10   Somasundaram 2007

11   Macy 1995

12   Somasundaram 2007

13   Somasundaram 2007

14   Audergon 2004. The Process Work approach was developed
     by A Mindell (Mindell 1995). The quote is from the
     International Tribunal for Yugoslavia, cited by Audergon.

15   Levine and Frederick 1997, p.228ff

16   http://en.wikipedia.org/wiki/Truth_and_reconciliation
     _commission accessed 8 July 2009

17   For information on the Yugoslavian Tribunal see
     http://www.icty.org/sections/AbouttheICTY; and for the
     Rwandan Tribunal see http://www.ictr.org/default.htm

18   Hollick 2006

19   Levine and Frederick 1997, p.231

20   Cyrulnik 2009

28. Meeting the Overwhelming Need

1   Oatley, Keltner, and Jenkins 2006

2   Perry 2000

3   Levine and Frederick 1997

4   Pert 1997

5   Reported in Chemistry World, Royal Society of Chemistry, 13
     Sept 2006 at
     http://www.rsc.org/chemistryworld/News/2006/Septem
     ber/1 3090603.asp accessed 10 July 2009

6   Anon 2009d

7   Aldhous 2009

8   Rothschild 2000

9   Ingerman 1991

10 Levine and Frederick 1997

11 Relevant books and CDs include (Gendlin 2003; Levine 2008; Bloom 2001; Katie 2002). Websites with free self-help information include www.emofree.com for EFT, www.trauma-healing.com for Peter Levine, www.focusing.org for Eugene Gendlin, and www.williambloom.com. Further resources are available for purchase.

12 Servan-Schreiber 2004

13 Servan-Schreiber 2004

14 Servan-Schreiber 2004

15 Fox 2008

16 For 5 Rhythms see http://en.wikipedia.org/wiki/5Rhythms, and http://www.gabrielleroth.com/GR/index.html; for Biodanza see http://biodanza.co.uk/website/. General information on music therapy and toning is given at http://www.answers.com/topic/sound-therapy

17 http://www.badth.org.uk/dtherapy/index.html

18 Nowak 2008

19 Anon 2009e. The letter appeared a few weeks later in New Scientist for 21 February, p.24.

20 Orme-Johnson, Dillbeck, and Alexander 2003; Orme-Johnson 2003. For summaries of research on the effects of TM in scientific journals see http://istpp.org/rehabilitation/index.html and http://permanentpeace.org/index.html

21 Walsh 1993

22 http://www.worldpeace.org/activities_teleconference.php

23 One of the more intriguing, first published in the British Medical Journal, involves the possibility of prayer enhancing healing retroactively (Olshansky and Dossey 2004)

24 For a brief review of the controversy surrounding parapsychological research, see Hollick 2006; Matthews 2004.

25 Many experiments have shown that as many as a third of people with a specific condition can benefit from sugar pills if they believe them to be powerful drugs. In some cases, this placebo effect, as it is called, rivals the real drugs in effectiveness.

26 Bond 2009b, 2009a

29. Evolving a Partnership Civilization

1 For an overview of decision-making processes in several ecovillage communities, see our earlier book (Hollick and Connelly 1998). This is available in electronic form from Praxis Education at http://www.praxiseducation.com/catalog/index.php/. For further information about intentional communities see http://www.ic.org/

2 Many other good suggestions are contained in the 'formal consensus' process (Butler and Rothstein 1991) (also available at http://www.ic.org/pnp/ocac/), and in the classic book *Getting to Yes* (Fisher and Ury 1991)

3 Heider 1985

4 http://www.findhorn.com/nfa/NFA/AboutUs. Also see http://www.findhorn.org

5 There is such a wealth of ideas, knowledge and experience in this field that it is hard to give guidance on where to go for further information. The best starting points may be information on intentional communities and ecovillages at http://www.ic.org/ and http://gen.ecovillage.org/. An excellent introduction to many of the issues discussed here is given in the Ecovillage Design Education curriculum (http://www.gaia.org/gaia/education/curriculum/), and also in the Ecovillage Training and other courses offered by the Findhorn Community in Scotland

(http://www.findhorn.org/whatwedo/ecovillage/eco village.php) For an analytical overview of several communities, see our earlier book (see note 1 in this chapter).

6   Eckersley 2009

7   Much of this section is based on the work of Evelin Lindner (2006)

8   Lindner 2006, p.60

9   Cited by Kornfield 1993, p.329.

Closure to Part VI

1   Diamond 2001

Part VII. Epilogue

1   Tolle 2005

2   Cited by Diamond 2001, p.115

3   Diamond 2001, p.86

4   Kornfield 1993, p.208

5   Kornfield 1993, p.166

6   Kornfield 1993, p.253

7   See http://alchemytechniques.com/

8   Diamond 2001, Prologue

Appendix A: Post-Traumatic Stress Disorder

1   Caplan 2007; Wyatt 2008

2   Bishop 2007

3   Bishop 2007

4   Harms 2005

5   http://www.psychnet-uk.com/dsm_iv/posttraumatic_stress_disorder.htm accessed 27 February 2009.

6   The source for this summary is: http://www.psychnet-uk.com/dsm_iv

Appendix B: Multiple Intelligences

1   Spiritual intelligence was proposed by Zohar and Marshall,

but may overlap with Gardner's existential intelligence (Zohar 2000); Mithen argues for the existence of physical and general intelligences (Mithen 1996)

References

Abram, D. 1996. *The Spell of the Sensuous*. NY: Vintage Books.

Alberts, B., A. Johnson, J. Lewis, M. Ruff, K. Roberts, and P. Walter. 2002. *Molecular Biology of the Cell*: Garland Science.

Aldana, J. 2009. *The 15-Minute Miracle*. Available from http://www.15minutemiracle.com/home.html.

Aldhous, P. 2009. The fog of war. *New Scientist* 202 (2707):40-43.

Amnesty International. 2009. *Stop violence against women: statistics*. Available from http://www.amnesty.org.uk/content.asp?CategoryID=10309.

Anon. 2007. Stress 'harms brain in the womb'. *BBC News*, 26 January.

— — —. 2008a. Here's to the baby. *New Scientist* 200 (2681):6.

— — —. 2008b. Obesity: in statistics. *BBC News*, 2 January.

— — —. 2008c. The abuse goes on. *New Scientist* 199 (2674):4.

— — —. 2008d. Understanding embryo implantation offers insight into infertility. *Medical Research Council News*, 29 September.

Anon. 2009. 'Christine' - A brave woman's fight for the future. *Amnesty Magazine* (153):21-22.

— — —. 2009a. Deteriorating home life puts kids at risk. *New Scientist* 201 (2701):14.

— — —. 2009b. 'Many girls' abused by boyfriends. *BBC News*, 31 August 2009.

— — —. 2009c. Umbilical cord. *Wikipedia* [Available from http://en.wikipedia.org/wiki/Umbilical_cord.

— — —. 2009d. Scary Associations Wiped for Good? *New Scientist* 201 (2695):14.

— — —. 2009e. Try Tetris to help treat trauma. *New Scientist* 201 (2691):12.

Anthony, D. W. 2007. *The Horse, the Wheel and Language: How Bronze-Age Riders from the Eurasian Steppes Shaped the Modern World*. Princeton: Princeton University Press.

Anthony, D. W., and D. R. Brown. *The Earliest Horseback-Riding and its Relation to Chariotry and Warfare* 2008. Available from http://users.hartwick.edu/anthonyd/harnessing%20horse-power.html.

Audergon, A. 2004. Collective Trauma: The nightmare of history. *Psychotherapy and Politics International* 2 (1):16-31.

Autism Research Centre. 2008. *Foetal Testosterone Longitudinal Study*. Available from http://www.autismresearchcentre.com/research/project.asp?id=13.

Badcock, C., and B. Crespi. 2008. Battle of the sexes may set the brain. *Nature* 454:1054-5.

Baron-Cohen, S. 2009. Fetal testosterone not only masculinises the body, it masculinises the mind. *New Scientist* 201 (2691):8.

Bateson, G. 1979. *Mind and Nature: A necessary unity*. London: Fontana.

Becker, D F, and et al. 2003a. Trauma and Adolescence I: The Nature and Scope of Trauma. *Adolescent Psychiatry* 27:143-163.

———. 2003b. Trauma and Adolescence II: The Impact of Trauma. *Adolescent Psychiatry* 27:165-200.

———. 2003c. Trauma and Adolescence III: Issues of Identification, Intervention and Social Policy. *Adolescent Psychiatry* 27:201-223.

Bishop, P. 2007. Angry soldier, unstable diagnosis, unholy muddle. *Human Givens* 14 (2):11-14.

Bloom, W. 2001. *The Endorphin Effect: A breakthrough strategy for holistic health and spiritual wellbeing*. London: Piatkus.

BMA Board of Science. 2007. Fetal Alcohol Spectrum Disorders: A guide for health professionals. London: British Medical Association.

Bogucki, P. 1999. *The Origins of Human Society*. Oxford: Blackwell.

Bond, M. 2009. Brain Shock. *New Scientist* 202 (2705):40-3.

———. 2009a. Be nice to people. *New Scientist* 203 (2726):32.

———. 2009b. Three Degrees of Contagion. *New Scientist* 201

(2689):24-27.

Brazier, C. 2009. The Heartbreak. *New Internationalist* (420):4-9.

Bronfenbrenner, U. 1972. *Two Worlds of Childhood: US and USSR.* NY: Simon & Schuster.

Brooks, N. 2006. Cultural Responses to Aridity in the Middle Holocene and Increased Social Complexity. *Quaternary International* 151:29-49.

Brown, P. 2006. Sobering news for pregnant women. *New Scientist* (2558).

Brown, T. Jr. 1978. *The Tracker.* NY: Berkley Books.

Butler, C T L, and A Rothstein. 1991. *On Conflict and Consensus: A handbook on Formal Consensus decisionmaking.* 2nd ed. Portland: Food Not Bombs Publishing.

Campbell, D. 2009. It's good for women to suffer the pain of a natural birth, says medical chief. *The Observer,* 12 July.

Caplan, P.J. 2007. Vets aren't crazy - War Is. *Tikkun* (Sept/Oct):44-48.

Carvel, J. 2008. Rising Divorce Tide Threatens 1 in 2 Couples. *The Guardian,* 28 March.

Champagne, F. A. 2008. Epigenetic mechanisms and the transgenerational effects of maternal care. *Frontiers in Neuroendocrinology* 29 (3):386-397.

Chapman, E., S. Baron-Cohen, B. Auyeung, R. Knickmeyer, K. Taylor, and G. Hackett. 2006. Fetal testosterone and empathy: Evidence from the Empathy Quotient (EQ) and the "Reading the Mind in the Eyes" Test. *Social Neuroscience* 1 (2):135-148.

Coghlan, A. 2009. Booze Control. *New Scientist* 201 (2701):22-3.

Cyrulnik, B. 2009. *Resilience: How your inner strength can set you free from the past.* London: Penguin.

de Waal, F. B. M. 1995. Bonobo Sex and Society. *Scientific American*:82-88.

———. *The empathic ape,* 8 October 2005. Available from http://space.newscientist.com/article/mg19125612.100.

———. *Bonobo's, Left and Right,* 8 August 2007. Available from

http://www.skeptic.com/eskeptic/07-08-08.html#feature.

de Waal, F. B. M., Lanting, F. 1998. *Bonobo: The Forgotten Ape*: University of California Press.

de Young, M. 2009. *Collective Trauma: Insights from a Research Errand*. American Academy of Experts in Traumatic Stress 1998. Available from http://www.aaets.org/article55.htm.

DeMeo, J. 2006. *Saharasia: The 4000 BCE origins of child abuse, sex-repression, warfare and social violence in the deserts of the old world*. 2nd ed. Ashland: Natural Energy Works.

Deng, B, A Deng, B Ajak, and with J A Bernstein. 2005. *They Poured Fire on Us from the Sky: The true story of three lost boys from Sudan*. NY: Public Affairs.

Diamond, J. 1992. *The Third Chimpanzee: The evolution and future of the human animal*. Harper Perennial ed. NY: HarperCollins.

— — —. 1998. *Guns, Germs and Steel: A short history of everybody for the last 13,000 years*: Vintage.

Diamond, L. 2001. *The Peace Book: 108 simple ways to create a more peaceful world*. 2nd ed. Berkeley: Conari Press.

Dingwall, E. J. 1931. *Artificial Cranial Deformation: A contribution to the study of ethnic mutilations*. London: John Bale, Sons, and Daniellson.

Disordered Eating. 2009. *Causes of Eating Disorders* 2009 [cited 2009].

Dutch Famine Study. *Dutch Famine Study* 2008. Available from http://www.hongerwinter.nl/index.php?option=com_content&task=view&id=12&Itemid=27.

Eating Disorders Association. 2009. *Understanding Eating Disorders* 2009. Available from http://www.b-eat.co.uk/AboutEatingDisorders/Whatisan Eatingdisorder.

Eckersley, P. 2009. Knowledge wants to be free too. *New Scientist* 202 (2714):28-29.

Eisler, R. 1987. *The Chalice and the Blade*. San Francisco: Harper & Row.

— — —. 2002. *The Power of Partnership*. California: New World Library.

— — —. 2007. *The Real Wealth of Nations: Creating a caring economics*. San Francisco: Berrett-Koehler.

Ellwood, W. 2008. This toxic life. *New Internationalist* (415):4-7.

Fehr, E. and Fischbacher, U. 2003. The Nature of Human Altruism. *Nature* 425:785-791.

Fisher, R, and W Ury. 1991. *Getting to Yes: Negotiation an agreement without giving in*. 2nd ed. London: Random House.

Fox, J. 2008. Poetic Medicine: A kind of magic. *Shift* (20):15-19.

Fry, D. P. 2006. *The Human Potential for Peace: An anthropological challenge to assumptions about war and violence*. Oxford: Oxford University Press.

Gardner, H. 1993. *Frames of Mind: The theory of multiple intelligences*. 2nd ed: Fontana.

Gaskin, I.M. 2002. *Spiritual Midwifery*. 4th ed: Book Publishing Company.

Geddes, L. 2009. Are successful traders born not made? *New Scientist* 201 (2691):11.

— — —. 2009a. Sedatives may slow trauma recovery. *New Scientist* 204 (2728):12.

Gendlin, E T. 2003. *Focusing: How to gain direct access to your body's knowledge*. Rev. ed. London: Rider.

Gerhardt, S. 2004. *Why Love Matters: How affection shapes a baby's brain*. NY: Routledge.

Gilbert, R., C.S. Widom, K. Browne, D. Fergusson, E. Webb, and S. Janson. 2009. Burden and consequences of child maltreatment in high-income countries. *The Lancet* 373 (9657):68-81.

Gilbert, S. E. 2000. *Developmental Biology*. 6th ed. Sunderland: Sinauer Associates.

Glover, V. *Fetal and Neonatal Stress Research Group* 2005. Available from

http://www1.imperial.ac.uk/medicine/research/research

themes/reprodscience/fetalstressgroup/.

Goleman, D. 1995. *Emotional Intelligence: Why it can matter more than IQ.* London: Bloomsbury Publishing.

Gopnik, A. 2009. *The Philosophical Baby: What children's minds tell us about truth, love & the meaning of life.* London: The Bodley Head.

Gorski, L., M. Sweet, and Sehring. 1990. In *Touch: The foundation of experience,* edited by K. E. Barnard and T. B. Brazelton.

Gosline, A. 2008. Nipping teen crime in the bud. *New Scientist* (2651):38-41.

———. 2009. The five ages of the brain: 3. Adolescence: Wired, and rewiring. *New Scientist* 202 (2702):28-30.

Grieg, J. 2009. Suicide psychology. *New Scientist* 201 (2701):24.

Grof, S. 1990. *The Holotropic Mind.* San Francisco: Harper Collins.

Grof, S., and C. Grof, eds. 1989. *Spiritual Emergency: When personal transformation becomes a crisis.* Los Angeles: Jeremy P. Tarcher.

Harlow, H. 1959. Love in infant monkeys. *Scientific American* 200 (6):68.

Harms, L. 2005. *Understanding Human Development: A multidimensional approach.* Melbourne: Oxford University Press.

Heider, J. 1985. *The Tao of Leadership.* Atlanta: Humanics New Age.

Henderson, M. 2008. Imprint of famine seen in genes of Second World War babies 60 years on. *Times Online,* 28 October.

Highfield, R. 2009. In your face. *New Scientist* 201 (2695):29-32.

Hollick, M. 2006. *The Science of Oneness: A worldview for the twenty-first century.* Ropley: O Books.

Hollick, M, and C Connelly. 1998. *Sustainable Communities: Lessons from aspiring eco-villages.* Perth, Australia: Praxis Education.

Horgan, J. 2009. The End of War. *New Scientist* 203 (2715):38-41.

Ingerman, S. 1991. *Soul Retrieval: Mending the Fragmented Self.* San Francisco: HarperCollins.

Kaplan, M. *Why bonobos make love, not war,* 30 Nov 2006. Available from

http://www.newscientist.com/article.ns?id=mg19225801.900.

Katie, B. 2002. *Loving What Is: Four questions that can change your life.* London: Rider.

Kornfield, J. 1993. *A Path with Heart: A guide through the perils and promises of spiritual life.* New York: Bantam Books.

— — —. 1993a. Even the Best Meditators Have Old Wounds to Heal: Combining meditation and psychotherapy. In *Paths Beyond Ego,* edited by R. Walsh and F. Vaughan. New York: Putnam.

Landau, E. *PTSD Linked to Higher Post-Surgery Death Rate.* 2009. Available from

http://edition.cnn.com/2009/HEALTH/10/20/ptsd.veterans.mortality/index.html?eref=igoogle_cnn.

Lerro, B. 2005. *Power in Eden: The emergence of gender hierarchies in the ancient world* Trafford Books.

Levine, P. A. 2008. *Healing Trauma.* Boulder: Sounds True.

Levine, P. A., and A. Frederick. 1997. *Waking the Tiger: Healing Trauma.* Berkeley: North Atlantic Books.

Lindner, E. G. 2006. *Making Enemies: Humiliation and International Conflict.* Santa Barbara: Praeger.

Lipton, B. H. 2005. *The Biology of Belief: Unleashing the power of consciousness, matter, and miracles.* Santa Rosa: Mountain of Love.

Loftus, E F, and J E Pickrell. 1995. The Formation of False Memories. *Psychiatric Annals* 25:720-725.

MacLean, P. D. 1974. *Triune Conception of the Brain and Behaviour.* Toronto: University of Toronto Press.

MacMillan, H.L., C.N. Wathen, J. Barlow, D.M. Fergusson, J.M. Leventhal, and H.N. Taussig. 2009. Interventions to prevent child maltreatment and associated impairment. *The Lancet* 373 (9657):250-66.

Macy, J. 1995. The Way to the Forest. Western Australia: The Gaia Foundation.

Malaspina, D., C. Corcoran, K.R. Kleinhaus, M.C. Perrin, S. Fennig, D. Nahon, Y. Friedlander, and S. Harlap. 2008. Acute maternal stress in pregnancy and schizophrenia in offspring: A cohort prospective study. *BMC Psychiatry* 8.

Marchant, J. 2004. Cell suicide is behind prenatal brain damage. *New Scientist* (2435).

Matthews, R. 2004. Opposites Detract. *New Scientist*:39-41.

McAnarney, E. B. 1990. Adolescents and Touch. In *Touch: The foundation of experience*, edited by K. E. Barnard and T. B. Brazelton.

McFetridge, G. 2004. *Peak States of Consciousness: Theory and Applications*. Vol. 1: Breakthrough techniques for exceptional quality of life. Hornby Island: Institute for the Study of Peak States Press.

———. 2008. *Peak States of Consciousness: Theory and Applications*. Vol. 2: Acquiring Extraordinary Spiritual and Shamanic States. Hornby Island: Institute for the Study of Peak States Press.

McGilvray, A. 2009. Researchers map human epigenome. *Australian Broadcasting Commission*, 15 October.

Mental Health Foundation. 2009. *Statistics on Mental Health* 2009. Available from http://www.mentalhealth.org.uk/information/mental-health-overview/statistics/#howmany.

Mindell, A. 1995. *Sitting in the Fire*. Portland: Lao Tse Press.

Mithen, S. 1996. *The Prehistory of the Mind: A search for the origins of art, religion and science*. London: Thames & Hudson.

———. 2003. *After the Ice: A Global Human History 20,000 - 5,000 BC*. London: Weidenfeld & Nicholson.

Montagu, A, ed. 1978. *Learning Non-Aggression: The experience of non-literate societies*. Oxford: Oxford University Press.

Motluk, A. 2009. Can Experiences before Conception be Passed on? *New Scientist* 201 (2694):12.

Mussen, P. and Eisenberg-Berg, N. 1977. *Roots of Caring, Sharing and Helping: The Development of Prosocial Behaviour in Children.* San Francisco: W. H. Freeman.

National Institute of Mental Health. 2008. *The Numbers Count: Mental Disorders in America.* Available from http://www.nimh.nih.gov/health/publications/the-numbers-count-mental-disorders-in-america/index.shtml.

Neugebauer, R. 2005. Accumulating Evidence for Prenatal Nutritional Origins of Mental Disorders. *J. Am. Med. Assoc.* 294 (5):621-3.

Nicholls, H. 2009. Taming the Beast. *New Scientist* 204 (2728):40-43.

Nowak, R. 2008. The e-Doctor will see you now. *New Scientist* 200 (2681):24-25.

Oatley, K, D Keltner, and J M Jenkins. 2006. *Understanding Emotions.* 2nd ed. Oxford: Blackwell.

Olshansky, B., and L. Dossey. 2004. Retroactive Prayer: An Outrageous Hypothesis? *Network: The Scientific and Medical Network Review* (84):3-11.

Orbach, S. 2009. The Unstable Body. *New Scientist* 201 (2694):28-29.

Orme-Johnson, D W. 2003. Preventing Crime Through the Maharishi Effect. *J Offender Rehabilitation* 36 (1-4).

Orme-Johnson, D W, M C Dillbeck, and C N Alexander. 2003. Preventing Terrorism and International Conflict: Effects of Large Assemblies of Participants in the Transcendental Meditation and TM-Sidhi Programs. *J Offender Rehabilitation* 36 (1-4).

Pariante, C. M. 2003. Depression, Stress and the Adrenal Axis: British Society for Neuroendocrinology.

Perry, B D. 1996. *An Interview with Bruce D. Perry by Lou Bank.* Available from http://www.childtrauma.org/CTAMATE-RIALS/loubank.asp.

– – –. 1997. Incubated in Terror: Neurodevelopmental Factors in the "Cycle of Violence". In *Children in Violent*

Society, edited by J. D. Osofsky.

— — —. 1999. Memories of Fear: How the brain stores and retrieves physiologic states, feelings, behaviors and thoughts from traumatic events. In *Splintered Reflections: Images of the body in trauma*, edited by J. Goodwin and R. Attias. NY: Basic Books.

— — —. 2000. Trauma and Terror in Childhood: The Neuropsychiatric Impact of Childhood Trauma. In *Handbook of Psychological Injuries: Evaluation, Treatment and Compensable Damages*, edited by I. Schulz, S. Carella and D. O. Brady: American Bar Association Publishing.

— — —. 2001. Bonding and Attachment in Maltreated Children: Consequences of Emotional Neglect in Childhood: Child Trauma Academy.

— — —. 2002a. Brain Structure and Function II: Special Topics Informing Work with Maltreated Children. In *Interdisciplinary Education Series*, edited by B. D. Perry: ChildTrauma Academy.

— — —. 2002b. Childhood Experience and the Expression of Genetic Potential: What childhood neglect tells us about nature and nurture. *Brain and Mind* 3:79-100.

Perry, J W. 1974. *The Far Side of Madness*. Englewood Cliffs, NJ: Prentice-Hall.

Pert, C. B. 1997. *Molecules of Emotion: Why you feel the way you feel*. NY: Simon & Schuster.

Powell, D. 2009. Treat a female rat like a male and its brain changes. *New Scientist* 201 (2690):8.

Ratnavale, D. 2007. An Understanding of Aboriginal Experience in the context of Collective Trauma: A challenge for healing: Aboriginal and Torres Islander Mental Health Services.

Rausch, P. 1990. In *Touch: The foundation of experience*, edited by K. E. Barnard and T. B. Brazelton.

Reading, R, S Bissell, J Goldhagen, J Harwin, J Masson, S Moynihan, N Parton, M S Pais, J Thoburn, and E Webb. 2009. Promotion of Children's Rights and Prevention of Child

Maltreatment. *The Lancet* 373:332-43.

Rhodes, R. 2000. *Why they Kill: The discoveries of a maverick criminologist.* NY: Vintage Books.

Rinpoche, Sogyal. 1992. *The Tibetan Book of Living and Dying.* London: Rider.

Robben, A C G M, and M M Suarez-Orozco, eds. 2000. *Cultures Under Siege: Collective Violence and Trauma, Publications of the Society for Psychological Anthropology.* NY: Cambridge University Press.

Roberts, N. 1998. *The Holocene: an environmental history.* 2nd ed. Oxford: Blackwell.

Robson, D. 2009a. Disorderly Genius. *New Scientist* 202 (2714):34-37.

Robson, D. 2009b. How to control your herd of humans. *New Scientist* 201 (2694):13.

Roseboom, T.J., J.H.P. van der Meulen, C.J. Ravelli, G.A. van Montfrans, C. Osmond, D.J.P. Barker, and O.P. Bleker. 1999. Blood pressure in adults after prenatal exposure to famine. *J. Hypertension* 17 (3):325-30.

Rothschild, B. 2000. *The Body Remembers: The psychophysiology of Trauma and Trauma Treatment.* NY: W W Norton.

Rowe, D. 2007a. *Beyond Fear.* Harper Perennial.

— — —. 2007b. Children are not mad or bad, they are just Scared. *New Scientist* (2608):24.

Rowlands, M. 2008. *The Philosopher and the Wolf: Lessons from the wild on love, death and happiness.* London: Granta.

Sarno, J. E. 1998. *The Mindbody Prescription.* NY: Warner Books.

Schlitz, M. M., C. Vieten and T. Amorok. 2007. *Living Deeply: The art and science of transformation in everyday life.* Oakland: New Harbinger Publications.

Schmookler, A.B. 1984. *The Parable of the Tribes: The problem of power in social evolution.* Boston: Houghton Mifflin.

Schore, A N. 1994. *Affect Regulation and the Origin of the Self: Neurobiology of emotional development.* Hillsdale: Lawrence

Erlbaum Assoc.

Scott, S., S.R. Duncan and C.J. Duncan. 1997. *Critical effects of malnutrition during pregnancy.* Available from www.localpopulationstudies.org.uk/PDF/LPS59/LPS59_1997_62-65.pdf.

Seery, M D, C S Silver, E A Holman, W A Ence, and T Q Chu. 2008. Expressing Thoughts and Feelings Following a Collective Trauma: Immediate Responses to 9/11 Predict Negative Outcomes in a National Sample. *J. Consulting and Clinical Psych.* 76 (4):657-67.

Seligman, M.E.P. 2002. *Authentic Happiness: Using the new Positive Psychology to realize your potential for lasting fulfillment.* London: Nicholas Brealey.

Servan-Schreiber, D. 2004. *Healing without Freud or Prozac: Natural Approaches to Curing Stress, Anxiety and Depression without Drugs and without Psychoanalysis* London: Rodale International.

Shaffer, D.R. 1979. *Social and Personality Development.* California: Brook/Cole Publishing Co.

Shonkoff, J P, and D A Phillips, eds. 2000. *From Neurons to Neighborhoods: The Science of Early Childhood Development, Committee on Integrating the Science of Early Childhood Development, Board on Children, Youth and Families, National Research Council and Institute of Medicine.* Washington: National Academy Press.

Siegel, G. J., B. W. Agranoff, R. W. Albers, S. K. Fisher, and M. D. Uhler, eds. 1999. *Basic Neurochemistry: Molecular, Cellular, and Medical Aspects.* Philadelphia: Lippincott, Williams & Wilkins.

Somasundaram, D. 2007. Collective Trauma in Northern Sri Lanka: A qualitative psychosocial-ecological study. *Int. J. Mental Health Sys.* 1 (5).

Spinney, L. 2008. Where are the bodies? *New Scientist* 200 (2681):40-43.

Steininger, T. *A Holocaust Healing Event in Berlin - Germany* 2008.

Available from http://www.globalawareness.info/aid=69.phtml.

Stephenson, P. 2002. *Billy*. London: HarperCollins.

Sternberg, E.M. 2009. *Healing Spaces: The science of place and well-being*. Cambridge, Massachusetts: Belknap Press.

Suomi, S. J. 1990. In *Touch: The foundation of experience*, edited by K. E. Barnard and T. B. Brazelton.

Szalavitz, M. 2008. Welcome to my world. *New Scientist* 199 (2674):34-37.

Taylor, S. 2005. *The Fall: The evidence for a Golden Age, 6,000 years of insanity, and the dawning of a new era*. Ropley: O Books.

Thomson, H. 2009. Suddenly I see. *New Scientist* 202 (2711):49.

Tolle, E. 2005. *A New Earth: Awakening to your life's purpose*. London: Penguin Books.

Torrence, R., and Grattan, J., ed. 2002. *Natural Disasters and Cultural Change*. London: Routledge.

Travis, A. 2009. Revealed: the hidden army in UK prisons. *The Guardian*, 24 September.

Turnbull, C. 1972. *The Mountain People*. NY: Simon & Schuster.

Updegraff, J A, C S Silver, and E A Holman. 2008. Searching for and Finding Meaning in Collective Trauma: Results from a National Longitudinal Study of the 9/11 Terrorist Attacks. *J. Personality and Social Psych.* 95 (3):709-22.

Vidal, J. 2009. 'Climate change is here, it is a reality'. *The Guardian*, 3 September.

Wade, N. 1974. Sahelian Drought: No victory for Western aid. *Science* 185:234-237.

Walsh, R. 1993. Meditation Research: The state of the art. In *Paths Beyond Ego*, edited by R. Walsh and F. Vaughan. New York: Putnam.

— — —. 1995. Asian Psychotherapies. In *Current Psychotherapies*, edited by R. J. Corsini and D. Wedding. Itasca: Peacock Publishers.

Weeks, A. 2007. *Umbilical Cord Clamping Should Be Delayed, Says*

Expert. Available from http://www.sciencedaily.com/releases/2007/08/070816193328.htm.

Werner, E. 1995. Resilience in Development. *Current Directions in Psychological Science* 4 (3):81-5.

Wesley-Esquimaux, C C, and M Smolewski. 2004. Historic Trauma and Aboriginal Healing: The Aboriginal Healing Foundation.

Whitfield, J. 2009a. Cruel to be Kind. *New Scientist* 202 (2708):42-45.

Whitfield, J. 2009b. Nature's Fabulous Freak Show. *New Scientist* 201 (2690):42.

Wiess, S. J. 1990. Parental Touching: Correlates of a Child's Body Concept and Body Perception. In *Touch: The foundation of experience*, edited by K. E. Barnard and T. B. Brazelton.

Wikramatunga, L. 2009. And then they came for me. *The Sunday Leader*, 11 January.

Wyatt, C. 2008. Coping with the trauma of warfare. *BBC News*, 26 November.

Zeanah, C. H. , and M. S. Scheeringa. 1997. The Experience and Effects of Violence in Infancy. In *Children in a Violent Society*, edited by J. D. Osofsky. NY: The Guilford Press.

Zimbardo, P. 2007. *The Lucifer Effect: How good people turn evil.* London: Rider.

Zohar, D. and Marshall, I. 2000. *SQ Spiritual Intelligence: The Ultimate Intelligence.* London: Bloomsbury.

Index

C

J

K

363-4

Antisocial Personality Disorder 34, 37, 149, 191, 201, 205, 217, 238-9

Anxiety 23-4, 26, 33-5, 37, 147, 182, 187, 189, 192, 201, 208, 219, 222-3, 230, 251-2, 260, 294-5, 297, 311, 314, 316, 321, 334-5, 338, 341, 362, 365, 371

Attention Deficit Hyperactivity Disorder (ADHD) 34-6, 190, 201, 223-4, 238-9

Bipolar Disorder 34-5, 251, 340

Conduct Disorder 201, 222-3, 230, 238, 260

Depression 23, 27, 33-5, 147, 177, 187-8, 193, 201, 206, 208, 217-9, 222-3, 230, 239, 251-3, 256, 260, 292, 296-7, 314-6, 334, 338, 340, 342, 359, 362, 365, 367, 371

Diagnosis, difficulties of, multiple 222-5

Fear as underlying cause (See under Fear)

Learning disability (See Learning disability)

Multiple Personality Disorder 25

Obsessive-Compulsive Disorder 27, 35, 193

Oppositional-defiant Disorder 223

Phobias (See Phobias)

Post-Traumatic Stress Disorder (PTSD) 13, 23-4, 29, 34, 43, 45, 48, 178, 208, 219, 221-4, 227-8, 230, 246, 248, 260, 264, 290-1, 295, 303-4, 316, 324, 335-6, 340, 371-3

Psychosis 23, 27, 181, 315, 371

Schizophrenia 34-5, 165, 190-1

Seasonal Affective Disorder 208

Psychiatry, psychiatrist (See under Therapy)

Psychic disharmony 148, 151, 297-8

Psychological defense mechanisms 26-7 (Also see Avoidance; Denial; Dissociation; Psychiatric disorders; Psychosomatic illness; Regression; Repression; Withdrawal)

Psychopath 8, 158, 200, 219

Psychosis (See under Psychiatric disorders)

Psychosomatic illness 33, 36-8, 314

Psychotherapy (See under Therapy)

PTE (See Potentially Traumatic Event)

Puberty (Also see Adolescence) 181, 236

Punishment
Of adults 153, 274, 330
Of children 9, 15, 215, 239, 276-8, 283-4

BOOKS

O is a symbol of the world, of oneness and unity. In different cultures it also means the "eye," symbolizing knowledge and insight. We aim to publish books that are accessible, constructive and that challenge accepted opinion, both that of academia and the "moral majority."

Our books are available in all good English language bookstores worldwide. If you don't see the book on the shelves ask the bookstore to order it for you, quoting the ISBN number and title. Alternatively you can order online (all major online retail sites carry our titles) or contact the distributor in the relevant country, listed on the copyright page.

See our website www.o-books.net for a full list of over 500 titles, growing by 100 a year.

And tune in to myspiritradio.com for our book review radio show, hosted by June-Elleni Laine, where you can listen to the authors discussing their books.